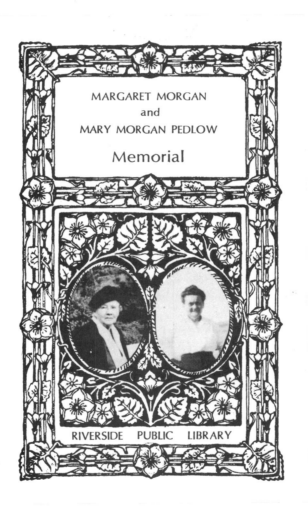

Africa

An Encyclopedia
for Students

GEOPOLITICAL

WESTERN SAHARA

MOROCCO

TUNISIA

ALGERIA

LIBYA

EGYPT

MAURITANIA

MALI

NIGER

CHAD

SUDAN

ERITREA

DJIBOUTI

SENEGAL

GAMBIA

GUINEA BISSAU

GUINEA

SIERRA LEONE

LIBERIA

BURKINA FASO

BENÍN

NIGERIA

CÔTE D'IVOIRE

GHANA

TOGO

CAMEROON

CENTRAL AFRICAN REPUBLIC

ETHIOPIA

SOMALIA

EQUITORIAL GUINEA

SÃO TOMÉ AND PRINCIPE

GABON

CONGO (Brazzaville)

CONGO (Kinshasa)

UGANDA

RWANDA

BURUNDI

KENYA

19,341 ft.

TANZANIA

COMOROS

ANGOLA

ZAMBIA

MALAWI

MOZAMBIQUE

ZIMBABWE

NAMIBIA

BOTSWANA

SWAZILAND

LESOTHO

SOUTH AFRICA

MADAGASCAR

ELEVATIONS OVER 1,640 FEET

Africa

An Encyclopedia for Students

John Middleton, Editor

Volume 1
Abidjan–Economic

CHARLES SCRIBNER'S SONS

GALE GROUP
™
THOMSON LEARNING

New York • Detroit • San Diego • San Francisco
Boston • New Haven, Conn. • Waterville, Maine
London • Munich

Developed for Charles Scribner's Sons by Visual Education Corporation, Princeton, N.J.

For Scribners
PUBLISHER: Karen Day
EDITORS: John Fitzpatrick, Brad Morgan
COVER AND INTERIOR DESIGN: Jennifer Wahi
PHOTO RESEARCH: Kelly Quin
PRODUCTION SUPERVISOR: Mary Beth Trimper

For Visual Education
PROJECT DIRECTOR: Darryl Kestler
WRITERS: John Haley, Charles Roebuck, Rebecca Stefoff, Joseph Ziegler
EDITORS: Noëlle Y. Child, Cindy George, Guy Austrian, Charles Roebuck
ASSOCIATE EDITOR: Cheryl MacKenzie
COPYEDITING SUPERVISOR: Helen A. Castro
ELECTRONIC PREPARATION: Fiona Torphy

Contributors
Nancy E. Gratton, Kevin van Bladel, Frank Griffel, Jeremy Raphael Berndt

Library of Congress Cataloging in-Publication Data

Africa: an encyclopedia for students / John Middleton, editor.   CHILDRENS ROOM
    p. cm
    Includes bibliographical references and index.
    ISBN 0-684-80650-9 (set : alk. paper) —ISBN 0-684-80651-7 (v. 1) —
ISBN 0-684-80652-5 (v. 2) —ISBN 0-684-80653-3 (v. 3) —
ISBN 0-684-80654-1 (v. 4)
    1. Africa–Encyclopedias, Juvenile. [1. Africa—Encyclopedias.] I. Middleton, John, 1921–

DT3 .A249 2001
960'03—dc21

2001049348

Table of Contents

List of Maps

Color Plates

Table of Contents

Volume 3

Table of Contents

Volume 4

Table of Contents

Preface

Understanding areas outside our own corner of the globe is always a challenge. This is particularly true in the case of Africa, a vast continent with a complex web of indigenous cultures. Yet Africans make up one-fifth of the world's population, and the continent lies at the crossroads between the Americas, Europe, and the Middle East. What happens in Africa affects us all.

Moreover, North America's links to Africa go back many centuries—first as a partner in the Atlantic slave trade and later as an ally of European colonial powers that ruled Africa. The slave trade had a lasting effect on the history of both North America and Africa. It brought millions of Africans to this side of the Atlantic as slaves, forming the basis for black populations in the Americas. At the same time, the slave trade divided Africa and deprived it of generations of young people who would have played a productive role in society.

A great deal of material about Africa—in textbooks, newspapers, novels, and films—is superficial, biased, or even invented. Most of it appears in bits and pieces and not as part of a comprehensive study of the region. This work, *Africa: An Encyclopedia for Students,* offers a more coherent picture of the continent. In its pages Africa emerges as a single continent with unique geographical features, a continuous, interrelated history, and similar economic, political, and social problems.

The Scope of the Encyclopedia. In its four volumes, *Africa: An Encyclopedia for Students* offers both a broad and a fairly detailed view of Africa's land and its peoples—from the Mediterranean Sea to the Cape of Good Hope and from the Atlantic Ocean to the Indian Ocean. Although it is not possible to provide a detailed treatment of all aspects of the continent in less than 1,000 pages, the work does bring together a great deal of vital information and careful analysis.

The student encyclopedia is based on the four-volume *Encyclopedia of Africa South of the Sahara,* published in 1997, of which I was editor in chief. The original work contains 896 articles by geographers, historians, anthropologists, linguists, philosophers, and other experts from Europe, North America, and Africa. In the past most scholarly research about the continent came from non-Africans. Now, however, scholars from Africa play a leading role in the field. Africans tend to see their continent in one way, while foreigners have other perspectives. Combining these different images of Africa brings us closer to an understanding of the continent.

Africa: An Encyclopedia for Students covers much of the same ground as the earlier work at a level suitable for middle and high school students. Many of the original articles have been adapted and updated, and a substantial amount of new material has been added on North Africa. In addition to articles on standard topics such as countries, cities, and historical individuals, the student encyclopedia contains entries on broad fields of knowledge, ranging from human origins to music and song, from colonialism to marriage systems, and from slavery to food and drink. All articles are arranged in alphabetical order to make it easy for students to find information.

Features of the Encyclopedia. Alongside the text column in the pages of *Africa: An Encyclopedia for Students* is a marginal column filled with helpful features. There readers will find time lines placing events in historical context, sidebars providing interesting information on a variety of topics, and definitions of difficult or unfamiliar words used in the text. Cross-references to related articles appear both within the text and at the end of entries. Fact sheets accompany each country article, providing significant data about the nation's people, geography, government, and economy in a convenient format.

The illustrations in the student encyclopedia bring the people and places discussed in the entries to life. Each volume has special full-color inserts

devoted to the themes of Peoples and Cultures, The Land and Its History, Art and Architecture, and Daily Life. The encyclopedia also includes more than 50 maps of modern nations, ancient kingdoms and colonial empires, trade routes, and various geographic features.

The original *Encyclopedia of Africa South of the Sahara* took six years to produce and *Africa: An Encyclopedia for Students* has taken nearly two more.

No single editor can do everything, and I wish to thank the publisher, Karen Day, and the senior editor, John Fitzpatrick, of Charles Scribner's Sons; Darryl Kestler of Visual Education Corporation; and the many members of their staffs. In addition, I thank the authors and the members of the original boards of associate editors, advisers, and consultants. This new student encyclopedia has been very much a cooperative effort.

John Middleton, Editor

A Time Line of Africa

4 m.y.a.*	Australopithecines *(early hominids) live in northern Rift Valley (Ethiopia, Kenya).*
2.5 m.y.a.*	*Early Stone Age;* Homo habilis *appears (Olduvai Gorge, Tanzania).*
1.5 m.y.a.*–150,000 B.C.	Homo erectus *appears.*
240,000–40,000 B.C.	*Middle Stone Age.*
80,000–20,000 B.C.	*Late Stone Age.*
20,000–10,000 B.C.	*Farming introduced in lower Nile Valley.*
10,000–6000 B.C.	*Cattle domesticated in northern Africa.*
	Millet and sorghum grown in western Africa.
6000–5000 B.C.	*Khoisan hunters of southern Africa create rock paintings.*
3000 B.C.	*King Menes unifies Lower Egypt and Upper Egypt.*
	Agriculture develops in Ethiopian highlands.
2000–1000 B.C.	*Horses introduced in Sahara region.*
	Bananas grown in central Africa.
332 B.C.	*Greeks occupy Egypt.*
200 B.C.	*Romans gain control of Carthage.*
32 B.C.	*Royal city of Meroë flourishes in what is now Sudan.*
A.D. 300s	*Aksum invades Meroë; Aksum king adopts Coptic Christianity.*
530s	*Byzantine empire takes Mediterranean ports.*
600s	*Muslim Arabs invade North Africa.*
ca. 1000	*Shona begin building Great Zimbabwe.*
1200s	*Portuguese voyage to northwest coast of Africa.*
	Sundjata Keïta founds Mali kingdom.

*m.y.a. million years ago

1312–1337	*Mansa Musa rules Mali and makes pilgrimage to Mecca.*
1400s	*Benin kingdom flourishes.*
1498	*Vasco da Gama sails around the southern and eastern coasts of Africa on the way to India.*
1505–1510	*Portuguese seize Swahili towns in eastern Africa and fortify Mozambique.*
	Kongo king Afonso I converts to Christianity.
1517	*Ottoman Turks conquer Egypt and port towns along the Mediterranean.*
1578	*Moroccans defeat Portuguese, remaining free of colonial control.*
1591	*Al-Mansur invades Songhai.*
1600s	*French, English, and Dutch establish trading posts along western coasts to export gold, ivory, and slaves.*
	Akan state emerges.
1650s	*Dutch settle at Cape of Good Hope in southern Africa.*
	Arab traders settle on East African coast.
1700s	*French and British establish network for slave trade in Central Africa.*
	Zanzibar prospers as Arab trading center.
1721	*French colonize Mauritius.*
1787	*British missionaries found Sierra Leone.*
1795	*British seize Cape Colony from Dutch.*
1798	*Napoleon leads French invasion of Egypt.*
1805	*Muhammad Ali takes power in Egypt, breaking free of Ottoman control.*
1807	*Britain and the United States abolish slave trade.*
1817	*Shaka emerges at head of Zulu kingdom in southern Africa.*
1821	*Freed slaves from the United States settle in what is now Liberia.*
1828	*Queen Ranavalona takes throne in Madagascar.*
1830s	*French rule proclaimed in Algeria.*
	Slave trade continues in western Africa.
1835	*Dutch settlers in southern Africa head north in "Great Trek."*
1840s–1880s	*Slave trade flourishes in East Africa.*
1847	*Republic of Liberia is established.*
1852–1873	*David Livingstone explores Central and East Africa.*
1858	*Portuguese abolish slavery in Central Africa.*

1855–1868	Emperor Téwodros rules Ethiopia.
1859–1869	Suez Canal is built.
1869	Diamonds are discovered at Kimberley in northern Cape Colony.
1880–1881	Afrikaners rebel against Britain in the First Anglo-Boer War, and British withdraw from Transvaal in southern Africa.
1885	Mahdist forces capture Khartoum.
1880s–early 1900s	European powers colonize most of Africa (present-day names of countries listed):
	Belgians in Congo (Kinshasa);
	British in Nigeria, Ghana, Sierra Leone, the Gambia, Uganda, Kenya, Somalia, Mauritius, Seychelles, Zambia, Zimbabwe, Malawi, Botswana, Lesotho, and Swaziland;
	French in Mauritania, Niger, Burkina Faso, Mali, Algeria, Tunisia, Morocco, Senegal, Guinea, Ivory Coast, Bénin, Central African Republic, Gabon, Congo (Brazzaville), Chad, Djibouti, Madagascar, Réunion, and the Comoro Islands;
	Germans in Togo, Cameroon, Namibia, Tanzania, Rwanda, and Burundi;
	Portuguese in Guinea-Bissau, São Tomé and Príncipe, Cape Verde, Angola, and Mozambique;
	Spanish in Western Sahara and Equatorial Guinea.
1893–1895	Africans in King Leopold's Congo revolt.
1895	France forms federation of colonies that becomes French West Africa.
1896	Ethiopian emperor Menilek defeats Italians, maintaining country's independence.
1899–1902	Afrikaners defeated by British in Second Anglo-Boer war.
1910	Union of South Africa formed.
1914–1918	World War I: French and British capture German Togo; Africans fight on the side of various colonial powers in Africa.
1922	Egypt gains its independence.
1930	Haile Selassie I crowned emperor of Ethiopia.
1935	Italians invade Ethiopia.
1936	Union party in South Africa revokes voting rights of blacks.
1939–1945	World War II: many major battles fought in North Africa; Africans in French and British colonies drafted to fight in Europe and Asia.
1940s	First nationalist political parties are formed in western Africa.

1944	William Tubman becomes president of Liberia.
1945	Arab League, an organization of Arab states, is founded in Cairo.
	Ethiopia regains its independence.
1948	Policy of apartheid introduced in South Africa.
1950s	Several independence movements against colonial rule develop.
1951	Libya declared an independent monarchy under King Idris I.
1952	Gamal Abdel Nasser seizes power in Egypt.
1953	Northern Rhodesia (Zambia), Southern Rhodesia (Zimbabwe), and Nyasaland (Malawi) join to form the Central African Federation.
1954	War breaks out in Algeria.
1956	Sudan, Morocco, and Tunisia become independent.
1957	Ghana achieves independence, with Kwame Nkrumah as president.
1958	Guinea, under Sékou Touré, becomes independent.
1960	Independence achieved in Cameroon (French Cameroun), Chad, Congo (Brazzaville), Congo (Kinshasa), Dahomey (Bénin), Gabon, Ivory Coast, Madagascar, Mali, Mauritania, Niger, Nigeria, Senegal, Somalia, Togo, and Upper Volta (Burkina Faso).
1961	Rwanda, Sierra Leone, and Tanganyika become independent.
1962	Independence achieved in Algeria, Burundi, and Uganda.
1963	Kenya (under Jomo Kenyatta) and Zanzibar become independent.
	Central African Federation ends.
	Organization of African Unity is founded.
	FRELIMO begins armed struggle for liberation of Mozambique.
1964	In South Africa, Nelson Mandela stands trial and is jailed.
	Tanganyika and Zanzibar join to form Tanzania.
	Malawi and Zambia become independent.
	Hutu overthrow Tutsi rule in Burundi.
1965	Rhodesia declares independence under Ian Smith.
	Mobutu Sese Seko takes power in Congo (Kinshasa) and renames it Zaire.
	King Hassan restores monarchy in Morocco.
	The Gambia gains independence.
1966	Independence achieved in Lesotho and Botswana.

1967–1970	*Biafra attempts to secede from Nigeria.*
1968	*Swaziland becomes independent.*
1969	*Muammar al-Qaddafi seizes power in Libya.*
1970	*Egypt/Sudan: Aswan Dam is completed.*
1974	*Guinea attains independence.*
1975	*Cape Verde and Angola become independent.*
	FRELIMO government gains independence in Mozambique.
1976	*Spain withdraws from Western Sahara; Morocco and Mauritania fight over territory.*
	Residents of Soweto and other South African townships begin violent protests.
1970s–1990s	*War erupts across the continent within the countries of Angola, Chad, Congo (Brazzaville), Congo (Kinshasa), Ethiopia, Guinea-Bissau, Liberia, Rwanda, Sierra Leone, Somalia, Sudan, and Western Sahara, and between the nations of Ethiopia and Eritrea, Ethiopia and Somalia, and Sudan and Uganda.*
1980	*Zimbabwe becomes independent.*
1990	*Nelson Mandela released from prison.*
	Namibia becomes independent.
1993	*Apartheid ends in South Africa.*
	Eritrea gains independence from Ethiopia.
1994	*Rwandan and Burundi presidents assassinated; ethnic violence between Hutu and Tutsi continues.*
	Nelson Mandela becomes first black president of South Africa.
1995	*Outbreak of deadly Ebola virus in Congo (Kinshasa).*
1997	*Laurent Kabila takes power in Zaire and renames it Democratic Republic of the Congo (Kinshasa).*
1999	*Libya hands over two suspects in 1986 airplane bombing over Lockerbie, Scotland.*
2000	*Ghana chooses president John Kufuor in free elections.*
	Paul Kagame is the first Tutsi to become president in Rwanda.
2001	*Congo (Kinshasa) leader, Kabila, is assassinated; Kabila's son, Joseph, succeeds him as president.*

Abidjan

With a population of about 2.8 million, Abidjan is the capital of IVORY COAST and one of the most important ports in French-speaking Africa. Situated along the edge of the Ebrié Lagoon on the Gulf of Guinea, its ocean port handles cargo for Ivory Coast, BURKINA FASO, MALI, and NIGER. Principal exports are cocoa, coffee, timber, and petroleum. Abidjan is also a banking center for West Africa.

The Krou and the Akan make up the two major ethnic groups living in Abidjan. The city's numerous educational institutions include the national university, archives, museum, and library. There is a research center for coffee and cocoa in addition to schools for marine science, communications, and administration.

Abidjan is clearly divided into modern and underdeveloped areas. The Hotel Ivoire, a tourist resort equipped with an ice rink, bowling alley, cinema complex, and casino, is one of the city's main attractions. Another landmark is the Italian-designed St. Paul's Cathedral, one of the most elaborate churches in Africa. The city is linked to other Ivory Coast cities by highway and to Burkina Faso by rail. (*See also* **Tourism, Transportation.**)

ABYSSINIA

See *Eritrea; Ethiopia.*

Accra

Accra, the capital of GHANA, lies on the Gulf of Guinea on the Gold Coast in West Africa. It is the commercial, educational, governmental, and cultural center of Ghana, the hub of the country's road and rail system, and the site of the Kotoka International Airport. The population is over 1.6 million.

The Portuguese, the first Europeans to visit the region, arrived in the early 1500s. They were followed in the 1600s by the Dutch and the British, who built two forts used in the SLAVE TRADE. The forts later grew into the city of Accra. Under the British, the city was the capital of the Gold Coast, which became Ghana in 1957. Present-day Accra is sharply divided into modern sectors and shantytowns*.

Industries in Accra include brewing and distilling, fish and fruit canning, clothing, shoes, and pharmaceutical products. The city has an ocean port, but Tema, to the east, surpasses it in importance. Accra is home to the University of Ghana as well as schools for communications, science, and technology. The national museum and archives and the National Theater are all located in the city. In addition, live music performances, movie theaters, and facilities for visitors have contributed to a growing tourist industry in Accra. (*See also* **Tourism.**)

* **shantytown** poor, run-down section of a city, often inhabited by immigrants

1

Achebe, Chinua

**1930–
Nigerian writer**

* **secede**   to withdraw formally from an organization or country

Chinua Cinualomogu Achebe is a Nigerian writer whose novels often explore the difficult choices faced by Africans in modern life. Achebe's first novel, *Things Fall Apart* (1958), is considered a classic and is one of the most widely read works of African literature. The hero of the book commits suicide, unable to choose between radically different ways of life shaped by traditional values and European values.

Achebe worked as a teacher and writer before serving as director of the Nigerian Broadcasting Corporation between 1961 and 1966. During the Nigerian civil war (1967–1970), he returned to his home territory of Igboland (renamed Biafra), which was attempting to secede* from NIGERIA. Achebe became a spokesperson for Biafra in Europe and North America. After the war he taught at several universities in Africa and the United States.

In addition to his novels, Achebe has written short stories and poetry inspired by his experiences during the war. He is also the author of several children's books intended specifically for use in African schools. (*See also* **Literature**.)

Nigerian author Chinua Achebe is known for his writings about the effects of colonialism and Western culture on traditional African societies.

Addis Ababa

Addis Ababa, the capital and largest city in ETHIOPIA, is located on a high plateau in the center of the country. As home to the ORGANIZATION OF AFRICAN UNITY, an organization devoted to the interests of African states, Addis Ababa is also the diplomatic capital of Africa.

Addis Ababa was founded in 1886 by Empress Taitu, the wife of Ethiopian emperor MENILEK II. An area of the city called Arada, which contained the palace, St. George's Cathedral, and the central market, became the center of Addis Ababa. The city grew as noblemen who received land grants from the emperor established military encampments around the center.

By 1892 Addis Ababa was the capital of the Ethiopian empire. However, a lack of firewood resulting from deforestation* in the area led Menilek to consider moving his capital to another location. The importation of fast-growing wattle (acacia) trees solved the problem.

A rail line joining Addis Ababa to the Red Sea port of DJIBOUTI was completed in 1917 and helped boost the prosperity of the city. Population also grew at that time, partly because of slave raiding in southwestern Ethiopia. Many of the people who were captured—and they numbered in the many tens of thousands—were sent to Addis Ababa.

Ethiopia was under Italian control between 1935 and 1941, and the Italians planned to rebuild Addis Ababa according to a European model. They made changes that shaped much of the modern city, including the construction of roads and factories in the city. Arada, renamed Piazza, became the central market and commercial district.

Today, Ethiopia's main roads, rail network, and air routes run through Addis Ababa. With a population of about 2.5 million, the city is also the country's financial, commercial, educational, and media center.

* **deforestation**   removal of a forest as a result of human activities

Africa, Study of

The study of Africa has a long history. People have been gathering information about the continent since ancient times. Early reports came mostly from travelers, explorers, missionaries, and merchants. Later, scholars in fields such as history, anthropology, geography, and the natural sciences began to conduct research there.

Early Contact. In ancient times, people living outside Africa knew little about it. The Greeks and Romans were quite familiar with parts of North Africa, but they had limited knowledge of sub-Saharan* Africa. Beginning in the A.D. 700s, the Arabs developed extensive contacts with peoples of the MAGHREB and began to explore areas south of the Sahara and along Africa's eastern coast. By the 900s Arabs had learned a great deal about the western and eastern parts of Africa through trade with the peoples of those regions.

European interest in sub-Saharan Africa began with voyages of exploration in the late 1400s. Explorers, missionaries, and merchants wrote about their visits to Africa, giving Europeans some basic information about the "dark continent." In the late 1800s, as Europeans became

* **sub-Saharan**   referring to Africa south of the Sahara desert

Africa, Study of

involved in a mad "scramble" for colonies in Africa, scholars began to turn their attention to the region.

Colonial and Postcolonial Eras. The creation of colonies led to a more systematic gathering of facts about Africa. At the same time, European museums and private collectors began to acquire African artifacts*. Explorers and geographers mapped the continent, and colonial authorities and social scientists began studying the customs, laws, and other aspects of African societies and cultures. Some colonial powers hoped to use the knowledge they gained to strengthen their control in Africa.

* **artifact** in archaeology, an ornament, tool, weapon, or other object made by humans

Throughout the colonial era, the interpretation of information about Africa generally reflected the ideas and viewpoints of Europeans rather than those of Africans. In the mid-1900s, as African nations gained independence, the study of Africa began to shift. New centers and associations dedicated to the study of Africa were established both on the continent and at universities around the world. Greater attention was paid to African points of view and research expanded into many different areas. From the 1960s to the 1980s, the Cold War* created a boom in African studies. The competition between the United States and the Soviet Union for political influence in Africa generated great interest in the region.

* **Cold War** period of tense relations between the United States and the Soviet Union following World War II

Today political instability in many African countries makes fieldwork difficult. Nevertheless, Western and African scholars have begun an increasing number of joint research projects in which they share data and resources. In some African nations, the need to devote scarce financial resources to more pressing economic, political, and social programs has resulted in cutbacks in African studies.

Range of Research. African studies include a broad range of fields, from African LANGUAGES, LITERATURE, ART, music, and culture to African history, biology, economics, political science, geology, anthropology, sociology, religion, and philosophy. Some African studies focus on one particular area of study, such as language and literature. Others take an interdisciplinary approach that combines different areas of study and focuses on the relationships and connections among them.

One goal of African studies is to gain a greater knowledge of the forces that have affected Africa and its people over the centuries. Scholars also focus on discovering the roots of the problems facing Africa, such as widespread poverty, lack of economic development, ethnic conflicts, and political instability. Attempting to understand the continent from an African point of view is often a key feature of their work. (*See also* **Archaeology and Prehistory, Economic History, Ethnic Groups and Identity, History of Africa, Maps and Mapmaking, Music and Song, Oral Tradition, Popular Culture, Travel and Exploration.**)

AFRICAN NATIONAL CONGRESS (ANC)

See *South Africa; Zambia.*

Afrikaner Republics

The Afrikaner Republics were independent states established in the 1850s by Dutch colonists (Afrikaners) from British-ruled SOUTH AFRICA. The two longest-lived of the Afrikaner Republics were the Orange Free State, located between the Orange and Vaal Rivers, and the South African Republic (or Transvaal), between the Limpopo and Vaal Rivers. Each state had a strong central government, a judicial system with limited powers, and voting rights restricted to adult white males. The black Africans who lived in these states had no civil liberties or rights of citizenship.

Troubled by conflicts with surrounding African communities and a weak economy, the Orange Free State was unstable. The economic situation improved dramatically when diamonds were discovered there in 1867. Although the Orange Free State lost ownership of some of its diamond fields four years later, its economy became more stable. Moreover, it increased its territory by conquering several small African states.

The South African Republic also experienced political turmoil as it tried to expand beyond its borders. In addition, the country was torn by infighting between Afrikaner groups. In 1877 the British declared the South African Republic a part of their colony in South Africa. The Afrikaners resisted the takeover, defeating the British army in the First War of Independence in 1881.

When gold was discovered in the South African Republic in 1886, thousands of fortune hunters flooded the land and European colonial mining companies tried to seize control of the country. Cecil RHODES, prime minister of the British Cape Colony, failed in an attempt to overthrow the South African Republic's government in 1895. Four years later the British declared war on the South African Republic in hopes of controlling the valuable gold mines. The Orange Free State joined the South African Republic in resisting the British, but the Afrikaner Republics lost the war and in 1902 became provinces of British-governed South Africa. (*See also* **Colonialism in Africa; Southern Africa, History**.)

AFRIKANERS

See *Afrikaner Republics; South Africa.*

Age and Aging

* **pastoralist** related to or dependent on livestock herding

Age has two significant roles in traditional African cultures south of the Sahara. First, respect for age and for the elderly is a universal social ideal. Second, many societies are organized into groups by age, and membership in such groups helps define a person's sense of identity and place in the community. Recent social changes have somewhat weakened these values and practices, but age is still a powerful shaping force in agricultural and pastoralist* areas, especially where local communities have a good deal of independence.

Age and Aging

cult group bound together by devotion to a particular person, belief, or god

diplomatic involved with conducting relations with other nations

ritual religious ceremony that follows a set pattern

assets property or other valuable goods or qualities

gerontocratic ruled by elders

Age and Respect. Older people claim a right to the respect of others based on their seniority—they have lived longer than others. They deserve respect because they have acquired wisdom and experience over the years. Younger people have a reason to accept this way of thinking. By showing respect to their elders, they hope to ensure that they will receive respect when they reach that stage of life.

The ideal of the respected elder shapes many African institutions. The extended family is dominated by the senior generation. Elders control property and also grant or withhold permission for younger people to marry. Religious beliefs also reflect respect for elders. Cults* that honor ancestors are the highest form of respect for seniority—ancestors are more senior than the oldest living family members. However, the elderly have power within the community because they are closer in age to the ancestors than anyone else.

The high status of older people in African cultures is related to the idea that family growth is good and fortunate. People see large families as a source of security in times of crisis, and they want to leave descendants who will honor them as ancestors. The position of older men in the community is closely tied to this concern with family size and fertility. The power held by older men is reinforced by their control over marriages and also over status of young men. By delaying the marriages of young men, the elders create a surplus of young women. If the elders take these women as second or additional wives, they create large families, which adds to their position in the community.

Another factor involved in the respect for elders is their control of information and resources. Not all older people are respected, however, especially once their abilities decline. But those who skillfully display their knowledge, diplomatic* skills, social connections, and ability to perform rituals* enjoy high regard. These skills are considered as community assets*.

The ideal of respect toward old age does not always match the reality of relations between the generations. Harsh treatment by older men can cause disrespect and anger among younger men, who may engage in behavior that the elders cannot completely control. In addition, where communities are dominated by older men, the women do not always accept their secondary status.

Women and men experience old age differently. Women may continue to gain status and power at an age when older men experience loss. Women build up supportive networks of influence within families and households. These continue throughout their lives. Men, who tend to operate in a more competitive public domain, must eventually give up some of their power in exchange for continued respect by the younger men.

Aging and Age Sets. Many African cultures view aging not as a steady process but as a series of jumps from one stage to another—often, from youth to adulthood to "elderhood." INITIATION RITES, ceremonies through which people acquire a new status, mark the transition from youth to adulthood. In some gerontocratic* cultures, initiation is a lifelong process during which the elders withhold knowledge and share it a little at a time. This delays the younger people's entry into the highest ranks. The content of the secrets is less important than the privileges that go with the possession of them.

Group initiation is one form of social organization based on age. As young people of similar age go through the process of initiation together, they form a bond or feeling of community that unites the group long after initiation, even into old age.

Another form of social organization is the age set, which involves dividing the community into groups based on age. Senior groups with-

In African cultures, elderly people are highly respected for their knowledge, skills, and experience. Older men, such as the Senegalese shown here, often hold considerable influence over the lives of younger members of the community.

in such systems dominate younger ones, reinforcing the connection between age and authority. In contrast, age mates, or people within a group, experience equality and bond as peers.

One typical example of a society based on age sets is that of the MAASAI people of eastern Africa. Their system was originally military in nature. It placed young men into warrior groups by age with their roles defined according to seniority. The system has survived as the basis of gerontocratic power over young men, the *moran,* or warriors. Boys must compete with those who are older to be accepted into the next age set of *moran.*

As *moran* they remain in limbo for extended periods, neither boys nor full adults. If the elders relaxed their restrictions and allowed the younger men to marry, the older men would lose their control over the women. Eventually, however, the *moran* are allowed to marry and are also admitted to the society of the elders in something like a second initiation. Not all elders are equal, however. Competition for power continues among the various groups as new sets achieve elder status and older ones are edged out of control.

Societies organized around age systems may regard their own history as a series of age sets. In these societies, the process of aging seems to be halted during periods when family, community, or age-set relations do not change. The occurrence of a significant change—such as a birth, initiation, marriage, or death—brings awareness that everyone is older. At such times, each age set moves forward and power shifts within the community. (*See also* **Death, Mourning, and Ancestors; Family.**)

Agriculture

* **subsistence farming** raising only enough food to live on

Agriculture plays a central role in the economies of nations throughout Africa, accounting for between 30 and 60 percent of all economic production. In many African nations, a majority of the people is engaged in farming, producing goods for domestic use and sometimes for export as well. Peasant and subsistence farming* is the basic form of agriculture in most parts of the continent.

Agricultural practices in Africa are extremely varied. Many of the differences are related to the continent's environmental diversity—its great range of landscapes and climates. Crops and farming methods suitable for the dry, desert regions of North Africa are quite different from those appropriate for the tropical rain forests of central Africa. In addition, the cultural tradition of a group or a region influences what crops are grown and the techniques used to grow them.

PRINCIPAL CROPS

There are two main types of farming in Africa: garden crops, grown primarily from the roots or shoots of plants that have been placed in the ground, and field crops, grown mainly from seeds. Africans also raise various animals as livestock.

Root Crops. One of the oldest and most important root crops in Africa is the yam, a starchy plant sometimes mistakenly referred to as the sweet potato. Grown primarily in tropical or subtropical regions, yams are a reliable staple crop that can be stored easily for later use. Although rather low in nutritional value, they are often grown in combination with vegetables and other foods that help provide an adequate balance of nutrients.

In some parts of Africa—especially western, central, and eastern Africa—cassava is an important food crop. This starchy root plant is the source of tapioca. Although once regarded as only an emergency crop for use during periods of famine, cassava is now planted extensively and has even replaced the cultivation of yams in some areas. Suitable for growing in a wide range of climates, cassava can be left in the ground in both wet and dry seasons much longer than most other crops.

Two other important African root crops are potatoes and plantains. Found mainly in the drier, Mediterranean-type climates of North Africa and southern Africa, potatoes are also grown in the higher elevations of other regions. Plantains, a relative of bananas, have been an important crop in Africa's tropical rain forests for centuries. Used mostly for cooking, some varieties of plantains are also brewed to produce beverages.

Another plant of the banana family, the enset, is sometimes called the false banana. The enset does not produce an edible bunch of fruit like its cousin, the banana. Instead, its stems are used to make fibers and ropes, while its seeds are used for ornamental and medicinal purposes. Found wild in several areas, the enset is cultivated only in the highland regions of ETHIOPIA, where its starchy stem is pounded, cooked, and served as a staple food.

A variety of root crops have been introduced into Africa from other parts of the world. Taro, a plant that grows near rivers and streams, came from Southeast Asia. Groundnuts, which are valued for their oil, and various types of beans have traveled to Africa from the Americas.

Seed Crops. Seed crops of grains and cereals are grown from seeds saved from the previous harvest. Raised in cultivated fields, these crops are found throughout Africa, particularly in the savannas* and regions of medium rainfall.

The most widespread of African grains—and the most important food in the history of the continent—is sorghum. Originally developed from wild grasses native to the savanna regions of northern Africa, sorghum has been grown for food for at least 7,000 years. In some areas, the cultivation of this grain probably developed in close association with LIVESTOCK GRAZING.

The spread of sorghum, however, is linked to the development of iron industries about 2,000 years ago. Iron tools proved especially useful for breaking and clearing the hard, dry soils of the savanna regions, as well as for weeding and harvesting crops.

Another important grain crop of the savanna regions of Africa is millet. Certain species of millet—including one called "hungry rice"—are especially important during times of famine because they can survive fairly long periods of little rainfall.

* **savanna** tropical or subtropical grassland with scattered trees and drought-resistant undergrowth

See color plate 6, vol. 4.

Agriculture

In some areas of Africa, the traditional cultivation of sorghum and millet has been replaced by the growing of maize, or corn. Brought from Central America, maize was grown in very limited amounts at first and only in a few coastal areas of West Africa. During the 1900s, however, the cultivation of maize spread and it became important as a staple food crop, especially in eastern and southern Africa. Maize is also grown extensively in parts of North Africa, primarily in areas under irrigation. Farmers who practice intensive cultivation of maize often use mechanical plows and artificial fertilizers.

Two other grain crops, wheat and barley, are raised on a limited scale. Once restricted to the lower Nile Valley and the highland regions of Ethiopia, wheat and barley have been introduced to highland areas of southern and eastern Africa. Irrigation and the development of new plant strains have also allowed wheat cultivation to spread to some savanna regions. Wheat and barley are grown primarily to make flour.

Two main species of rice are grown in Africa. Common rice originated in Southeast Asia and probably reached eastern Africa more than 1,000 years ago by Indian Ocean shipping routes. The other species, Guinea rice, is native to wet areas of the Guinea coast and upper Niger River region of West Africa. Rice does not require grinding and can be stored and transported quite easily. In towns along the eastern coast of Africa, rice gained prestige as a food for travelers and guests. Among the most important rice-producing countries in Africa today are Egypt, Guinea, Senegal, Sierra Leone, Ivory Coast, Nigeria, and Tanzania.

Other Crops. In addition to the main root and seed crops, Africans grow various legumes*, fruits and vegetables, and plants used to make beverages. Protein-rich legumes—such as beans, cowpeas, and soybeans—are produced widely throughout Africa, generally in combination with other crops. Such crops are typically grown in garden plots tended by families.

* **legumes** vegetables such as peas and beans

Among the most important fruits raised in Africa are dates, figs, olives, bananas, and pineapples. Dates, figs, and olives are cultivated primarily in the desert oases of North Africa. Bananas are grown throughout the tropical regions of Africa; pineapples are produced mainly as a cash crop* in South Africa, Ivory Coast, the Congo basin, and Kenya. Citrus fruits, including oranges and grapefruit, are grown for export primarily along the southern coast of South Africa and the Mediterranean coast of North Africa.

* **cash crop** crop grown primarily for sale rather than for local consumption

A number of vegetables—including tomatoes, onions, cabbages, peppers, okra, eggplants, and cucumbers—are raised in Africa. Tomatoes and onions, the most common vegetables, grow in large quantities along the coast of North Africa.

The principal beverage crops of Africa are tea, coffee, cocoa, and grapes. The largest producers of tea, grown mainly in highland regions, are Kenya, Tanzania, Malawi, Zimbabwe, and Mozambique. Major coffee producers include Ethiopia, Uganda, Kenya, Tanzania, and Madagascar. Cocoa, best suited to tropical regions, is cultivated in West Africa. Grapes, produced in northern Africa and South Africa, are used primarily for making wine. These are all important cash crops, grown mainly

See color plate 3, vol. 4.

for export. Other cash crops include palm oil, coconuts, cashews, rubber, tobacco, cotton, and sugarcane.

CULTIVATION AND TECHNOLOGY

African farmers often struggle to make a living off the land. In many countries, between 70 and 90 percent of the people engage in farming on very small parcels of land, growing just enough to meet their own needs. Although the environment largely determines which crops are grown, local cultural, social, and economic conditions shape methods of cultivation.

Systems of Cultivation. Traditionally, Africans in savanna regions and in tropical forest areas have practiced a method of farming known as shifting cultivation. Farmers clear trees and shrubs from a small patch of land, burn the vegetation to enrich the soil with nutrients, and then plant crops. After two or three years of use, the soil becomes exhausted and the patch of land is left fallow* for anywhere from 4 to 20 years until natural processes restore the fertility of the soil. Meanwhile, farmers move on to clear and plant another parcel of land, and in this way prevent soil erosion.

* **fallow** plowed but not planted during the growing season

While modern tractors are found throughout Africa, animals such as oxen are often used on small farms. Here, farmers in Burkina Faso plow a field to prepare it for planting.

Agriculture

Shifting cultivation requires large amounts of land. In recent decades, African populations have grown dramatically and expanded onto much of the available land. As a result, this system of cultivation has begun to disappear in many parts of Africa.

The increasing scarcity of land has led a lot of farmers to adopt a system of rotational cultivation. This means that they plant different crops in the same fields, leaving some areas fallow for short periods. Much rotational cultivation relies on the use of fertilizers and other agricultural techniques to maintain the fertility of the soil.

In most of North Africa, and many areas south of the Sahara, farmers continuously plant crops in the same fields. This system of permanent cultivation is used where population densities are very high, farmland is very scarce—as in North Africa—or where the soils are naturally very rich—as with the volcanic soils of east Africa. To maintain crop yields and fertility, farmers use modern techniques such as commercial fertilizers, special seed varieties, and irrigation.

In many regions south of the Sahara, these different systems of cultivation overlap. For example, rotational cultivation is often combined with the permanent cultivation of household gardens. Permanent cultivation of cash crops occurs alongside subsistence crops grown under shifting cultivation.

Agricultural Technology and Labor. The majority of farmers in Africa have very little money to invest in modern technology. As a result, most agriculture is very labor intensive, with individuals performing the work on their small plots of land using hoes, hand plows, and other simple tools. Mechanized farm machinery such as tractors and harvesting machines generally are found only on large commercial farms that produce cash crops for export. The price of oil has become far too high for ordinary farmers to use these machines.

In some areas of Africa, especially densely populated regions, farming is often closely connected with livestock grazing. Some farmers use cattle as draft animals to pull plows and spread animal wastes on fields as fertilizer. In other areas—including parts of Nigeria and Kenya—nomadic herdsmen usually live apart from settled farmers, resulting in a lack of access to draft animals and natural fertilizers.

Irrigation and terracing are two agricultural technologies used in Africa. Irrigation is especially important in the desert regions of North Africa, enabling farmers to cultivate land that would normally be unsuitable for agriculture. In some hilly regions—such as in northern Nigeria, CAMEROON, SUDAN, and Ethiopia—farmers have built terraces on hillsides to create fields and protect the soil from erosion.

The division of labor in African agriculture is flexible and diverse. The ways in which different societies organize farm work vary so much from region to region that it is difficult to make generalizations. As a rule though, particularly in subsistence and peasant farming communities, men prepare the land and women plant and harvest the crops and perform most other agricultural tasks. Besides growing food for the family, women also plant vegetables to take to the market, prepare cooked food to sell on the streets of towns and cities, and work as day laborers.

Women in Cameroon remove the husks from ears of maize, or corn. Originally from the Americas, maize has become an important staple food in Africa.

Rice Research

A new type of rice developed in the 1990s has been transforming farming methods in West Africa. The new rice is a cross between Asian rice and traditional varieties grown for more than 3,000 years in Africa. The African rices, with wide, droopy leaves that prevent weeds from sprouting, are resistant to drought and pests. However, many farmers in the region were planting Asian rice, which is less resistant to weeds, drought, and pests but has higher crop yields. The new rice, developed by the West Africa Rice Development Association, combines the best features of both species. It was achieved through the use of biotechnology techniques and a gene bank containing seeds of 1,500 African rices.

LAND REFORMS AND PROBLEMS

Throughout Africa, land traditionally was distributed and assigned according to age-old political and social customs. In some places, decisions about land were made by village chiefs; in others, by democratic village institutions, religious leaders, or elders. Much of the land was owned in common by all the people of a particular village, region, or group.

During the second half of the 1900s, many governments in Africa began to introduce land reforms aimed at changing the traditional land and labor systems. The goal was to create landholdings owned and operated by individuals rather than by groups. It was hoped that such reforms would increase farm production and create more stable agricultural economies. Along with land reform, African governments also encouraged farmers to grow cash crops that could create export income for their countries.

Such policies have contributed to serious problems in African agriculture. Land reform led to confusion and conflicts, as different ethnic and social groups struggled over ownership of land. In some areas, the reforms left some farmers without any land. In others, government attempts to force people to settle elsewhere disrupted traditional societies. This occurred in Tanzania under President Nyerere when farmers were forced to live in large communal settlements based on the Chinese model.

The increased emphasis on cash crops has contributed to shortages of basic food crops, making it difficult for African countries to feed their populations. As a result, many countries now import food. Rapid population growth has added to the problem, creating a demand for larger quantities of food. At the same time, the migration of Africans from rural areas to cities has reduced the number of people engaged in subsistence farming who grow enough to feed themselves.

Environmental conditions and crop failures have added to the problems of agricultural production. Africa has always experienced periods of drought and famine. However, as populations have risen, it has become increasingly difficult for African nations to cope with crop shortages. This situation has been made worse by the lack of cheap long-distance transportation.

High population growth rates, environmental circumstances, and failed economic policies have created an agricultural crisis in many African countries. Forced to import food, governments have had to spend money that could be used to improve their economies and the lives of their people. Instead, they must struggle just to provide for the basic needs of their populations. The challenge of the future will be for African countries to develop more productive, profitable, and dependable agricultural systems. (*See also* **Animals, Domestic; Development, Economic and Social; Hunger and Famine; Irrigation and Flood Control; Labor; Land Ownership; Peasantry and Land Settlement; Plantation Systems; Plants: Varieties and Uses; Women in Africa.**)

AIDS

sub-Saharan referring to Africa south of the Sahara desert

AIDS (acquired immunodeficiency syndrome) is a fatal disorder affecting millions of people around the world. A leading cause of death among adults in sub-Saharan* Africa, AIDS threatens to overwhelm many African nations and disrupt their social and economic development.

AIDS is caused by HIV, a virus that attacks and destroys the body's immune system, making the infected person susceptible to disease. The virus is transmitted primarily through sexual intercourse, transfusions of contaminated blood, and sharing of needles by drug users. Mothers can pass HIV to infants during birth and while breast-feeding them. Each year nearly 500,000 African children are born with HIV.

Figures released by the United Nations in 2000 showed that nearly 14 million Africans had died of AIDS-related illnesses, and 25.3 million were infected with HIV. However, the impact of AIDS is not the same throughout the continent. Although it surfaced first in East Africa, southern Africa is now the hardest hit area. The percentage of people infected with HIV there ranged from about 20 percent in SOUTH AFRICA to about 36 percent in BOTSWANA. The rate of infection was lower in East and West Africa and much lower in North Africa—though the disease is gaining ground in some of those areas as well.

In the early years of the AIDS epidemic, the disease struck mainly in African cities. In recent years, however, the rate of infection in rural areas has been rising dramatically. One reason is the increased movement of people between urban and rural areas. Many rural residents migrate to cities to work, become infected, and then spread the disease when they visit their villages. Rates of infection have been highest in areas along long-distance trucking routes.

A number of other explanations have been advanced for the rapid spread of HIV in sub-Saharan Africa. For one thing, Africans tend to begin sexual activity at a fairly young age and often have sex outside marriage. Lack of education has limited the acceptance of safe sex practices. Experts also note that individuals who have other sexually transmitted diseases (STDs) are more likely to contract HIV. In many parts of Africa, people with STDs may not receive proper treatment because of a shortage of health care services and the high cost of medications produced by Western drug companies.

AIDS poses a tremendous danger to the future of African nations. By reducing the number of productive workers, the disease will create severe labor shortages in industries and agriculture. Schools and hospitals will be understaffed. Large numbers of children will lose their parents to AIDS. Already, the disease has left more than 13 million African children orphaned, and it is estimated that this number will rise to 40 million by 2010. As a result, vast numbers of children may grow up in poverty with few opportunities and little hope.

At present, the prospects for controlling HIV and AIDS in Africa appear dim. Many countries lack the funds for massive education and health care programs. In some nations, officials have failed to acknowledge the scope of the problem. Although some treatments can prolong

the lives of people with AIDS, the cost is beyond the reach of most Africans. Researchers are currently working on a vaccine to prevent HIV infection, but such a remedy may not be available for many years. In the meantime, the best hope is to educate people about the disease and make treatment more widely available. Western drug companies have been criticized for the high prices they charge for drugs used to treat HIV and AIDS. (*See also* **Diseases, Family, Gender Roles and Sexuality, Health Care, United Nations in Africa.**)

Akan Region

* **clan** group of people descended from a common ancestor

The Akan region, an area on the coast of West Africa's Gulf of Guinea, lies between the Bandama River in IVORY COAST and the Volta River in GHANA. During the 1600s, separate, competing states were formed in the northern and southern parts of the region.

Before the 1400s, the region consisted of small communities of Akan clans*. These people lived in relative isolation until traders from the north arrived, attracted by the gold and kola nuts to be found in the Black Volta River region and the Akan forest. This new trade led some Akan people to move north and eventually to found several important states and trading towns.

Europeans arrived on Ghana's coast in the late 1400s, stimulating trade in gold and slaves. The Portuguese arrived first, and were followed by the French, English, and Dutch in the sixteenth century. Later, the Danes, Swedes, and Brandenburgers (traders on the Gold Coast from the Brandenburg Africa Company) arrived in the seventeenth century. Some Akan clans moved south to the coast, where they established a loose confederation known as the Fante states. These states competed for trade with the northern Akan clans. In the 1600s several different Akan states tried to gain control of the region. The most powerful to emerge were the Denkyira, who conquered a large portion of the southern and western Akan region.

In the late 1600s a group of northern Akan chiefs formed the ASANTE state. Over the years, the Asante took over territories in the region and established an empire. They expanded their trading routes and became an important source of slaves for the slave trade.

In 1807 the Asante attacked the Fante, and warfare between the two peoples continued for 11 years. This conflict brought the Asante into contact with the British, who had traded with the Fante for many years. Opposed to the Asante's slave trade, the British sided with their long-time trading partners. In 1824 the British and the Fante attacked the Asante but were badly defeated. The allies had more success two years later, and the conflict was settled in 1831 by a treaty that recognized the independence of the Fante states. To enforce the treaty, Britain expanded its political and economic presence in the area.

In the 1860s a new Asante king tried to conquer the Fante, but the British invaded and defeated the Asante. Britain declared the Fante area a British colony, and in 1896 the Asante state also became part of the British Empire. (*See also* **Colonialism in Africa.**)

Aksum

Aksum

Aksum was a kingdom located in present-day ERITREA and northern ETHIOPIA between about 200 B.C. and A.D. 650. Its capital city of Aksum sat on the western edge of the Eritrean highlands and was for several centuries a powerful and wealthy city.

Historians take a particular interest in Aksum because its ruler, Ezana, converted to Christianity in 340, shortly after the Roman emperor Constantine became a Christian. The form of Christianity practiced in Aksum, called Monophysite, was based on the belief that Jesus Christ was completely divine and not human. When the Catholic Church condemned this view in 451, many Monophysite Christians fled the Byzantine Empire (the eastern portion of the Roman Empire) and settled in Ethiopia. This group probably helped spread the faith among the local population. In fact, the modern city of Aksum still exercises a great deal of influence in the affairs of the ETHIOPIAN ORTHODOX CHURCH.

Although the economy of ancient Aksum was based on farming and the tribute* received from other lands, the main source of the kingdom's wealth was international trade. Archaeological* evidence and written records indicate that by 100 B.C. a series of towns connected the inland capital to the port of Adulis on the Red Sea coast. These towns formed an overland trade route for valuable goods such as ivory, tortoiseshell, and rhinoceros horn. Aksum grew wealthy from exporting these goods to trading partners along the shores of the Red Sea and the Indian Ocean.

* **tribute** payment made by a smaller or weaker party to a more powerful one, often under the threat of force

* **archaeological** referring to the study of past human cultures and societies, usually by excavating ruins

By the late A.D. 200s Aksum began to mint coins of gold, silver, and copper that made it easier to trade with other lands. Most of these coins have been found in southern Arabia, one of the territories that Aksum controlled.

Aksum reached the height of its power and influence in the 500s under King Kaleb. Thereafter, the kingdom suffered a rapid decline and within 100 years of Kaleb's death had lost its trading partners and the territories it had ruled. At the same time soil erosion and the people's overuse of its natural resources weakened Aksum's local economy. All that is left of ancient Aksum are the ruins of the capital, with its giant carved stone columns. These columns were probably grave monuments for the tombs of Aksum's pre-Christian kings.

ALCOHOL

See *Food and Drink.*

Alexandria

Located on a spit of land near the NILE RIVER delta, Alexandria is the second largest city in EGYPT and the country's main port. It was founded in 332 B.C. by Alexander the Great and quickly emerged as the leading city of the Mediterranean region. Renowned in the ancient world as a center of learning, Alexandria possessed the greatest library of the time and attracted scholars from near and far. Although the city remained a major port and trading center after the Arab conquest of Egypt in A.D. 642, it slowly declined over the next several hundred years.

The French occupied Alexandria from 1798 to 1801. Then in the early 1800s the Ottoman viceroy Muhammad Ali brought new life to the city by building a canal to the Nile River and by encouraging foreign traders to settle there. Alexandria thrived as a result of the newly established cotton trade. After the Suez Canal opened in 1869, the city once again became a major trading post between Europe and Asia. During the late 1800s and early 1900s, the population expanded and came to include many nationalities, cultures, and religions.

When Gamal Nasser became Egypt's leader in 1952, however, most of the foreign residents left the city. In recent years Alexandria has developed into a major center of industry and commerce. It is currently home to more than 3 million people.

Algeria

* **fundamentalist** member of a group that emphasizes a strict interpretation of religious beliefs

* **secular** nonreligious; connected with everyday life

A t the end of the 1900s, the North African republic of Algeria was locked in a civil war between Islamic fundamentalists* and the government, which had broad popular support. At the heart of the conflict was a struggle for control over the nation's future—should Algeria remain a secular* state or adopt strict Muslim rule? The war was the most recent chapter in the country's turbulent history, which has included periods of invasion, foreign rule, and internal division.

THE LAND AND ITS PEOPLE

The second largest nation in Africa, Algeria consists of 920,000 square miles of territory. It is bordered on the north by the Mediterranean Sea, with Morocco and Mauritania to the west, and Tunisia and Libya to the east. The land has three distinct climate and geographical zones: the Tell, the Highland Plateau, and the Algerian Sahara desert.

The Tell. A region of fertile hills and valleys, the Tell (from the Arabic word for "hill") runs across the country from Morocco to Tunisia. It has a Mediterranean climate with mild winters and summers and enough rainfall to support crops of grain, citrus fruits, and grapes.

Approximately 90 percent of Algeria's people live and work in the Tell, mostly in agriculture. In addition, the country's principal cities, including Algiers—the capital, Oran, and Annaba, are in the Tell. These modern cities blend Islamic and European influences. The Algerians who live in the cities tend to be more highly educated, more secular in outlook, and more open to Western culture than those from rural areas.

* **savanna** tropical or subtropical grassland with scattered trees and drought-resistant undergrowth

The Highland Plateau. South of the Tell are the Tell Atlas Mountains, which stretch eastward from Morocco. Beyond these mountains is the Highland Plateau. Mostly savanna*, the plateau is marked by shallow depressions that fill with water in the rainy season to form salt lakes called *chotts*. During the dry season, the water in these lakes evaporates, leaving behind salt deposits. Highly prized in ancient times, salt was the original source of Algeria's wealth. Today, the Highland Plateau is home to nearly 7 percent of Algeria's population, and most of the inhabitants make a living by keeping herds of sheep, goats, and cattle.

Algerian Sahara Desert. Along the southern edge of the Highland Plateau lie the Saharan Atlas Mountains. Beyond the mountains is the vast Algerian Sahara. At the heart of this desert loom the Ahaggar Mountains, a volcanic chain that includes Mount Tahat, the highest peak in the country (9,573 feet).

Although the desert includes more than 80 percent of the country's total area, only about 3 percent of the population lives there. Most inhabitants have settled near oases, where deep wells tap into underground springs to provide irrigation for crops of grain and dates. In the desert's harsh climate, temperatures can soar as high as 120ºF. A hot, dusty wind called the sirocco blows northward across the desert to parch the Highland Plateau (for 40 days each summer) and the Tell (for 20 days) before it meets moister, cooler air over the Mediterranean.

Economy. Algeria's wealth has always been tied to its minerals. In the heyday of the trade routes that crossed the Sahara, merchants carried salt south of the desert to exchange it for gold. Today, oil and natural gas buried beneath the desert sands provide the basis for the Algerian economy. Oil and gas bring in 95 percent of Algeria's export earnings and make up a quarter of the country's gross domestic product (GDP)*. Reliance on oil exports, however, has made the economy unstable. In

See map in Minerals and Mining (vol. 3).

* **gross domestic product (GDP)** total value of goods and services produced and consumed within a country

1986 the collapse of worldwide oil prices plunged the nation into a severe economic slowdown from which it has yet to recover.

Throughout history, agriculture—largely in the Tell—was the livelihood of most Algerians. Today, many people work in factories, the government, and service industries. Concentrated in and around the cities, these sectors* attract rural people seeking work. Overall, there is a shortfall of jobs; in the late 1990s, the unemployment rate was about 30 percent.

HISTORY

From earliest times, Algeria's location along the shores of the Mediterranean made it a prime attraction for invaders and settlers from the Middle East and Europe. Controlled by the Roman and Ottoman Empires for various periods of its history, Algeria was ruled by the French for more than 100 years before gaining independence in 1962.

Early History. The original inhabitants of Algeria lived in the Ahaggar region as early as 40,000 years ago, before the Sahara became a desert. Rock paintings dating back about 6,000 years show the diverse wildlife once found in the region: elephants, hippopotamuses, and crocodiles. These are gone today, replaced by species that are more suited to the desert climate.

As the Sahara became a desert, the peoples of the region moved away to find better land for their farms and herds. Some made their way to the coast, founding settlements there by 3000 B.C. About 500 years later, the Phoenicians, a seafaring people from the Middle East, established outposts along the North African coast, including what would later become Algiers.

As the Phoenicians expanded their trade throughout the Mediterranean and into Europe, Rome was drawn by their wealth. In the Punic Wars of the 200s and 100s B.C., the two powers fought in North Africa, Spain, and Sicily. Eventually, Rome gained control of the region.

The Roman era, which lasted until the early A.D. 400s, was a time of relative peace and prosperity. The Romans built roads and military posts, introduced Christianity, and provided a market for Algerian grain. But as the Roman Empire declined, its control over Algeria weakened.

For a time the members of a Christian group known as the Donatists led an independent state in Algeria. This fledgling state fell to the Vandals, who invaded North Africa from Europe. The Vandals, in turn, were driven out of Algeria by the Byzantine Empire, the eastern part of the former Roman Empire.

Arab Invasion. In the 600s invaders from the Arabian peninsula attacked and conquered Algeria. Arab settlers sent to rule the coastal cities mixed with the indigenous* BERBER peoples, producing the Arab-Berber ethnic groups found in the country today. The Arabs also brought Islam, which quickly became the dominant religion of the region, as well as Islamic law and the Arabic language.

In the 1500s, under attack by invaders from Christian Spain, Algeria's Muslims turned to the Ottoman Empire in Turkey for assistance. The

Barbary Pirates

In the 1500s Algeria was a province of the Ottoman Empire, based in Turkey. Algiers became a center for pirates, led by two brothers who were captains in the Turkish navy. The pirates roamed the Mediterranean Sea, launching raids on passing ships. Famous for their fierceness, they were known as the Barbary pirates (from the Latin word for "foreign"). Piracy in the Mediterranean continued into the early 1800s, when navies of the United States and Europe joined forces to bring it to an end.

* **sector**   part; subdivision of society

See map in Archaeology and Prehistory (vol. 1).

* **indigenous**   native to a certain place

19

Algeria

Turkish fleet succeeded in turning back the Spanish, and Algeria came under the control of the Ottoman Empire.

French Colony. The Ottomans ruled Algeria for 300 years. During this time Algeria carried on trade with European countries, particularly France, which was a major importer of Algerian grain. In 1830 France decided to take over Algeria. Using the excuse of a trade dispute, the French attacked Algiers.

The Algerians resisted, but by 1847 France had gained control of the country. To strengthen its hold, France began sending settlers to the region. By 1912 nearly 800,000 had arrived. The French also imposed social and political order on Algeria, replacing Arabic with French as the official language and suppressing Islamic culture. Only French citizens and Algerians who converted to Catholicism enjoyed the rights of citizenship. Most Algerians were excluded from the best land and jobs and denied political rights. It was only a matter of time before the situation exploded into violence.

Independence Movements. The first steps toward an Algerian independence movement occurred in the 1930s, when a group of Algerians

During the 1950s French troops crisscrossed the Algerian countryside in an effort to put down uprisings by rebel bands fighting for independence.

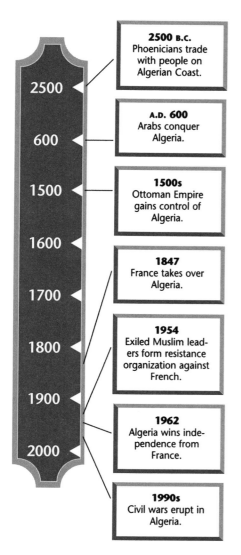

2500 B.C.
Phoenicians trade with people on Algerian Coast.

A.D. 600
Arabs conquer Algeria.

1500s
Ottoman Empire gains control of Algeria.

1847
France takes over Algeria.

1954
Exiled Muslim leaders form resistance organization against French.

1962
Algeria wins independence from France.

1990s
Civil wars erupt in Algeria.

* **nationalize** to bring land, industries, or public works under state control or ownership

* **coup** sudden, often violent overthrow of a ruler or government

* **guerrilla** type of warfare involving sudden raids by small groups of warriors

demanded that Muslims be granted greater rights. The French colonists, recognizing the threat that this posed to their way of life, strenuously opposed any such action. The situation gradually worsened. Relations between Algerian Muslims and French colonists hardened into mutual hatred, and Muslim leaders began to call for armed revolution.

In 1954 several exiled Algerian Muslim leaders, including Ahmed BEN BELLA, met in Egypt to form the National Liberation Front (FLN). In November of that year they launched an attack on government and military sites throughout the country. A fierce and bloody war followed. In 1958, General Charles de Gaulle of France was called in to resolve the crisis. Recognizing that no military solution was possible, de Gaulle announced a referendum in Algeria on independence and opened the vote to Muslims. The French colonists responded with violence, but they had no hope of success. In the referendum, held in 1962, Algeria's population voted nearly unanimously for independence and elected Ben Bella as the first president. By the end of the year, most of the French had fled the country.

Post Independence. President Ben Bella had to deal with a devastated economy and a nation exhausted by decades of war. He promptly nationalized* the oil and natural gas companies and redistributed lands that had been held by the French colonists. He also sought to build ties with other African nations and with other revolutionary governments— such as Cuba, led by Fidel Castro. However, in 1965 Ben Bella was overthrown by a miliary coup* and Colonel Houari BOUMÉDIENNE was installed as president.

When Boumédienne took power, the Algerians were impatient for change. The urban centers were bulging with refugees from the countryside who lacked the skills and the education needed to obtain jobs in the cities. Boumédienne proposed programs to improve services and living conditions for the people. In 1978 he introduced a new constitution, establishing the FLN as the sole legal party. However, Boumédienne died suddenly and was replaced by Colonel Chadli Benjedid in 1979.

When Benjedid assumed leadership, many Algerians felt that the promise of independence remained unfulfilled. The FLN lost much of its popular support as people turned to leaders drawn from Islamic fundamentalist groups. After a series of increasingly violent protests in the 1970s and 1980s, a mass demonstration erupted in 1988 calling for multiparty elections. Benjedid was forced to allow free elections in 1991, with more than 20 political parties participating.

The Islamic Salvation Front (FIS), a radical fundamentalist party, won the majority of seats in the legislature. The FIS leaders announced their plan to impose rigid Islamic rule, patterned after the government then in power in Iran. This touched off a new round of demonstrations, particularly among the trade unions, professional classes, and women, all calling for the election results to be overturned. The military, with support from France and the United States, suspended the constitution and set up a five-member military council to rule the country. The FIS responded by adopting guerrilla* tactics in an effort to regain power.

Algeria

 The Democratic and Popular Republic of Algeria

POPULATION:
31,193,917 (2000 estimated population)

AREA:
919,595 sq. mi. (2,381,740 sq. km)

LANGUAGES:
Arabic (official); French, Berber dialects

NATIONAL CURRENCY:
Algerian dinar

PRINCIPAL RELIGIONS:
Muslim (Sunni) 99%, Christian and Jewish 1%

CITIES:
Algiers (capital), 4,200,000 (1999 est.); Oran, Constantine, Annaba, Batna

ANNUAL RAINFALL:
Varies from 30 in. (760 mm) along the coast to less than 4 in. (100 mm) in the Sahara

ECONOMY:
GDP per capita: U.S. $4,650

PRINCIPAL PRODUCTS AND EXPORTS:
Agricultural: wheat, barley, oats, citrus fruits, olives, grapes, wine, dates, figs, sheep, cattle
Manufacturing: electrical, petrochemical, food processing, light industries
Mining: petroleum, natural gas, iron ore, phosphates, uranium, lead, zinc

GOVERNMENT:
Independence from France, 1962. Multiparty republic. President elected by universal suffrage. Governing bodies: Assemblée Populaire Nationale (legislative house), prime minister and cabinet of ministers appointed by president.

HEADS OF STATE SINCE INDEPENDENCE:
1962–1965 Ahmed Ben Bella
1965–1978 Houari BoumÉdienne
1979–1991 Chadli Benjedid
1991–1998 Liamine Zeroual
1999– Abdelaziz Bouteflika

ARMED FORCES:
122,000

EDUCATION:
Compulsory for ages 6–15; literacy rate 62%

Civil War. The conflict between educated, westernized Algerians who sought a secular, multiparty state and poorer, more religiously centered citizens touched off a civil war. The FIS targeted leaders who spoke against it, including Mohammad Boudiaf, president of the State Council, who was assassinated in 1992. The government's response was equally harsh, imprisoning suspected FIS sympathizers without trial, and resorting at times to torture and execution of such prisoners.

In 1994 General Liamine Zeroual assumed control of Algeria and made some attempts to resolve the conflict. He called for elections to be held in 1997, but barred political parties that based membership on religion or language from participating. This enraged the FIS and other Islamic parties. The Armed Islamic Groups (GIA) called for a jihad, or holy war, against the government. A new and even bloodier phase of civil war began, as GIA supporters embarked on a campaign of terror and violence against anyone thought to be collaborating with the government.

In 1999 new presidential elections were held, and Abdelaziz Bouteflika won. However, charges of fraud accompanied the election. Bouteflika's presidency has failed to reduce the violence raging throughout the country.

Unable to achieve peace, the government provided arms to villagers to use for self-defense. Local units, called *les patriotes,* formed to protect their communities. However, many of these groups have used their weapons to launch revenge attacks against neighboring villages. The violence, which continues to escalate, underscores the profound differences dividing Algerian society. (*See also* **Arabs in Africa, Atlas**

Mountains, Colonialism in Africa, Independence Movements, Islam in Africa, Maghreb, North Africa: Geography and Population, North Africa: History and Cultures, Sahara Desert.)

Algiers

Algiers, the capital of ALGERIA, is situated on a hillside overlooking the Mediterranean Sea. Home to 3.7 million people, it is one of the major cities of North Africa. The various sections of the old city show the different cultures that have influenced Algiers: French-style districts of wide boulevards alternate with Arab sections such as the Casbah, a neighborhood of narrow winding passageways. On the plain spreading to the south and east lies a growing industrial area and new suburbs.

First settled by the ancient Phoenicians, Algiers was destroyed by the Vandals in the A.D. 400s. Rebuilt by BERBERS in the 900s, the city later belonged to the Ottoman Empire. In 1830 the French captured Algiers; they controlled it until 1962, when Algeria won its independence.

After independence, the Algerian government made efforts to modernize the capital. Many rural people migrated to Algiers, replacing departing French settlers who had lived and worked there. By the mid-1960s, Algiers claimed Algeria's highest literacy rate and had the most cars, buses, hospitals, theaters, libraries, museums, and sports complexes. Over the next few decades, industries in the Algiers region produced increasing amounts of agricultural goods, textiles, wood, paper, and mechanical and electrical machinery. Unchecked industrial growth, however, began to damage the surrounding farmland. In the 1980s the government ordered an end to expansion and relocated large numbers of new residents. (*See also* **Architecture**.)

AL-MAHDI

See *Mahdi, al-*.

AL-MANSUR

See *Mansur, al-*.

Amhara

The Amhara and the Tigrinya, indigenous* peoples of ETHIOPIA, make up the group commonly known as Abyssinians. Both the Amhara and the Tigrinya are descendants of the founders of the ancient kingdom of AKSUM, and both speak Semitic languages.

Originally based in the Ethiopian highlands, the Amhara gradually spread out to settle a large area of central Ethiopia. The Tigrinya live

* **indigenous**   native to a certain place

Amhara

mainly in Tigre province and ERITREA. Largely agricultural, both peoples cultivate crops and, to a lesser extent, raise livestock.

Over the centuries the Amhara have dominated the region politically and their culture has spread to neighboring peoples. Most Amhara are followers of Monophysite Christianity, the religion of the old Aksumite kingdom that holds that Jesus Christ is solely divine and not human in nature. Contact with the Amhara has led some Islamic inhabitants of the Ethiopian highlands to adopt Christian customs.

Until modern times, a continuous line of Amhara royalty ruled Ethiopia. These rulers considered themselves to be descendants of Menilek I, who was said to be the son of King Solomon of Jerusalem and the queen of Sheba. The last Ethiopian emperor of this dynasty, HAILE SELASSIE I, was overthrown in 1974. (*See also* **Christianity in Africa**.)

Amin Dada, Idi

ca. 1925–
Ugandan dictator

* **coup** sudden, often violent overthrow of a ruler or government

* **Islam** religion based on the teachings of the prophet Muhammad; religious faith of Muslims

Idi Amin Dada, a member of the Nubi people, ruled UGANDA from 1971 to 1979. Regarded as one of Africa's most ruthless leaders, Amin used murder as a political tool, and may have killed as many as 300,000 people during his reign.

Enlisting in the military as a young man, Amin advanced rapidly. He was one of the few black Ugandans to become an officer before Uganda won its independence in 1962. During the next six years, he reached the rank of major general and was named commander of both the army and the air force. Amin also became a close ally to Uganda's first president, Milton OBOTE. After both men were accused of gold smuggling in 1966, Obote took total control of the country with the support of Amin and the military. However, Obote did not trust Amin and arrested him four years later.

In 1971, while Obote was out of the country, Amin led a coup* and took over the office of president. Amin began by ridding the army of soldiers from Obote's area of northern Uganda, replacing them with loyal troops. He seized foreign-owned businesses (mainly those owned by Indians) and gave them to his supporters. But the new owners looted the companies, leading to the ruin of Uganda's economy. To maintain his power, Amin sought support from traditionally Muslim Arab countries and declared Islam* Uganda's official religion, though few Ugandans were Muslims.

In 1976 Amin gained international attention when he allowed Palestinian hijackers to land a plane full of Israeli hostages at the capital of Entebbe. Israeli commandos later rescued the hostages. He received further attention a year later when several prominent people in Uganda were killed in suspicious circumstances.

In 1978 Amin invaded and seized Tanzanian territory, which led TANZANIA to attack Uganda the following year. Meanwhile, various groups in Uganda that opposed Amin united against him. These rebels joined with the Tanzanian army to defeat Amin's troops, forcing him to flee the country in April 1979. Amin went into exile in Saudi Arabia.

ANCESTORS — See *Death, Mourning, and Ancestors.*

The Republic of Angola is located on the southwestern coast of Africa on the Atlantic Ocean. This former colony of Portugal has had a tumultuous history since gaining independence in 1975. Torn by a long, bitter, and destructive civil war, the nation is still trying to find an end to that conflict.

GEOGRAPHY AND ECONOMY

Angola is the seventh largest country in Africa, with an area greater than Texas and California combined. A small part of the nation—a coastal area called CABINDA—is separated from the rest of Angola by a strip of territory belonging to the neighboring country of CONGO (KINSHASA). Rich in natural resources, Angola has great potential for industry and economic prosperity. However, since independence, frequent civil unrest has slowed Angola's development.

The capital of Angola is Luanda, a coastal city that was once a major slave-trading port for the Portuguese. Although it boasts modern skyscrapers, an international airport, and a state-run university, Luanda has been severely damaged by the civil war. In addition, refugees fleeing the fighting in the countryside are crowding the city's poorer sections and overwhelming public services.

Landforms. Nearly two thirds of Angola consists of vast interior plateaus and highlands—including the Kongo Highlands, the Malanje Plateau, and the Central Highlands. These features average 3,150 to 4,430 feet in elevation, with some peaks as high as 8,465 feet.

To the west of these areas, the land falls in a series of dramatic escarpments* to a narrow coastal plain, cut by fertile river valleys and dotted with natural harbors. Most of Angola's rivers start in the interior highlands and flow through the coastal plain to the sea. Only a few of these are navigable* for any distance inland. Several rivers are tributaries* of the CONGO RIVER and the ZAMBEZI RIVER. One of Angola's major rivers, the Kubango, flows into the Okavango Swamp—a vast swampland in northern BOTSWANA.

Climate. With the exception of the temperate Central Highlands, Angola's climate is primarily tropical. Rainfall in the tropical regions is seasonal, occurring mainly between October and May. Parts of southern and eastern Angola have a drier climate, and the southernmost part of the country borders the great KALAHARI DESERT. The Benguela Current—a cold, northward-flowing ocean current—brings both a dry climate and rich fishing grounds to Angola's coastal region.

Vegetation and Wildlife. Much of Angola is covered with savanna*. In the north these grasslands have scattered trees, while in the south the

* **escarpment**   long, clifflike ridge of land or rock

* **navigable**   deep and wide enough to provide passage for ships

* **tributary**   river that flows into another river

* **savanna**   tropical or subtropical grassland with scattered trees and drought-resistant undergrowth

25

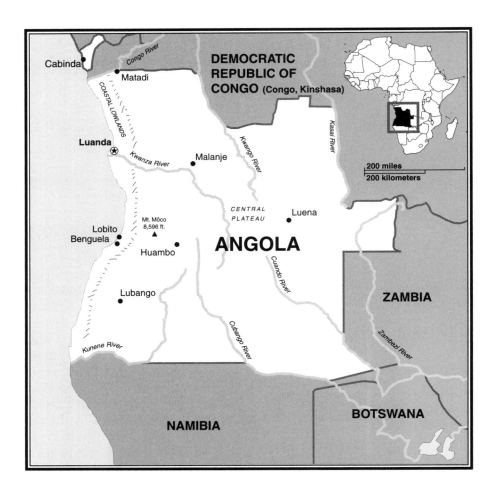

See map in Archaeology and Prehistory (vol. 1).

savanna consists of low, thorny shrubs. Dense rain forests are scattered through the northern half of the country, primarily in Cabinda. Angola once had more extensive rain forests, but since colonial times many have been cut down by the logging industry and to make way for agriculture. One of the few plants that survive in the desert regions of far southwestern Angola is the tumboa, an unusual plant with a very deep root and two wide 10-foot-long leaves that spread along the ground.

The wildlife of Angola is typical of other grassland regions of Africa. Mammals include elephants, hippopotamuses, rhinoceroses, giraffes, zebras, wildebeests, leopards, lions, and various types of antelopes and monkeys. Angola is also home to many species of birds and a great variety of reptiles, including crocodiles. Among the most dangerous animal species in Angola is an insect—the tsetse fly, which carries diseases that harm both humans and livestock. Marine life thrives in the ocean off Angola's coast, especially in the waters swept by the Benguela Current.

Agriculture, Forestry, and Fishing. Farming is the main economic activity in many areas of Angola. About 80 percent of the Angolan people are engaged in subsistence farming, in which families grow only enough food for their own use. One of the principal food crops is manioc (or cassava), a plant with thick, starchy roots that are cooked and

* **maize**   corn

* **cash crop**   crop grown primarily for sale rather than for local consumption

See map in Minerals and Mining (vol. 3).

* **first millennium** A.D.   years from A.D. 1 to 1000

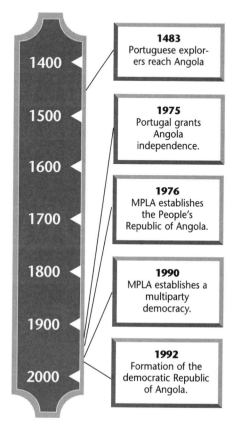

1400	**1483** Portuguese explorers reach Angola
1500	**1975** Portugal grants Angola independence.
1600	
1700	**1976** MPLA establishes the People's Republic of Angola.
1800	**1990** MPLA establishes a multiparty democracy.
1900	
2000	**1992** Formation of the democratic Republic of Angola.

eaten like potatoes. Other major crops include maize*, potatoes, beans, millet (a type of grain), bananas, peanuts, rice, and wheat.

During the colonial period, Angola grew several profitable cash crops* for export, including cotton and coffee. These commercial crops declined dramatically after independence as a result of changing economic policies and years of civil war. Nevertheless, crops such as tobacco, coffee, bananas, sisal, cocoa, sugarcane, and cotton are still grown commercially.

Subsistence farmers in Angola raise a variety of livestock, including sheep, goats, pigs, and poultry. Cattle raising is most successful in southern Angola, where the disease-spreading tsetse fly is less of a problem than in other areas of the country.

Forestry is concentrated in Cabinda, where the dense rain forests provide valuable lumber. Portuguese colonists developed a thriving fishing industry off the coast of Angola, which supplied fish for both export and local markets. However, after 1975, the local fish population shrank and Angola's fishing industry became less significant.

Industry and Mining. Prior to independence, Angola enjoyed expanding industrial activity, especially manufacturing and construction. As with commercial agriculture, the upheavals following independence disrupted Angolan industry and caused it to decline.

Manufacturing in Angola today is focused on fulfilling domestic needs rather than on producing goods for export. The principal manufacturing activities are oil refining, food processing, brewing, textile making, and the production of construction materials. One major manufacturing center is the city of Luanda. The electricity needed to run Angolan industry comes from hydroelectric plants that harness the energy of the country's great rivers.

Mining plays a very important role in Angola's economy. The country's principal exports are petroleum and diamonds. Petroleum alone, most coming from Cabinda, accounts for more than 90 percent of Angola's export income. Although Angola's iron mines have been inactive since 1975, the nation produces other minerals including phosphates, manganese, and copper. The country also has deposits of natural gas.

HISTORY AND GOVERNMENT

In ancient times, hunting and gathering societies inhabited the area that is now Angola. Sometime during the first millennium A.D.* large migrations from other parts of southern Africa brought Bantu-speaking peoples to the region. These groups eventually established a number of independent, centralized kingdoms, the most important of which was the Kongo. Angola later took its name from another early kingdom, known as Ngola.

The Colonial Period. Portuguese explorers reached Angola in 1483. They traded with the inhabitants and worked to convert them to Christianity. Over the next few centuries Portugal became increasingly involved in the African SLAVE TRADE, and several Angolan kingdoms were

Angola

* **nationalist** devoted to the interests and culture of one's country

* **guerrilla** type of warfare involving sudden raids by small groups of warriors

* **communist** relating to communism, a system in which land, goods, and the means of production are owned by the state or community rather than by individuals

* **Cold War** period of tense relations between the United States and the Soviet Union following World War II

eventually destroyed because they resisted SLAVERY. Portuguese settlers soon dominated the coast of Angola and organized the local economy around supplying slaves to Brazil, Portugal's South American colony.

Portugal's claims to rule the lands and people of Angola were officially recognized by other European governments in 1891. Then Portugal extended its authority beyond the coastal region of Angola. This expansion led to a dramatic growth in export products, primarily cash crops grown by Portuguese settlers. Some Angolan groups were fairly successful in competing economically with the Portuguese colonists. Nonetheless, all came under Portuguese control between 1890 and 1922.

The further extension of Portuguese colonial power in the early 1900s created great hardship for both Africans and Afro-Portuguese—people of both African and Portuguese ancestry. Many of these people were pushed out of the administrative and commercial activities they dominated in earlier years, and they had few opportunities to achieve economic success. As a result, nationalist* movements emerged in Luanda and other coastal cities. Nationalist leaders spoke out against forced labor, racism, and other abuses, and called for Angolan independence.

When Angola officially became an overseas province of Portugal in 1951, the Angolan people faced more mistreatment by Portuguese authorities. Tensions mounted and led to a serious rebellion against Portuguese rule in 1961. This proved to be a turning point in Angola's history, as increasing numbers of people were drawn into the struggle for independence. By the end of the 1960s several nationalist groups had launched guerrilla* operations against the Portuguese government. Each group also competed for power.

An Independent Angola. Portugal yielded Angola its independence on November 11, 1975. However, it did not formally transfer power to any one of the competing nationalist groups. One group, the Popular Movement for the Liberation of Angola (MPLA), gained control of most of the country and founded a communist* state called the People's Republic of Angola in 1976.

Rivalries continued between the three main groups—the MPLA, FNLA (National Front for the Liberation of Angola), and UNITA (National Union for the Total Independence of Angola)—fueling a long and bitter civil war. Cold War* politics contributed to the strife because the MPLA had support from the Soviet Union and Cuba, while UNITA had the backing of SOUTH AFRICA and the United States. In addition, the Angolan government was aiding the neighboring country of NAMIBIA in its fight for independence from South Africa. As Angola's complex struggle dragged on, it hindered economic progress and efforts to move ahead with social programs.

Signs of hope for an end to the fighting appeared in the late 1980s. Talks between Angola, Cuba, South Africa, and the United States led to a series of agreements concerning Namibian independence and the withdrawal of Cuban troops that had been supporting the MPLA. When the last Cuban forces left Angola in 1991, peace finally seemed possible.

In 1990 the MPLA had voted to turn itself into a democratic party, establish a multiparty system, and create policies that gave individuals and companies a larger role in the economy. These changes led to the establishment of a new democratic government and to the birth of the Republic of Angola in 1992. Since 1979 Angolan politics have been dominated by two individuals—José Eduardo dos Santos, the nation's president and MPLA leader, and Jonas Savimbi, the leader of UNITA. Each enjoys support from different ethnic groups within the country.

Despite the establishment of a democracy, progress in Angola has not come easily. The economy has been slow to develop and improve, and smuggling—mainly of diamonds—has caused great damage. Education and medical care are inadequate, malnutrition is widespread, and infant deaths are common. Moreover, the MPLA and UNITA continue to compete fiercely for control. Since 1992 fighting has broken out several times in various parts of the country, and a return to full-scale civil war remains a possibility. Even in times of relative peace, many Angolans are killed or injured by the millions of land mines still hidden in the ground.

PEOPLE AND CULTURES

The majority of Angolans are members of various Bantu-speaking groups, each with a distinctive culture and language. Other Angolans are of Portuguese or other European ancestry, and a few isolated bands of a Khoisan group known as the !Kung live in the remote southeastern corner of the country. Portuguese is the official language and is spoken by

A parade held in Luanda, the Angolan capital, in 1975 to celebrate the country's independence from Portugal.

Angola

 Republic of Angola

POPULATION:
10,600,000(estimated population)

AREA:
481,351 sq. mi. (1,246,700 sq. km)

LANGUAGES:
Portuguese (official); Bantu languages (at least 55)

NATIONAL CURRENCY:
Kwanza

PRINCIPAL RELIGIONS:
Traditional 47%, Roman Catholic 38%, Protestant 15%

CITIES:
Luanda (capital), 2,677,000 (2000 est.); Lobito, Benguela, Malanje, Huambo, Cabinda, Lubango

ANNUAL RAINFALL:
Varies from 0 in southwestern coastal desert to 70 in. (1,780 mm) in extreme north

ECONOMY:
GDP per capita: U.S. $1,000

PRINCIPAL PRODUCTS AND EXPORTS:
Agricultural: coffee, sisal, cotton, tobacco, sugarcane, bananas, manioc, corn, timber, fish, livestock
Manufacturing: food and beverage processing, textiles, cement, petroleum refining, fish processing, brewing, tobacco products
Mining: petroleum, diamonds, iron ore, copper, feldspar, phosphates, gold, bauxite, uranium

GOVERNMENT:
Independence from Portugal, 1975. President elected by universal suffrage. Governing bodies: 220-member Assembleia Nacional (elected), Council of Ministers appointed by President.

HEADS OF STATE SINCE INDEPENDENCE:
1975–1979 Antonio Agostinho Neto
1979– José Eduardo dos Santos

ARMED FORCES:
114,000 (2000 est.)

EDUCATION:
Compulsory for ages 7–15; literacy rate 40%

See color plate 7, vol. 3.

many Angolans. However, most groups also speak their own native languages.

As Bantu-speaking groups settled throughout present-day Angola, each formed a culture based on the particular type of environment in which they lived. The largest group is the Ovimbundu. They live mainly in the Central Highlands of Angola, where the climate is well suited to farming. Over time, the Ovimbundu have developed extensive agricultural communities with large populations. Those living in drier areas to the south raise cattle as well. Many Ovimbundu have migrated to the cities of Benguela, Lobito, and Luanda.

The second largest group in Angola, the Mbundu, dominates the capital city of Luanda and other coastal towns as well as the Malanje highlands to the east. The culture of the Mbundu has its roots in the ancient warrior state called Ngola. Among the many other groups in Angola are the Ngangela, Ovambo, and Chokwe.

Although some Angolans continue to follow traditional religions, most have adopted Christianity. Roman Catholicism is particularly well established among the Ovimbundu. Various Protestant faiths have strong followings among other Bantu groups.

Despite the influence of European culture and Christianity, most Angolan peoples still share certain Bantu traditions. Extended families are central to social life, polygamy* is common, and ancestors are deeply respected. Forms of witchcraft are still practiced in many areas, even among people who have converted to Christianity. Another ancient tradition that survives today is Angola's rich oral literature—stories that have been passed down for many generations.

* **polygamy** marriage in which a man has more than one wife or a woman has more than one husband

The country's rural inhabitants often follow the same traditions and ways of life their ancestors did. Others, especially city dwellers, have adopted more modern lifestyles. In every region and walk of life, Angolans retain long-standing ethnic loyalties and distinctions. The many differences that enrich Angola's culture also continue to fuel the nation's political unrest. (*See also* **Bantu Peoples; Colonialism in Africa; Diseases; Ethnic Groups and Identity; Forests and Forestry; Independence Movements; Languages; Livestock Grazing; Minerals and Mining; Neto, Agostinho; Religion and Ritual**.)

Animals, Domestic

* **domesticated** raised by humans as farm animals or pets

* **evolution** changes in groups of organisms that occur over time

Africans have been raising animals for their own use for thousands of years. Species of domesticated* animals spread slowly southward through Africa, beginning around 3000 B.C. or earlier, and livestock herding became a traditional way of life across broad regions of the continent. Cattle, in particular, have played a central role in the social, economic, and religious lives of many African peoples.

Domestication. The process of domestication begins with wild animals. The definition of domestication states that animals have been domesticated when they have been worked into the social structure of a human community as objects that people can own, exchange, buy, sell, and inherit. In biological terms, domestication is something like evolution*. A small number of wild animals are separated from the other members of their species. Over time, these animals become used to living with humans, who may control their breeding to emphasize certain characteristics.

In order to be domesticated, an animal must have a temperament that allows it to accept human control and to live in close contact with people and other animals. It must also breed well in captivity. Cattle, sheep, and goats have these qualities. In addition, elephants are occasionally trained for work, and in ancient times they were used in war. Other potentially useful animals—such as antelope—do not have these traits, which probably explains why they have remained wild.

Although a few types of animals seem to have been domesticated in Africa, many species became part of the human community first in Asia and entered northeastern Africa from the Near East or Arabia. The ancient Egyptians had dogs, cats, and all of the kinds of domestic livestock now found in Africa. It took a long time for domesticated species to spread southward, however. Most African groups probably did not adopt such animals until their populations had grown too large to be supported by hunting. Disease, especially sleeping sickness (trypanosomiasis) carried by the tsetse fly, kept some animals from thriving very far south of the Sahara.

African Cattle. Africa has long been a melting pot for different kinds of cattle. Rock paintings found in mountains of the central Sahara suggest that people were herding and milking cattle there as early as 6,500 years ago, when the region was wetter and greener than it is today. A

Animals, Domestic

* **pastoralist** related to or dependent on livestock herding

* **ritual** religious ceremony that follows a set pattern

* **bridewealth** property paid by a groom's family to that of his future wife

* **vulnerable** open to harm or attack

thousand years later, livestock herding was well established in the Sahara. Pastoralist* groups tended longhorn and shorthorn cattle originally domesticated in Europe and Asia, as well as native shorthorn cattle domesticated in North Africa. Beginning around 5,000 years ago, the growing dryness of the Sahara drove these peoples south and east. They introduced cattle to the Nile Valley, Ethiopia, and northern Kenya.

Around the same time zebu, or humped cattle, from India and western Asia were brought to Ethiopia. They crossbred with the longhorn and shorthorn cattle, producing a new breed called the sanga, which spread through central and southern Africa. Since then, crossbreeding has created dozens of varieties of cattle, including newer zebu breeds that are replacing the sanga in parts of northern and eastern Africa. Tsetse flies and parasites have kept cattle from becoming numerous in Africa's rain forest regions, although efforts are being made to introduce breeds that are resistant to sleeping sickness.

The many breeds of African cattle are put to various uses. Some herding peoples keep the animals mainly for milk, while other groups eat the meat as well. Cattle are frequently used to pull plows, turn waterwheels or grain mills, and carry loads. Sometimes cattle are ridden. In many herding societies, cattle are regarded not only as a convenient source of food but also as a living symbol of well-being and prosperity—both spiritual and economic. The pastoral peoples of Kenya do not kill their cattle for food, although they consume milk and blood from living animals and use the hides of dead ones. Cattle are important in many old African rituals*, including sacrifice and the giving of bridewealth* from a groom's family to a bride's family.

Beasts of Burden. The dromedary, or one-humped Arabian camel, is found across the North African desert and the lands along its southern edge. All dromedaries are domesticated. About 70 percent of the world's camels live in the Sahel, northern Kenya, and the lowlands of northeastern Africa, including Egypt. Because camels are extremely vulnerable* to diseases such as sleeping sickness, they cannot survive in wetter regions inhabited by the tsetse fly. In the Sahel and in the northeastern lowlands, nomadic herders raise camels almost entirely for their milk production, while in western Sudan and parts of Kenya, camels are used for meat and transport.

In northern Sudan and North Africa, camels are used primarily for riding and carrying loads. The main advantage of these animals is that they require much less water than cattle. They can tolerate desert conditions and carry loads of up to 350 pounds over long distances. For hundreds of years caravans—groups of traders and travelers journeying together—have crossed the Sahara with the help of camels. As recently as the early 1900s, traditional salt-trading caravans included as many as 20,000 animals.

Horses came to Egypt from western Asia about 3,500 years ago. In many parts of the continent they suffer both from sleeping sickness and from African horse disease—an illness that can kill 90 percent of a herd. Most horses are found in North Africa, the Saharan and Sahelian regions, and parts of western Africa. Horses that were originally brought by European settlers live in South Africa.

Unlike horses, donkeys were domesticated in Africa in the Nile Valley around 6,000 years ago. More than half the donkeys in Africa today are located near the Nile region, in northeastern Africa, and the Sahel. People ride donkeys and use them to pull plows and carry firewood, water, and other loads.

Animals Raised for Food and Other Products. Domestic sheep from western Asia were brought to Egypt 5,000 years ago. African sheep today are descended from several basic types, some of which have fat tails or rumps that are an extremely valuable food resource. Sheep throughout Africa produce milk and meat. Pastoralist groups in northwestern and northeastern Africa favor indigenous* breeds that tolerate dry conditions. In southern Africa, European settlers introduced breeds such as the merino and Blackhead Persian sheep for fine wool production.

Goats—also first domesticated in western Asia—have evolved over the centuries into various African breeds. All of them are used for meat and skins, although some are milked as well. In the Sahel region on the

* **indigenous**   native to a certain place

Dromedaries (one-humped camels) like this one can survive without water longer than any other mammal. This trait makes them ideally suited for life in the desert regions of northern Africa.

Animals, Domestic

See color plate 2, vol. 4.

fringes of the Sahara, medium-sized goats have adapted to the area's very dry grazing lands. One such goat breed, the Red Sokoto, has a very fine hide prized by the leather workers of Morocco and Nigeria. In wetter areas of western Africa and Sudan, farmers raise smaller animals called dwarf goats. Angora goats were brought to southern Africa in the 1800s, and since then the region has become a major producer of mohair—the Angora goat's long, wooly hair.

In the past, pigs have not been very important in Africa. Muslim peoples have religious restrictions against eating their meat. In addition, pigs are better suited to life on a farm than to the pastoral lifestyle of many African peoples. Pigs are also vulnerable to many African diseases and parasites. Most of the continent's domestic pigs are raised on large, European-style commercial farms. However, pigs are gradually being introduced into the farming systems of indigenous peoples, where they provide meat in areas that lack other meat sources.

Various smaller animals are also raised for food in Africa. The guinea fowl, a chicken-like bird, is native to Africa and was domesticated there. European explorers later carried it to other parts of the world. Africans also raise chickens. In some parts of western Africa, people have bred the giant African rat and the cane rat as food animals.

Many domesticated animals in Africa, like this donkey, are used to pull carts or carry passengers.

Crossbreeding. Over the last 2,000 years, African domestic animals have been crossbred with foreign breeds brought by Arab and Asian traders and, more recently, by colonial settlers from Europe. The combination of evolution and controlled breeding produced many new breeds with distinctive features, such as the rounded horns of cattle from the region of Lake Chad in the Sahel.

During the twentieth century, Africans called for improved livestock—animals that would be more productive than African breeds and better suited to the African environment than foreign livestock. This demand led to many experimental breeding programs. For example, the native cattle of southern Ethiopia, which can survive in a semidesert environment, were crossbred with cattle from northern Europe that produce large quantities of milk and beef. Such practices increase production of beef and milk in the short term, but crossbreeding may have serious long-term effects on the ecosystem. The unique genetic makeup of local breeds of livestock may be lost in the process, and new breeds may have less resistance than the native animals to diseases or to environmental stresses such as drought.

People now recognize that long-established domestic species are as much a part of the African environment as wildlife. As a result, some livestock "improvement" projects have been halted, and Africans are making an effort to preserve the remaining herds of purely indigenous livestock. (*See also* **Agriculture, Climate, Diseases, Ecosystems, Livestock Grazing, Pests and Pest Control, Wildlife and Game Parks.**)

ANIMALS, WILD

See *Wildlife and Game Parks.*

Annan, Kofi

1938–
Ghanaian diplomat

Elected Secretary-General of the United Nations (UN) in 1997, Kofi Annan is the first Secretary-General from Africa south of the Sahara. This diplomat from GHANA has worked for the UN since 1962, except for a brief period in the 1970s when he served as Ghana's director of tourism.

Before embarking on his career in diplomacy, Annan attended colleges and graduate schools in Ghana, the United States, and Switzerland. He holds a bachelor's degree in economics and a master's degree in management. He is fluent in English, French, and several African languages.

Over the years, Annan has held several posts within the UN. He began as a budget officer with the World Health Organization in Geneva, Switzerland. Later, he served with the UN Economic Commission for Africa in Addis Ababa, ETHIOPIA. While Under Secretary-General in the mid-1990s, he oversaw UN peacekeeping operations in SOMALIA and Bosnia and Herzegovina.

As Secretary-General, Annan has focused on the international community's commitment to help Africa's developing nations. Annan has

also worked at improving relations between the UN and the United States, which were strained in the early 1990s. (*See also* **United Nations in Africa**.)

Antananarivo

Located on hills overlooking the Ikopa and Betsiboka Rivers, Antananarivo is the capital and largest city of MADAGASCAR. A king of the Merina people called Andrianjaka conquered the site in the early 1600s. Antananarivo, which means "city of a thousand," was named for the guard of 1,000 men who defended it after Andrianjaka's conquest.

By 1800 the Merina kingdoms established control over Madagascar, and Antananarivo became the center of the most important of those states. The Merina restricted access to the city by refusing to build roads and sometimes banning Westerners. Nevertheless, missionaries, traders, and architects eventually made their way to the city and brought European influence with them.

When the French made Madagascar a colony in 1896, they renamed the city Tananarive. During the early 1900s they renovated the city, widening its streets and building roads and rail lines to connect it to the coast. While under French rule, the city's population increased by almost 200,000 people.

Madagascar achieved independence in 1960, and the city regained its original name after a revolution in 1972. Today Antananarivo is home to nearly one million people, and it remains the economic and political center of the country.

Apartheid

* **discrimination** unfair treatment of a group

Apartheid, a system of racial segregation, was official government policy in the Republic of SOUTH AFRICA from 1948 to 1994. Under apartheid, South African blacks, Asians, and people of mixed ancestry called "Coloureds" were systematically separated from white society, deprived of any participation in government, and subjected to all forms of discrimination*.

The idea of white supremacy and racial discrimination had been accepted in South Africa before 1948, and white South African governments had put various segregationist policies into effect. However, it was not until after the 1948 elections, won by the pro-segregation National Party, that these policies became law.

During the 1950s and 1960s, the South African government passed a number of laws that classified people by race. These laws deprived blacks, Coloureds, and Asians of most basic rights—taking away their property, restricting their movement and activities within the country, and forcing blacks to relocate to special "reserves" apart from white society. The laws affected millions of people. They segregated South Africans in every aspect of life and gave a tiny white minority total control over the nation.

By the 1960s other nations had begun to criticize South Africa for its apartheid policies. At the same time, increasing numbers of black South

Africans started to protest against apartheid laws. Partly in response, the government accelerated a policy for creating independent, self-governing "homelands" where black South Africans could develop their own societies. This policy, designed to further the separation of blacks, proved a failure. The homelands consisted of poor quality lands, often broken up into small blocks of territory. They did not have the resources to become economically self-sufficient and truly independent.

As a result of international pressure, increasing unrest within South Africa, and the worsening of economic conditions in the homelands, the South African government was forced to abandon its apartheid policies. In 1991 the government under President De Klerk repealed* the basic apartheid laws. Three years later, the adoption of a new constitution gave equal rights to all South Africans. Despite this change, apartheid has left behind a history of racial conflict, poverty, and inequalities in education, housing, and welfare that will affect South Africa for many years to come. (*See also* **Afrikaner Republics; Biko, Steve; Cape Coloured People; De Klerk, Frederik Willem; Mandela, Nelson; Southern Africa, History; Tutu, Desmond Mpilo; Verwoerd, Hendrik Frensch.**)

* **repeal**   to undo a law

Arabs in Africa

Arabs have lived in Africa since at least the A.D. 600s, when people from the Arabian peninsula conquered EGYPT and LIBYA. Arabs eventually controlled much of North Africa. Arab culture—including the Arabic language and the practice of Islam—has been so widely adopted that Egypt, Libya, ALGERIA, TUNISIA, and MOROCCO are now considered to be part of the Arab world. Other regions of Africa have also been influenced by contacts with Arab culture, primarily through trade.

North Africa. In 640 an Arab force invaded Egypt, then part of the Byzantine Empire (the eastern portion of the Roman Empire). From Egypt, various Arab generals moved to the west taking over the northwest African coast. This territory, known as the MAGHREB, was inhabited by the BERBERS, who surrendered in large numbers to the invaders and adopted Islam. By 705 the Maghreb had become a province under the control of the Muslim Umayyad dynasty. As colonial rulers, the Arabs brought their religion, customs, and language to the region.

Eastern Africa. Eastern Africa lies across the Red Sea from the Arabian peninsula, the birthplace of Islam and much of Arab culture. People and goods traveled between the two regions well before the rise of Islam in the 600s.

ETHIOPIA was one of the first areas in eastern Africa to be influenced by Arab culture. By about A.D. 100, people from southern Arabia had reached Ethiopia by sea, bringing their language and their ability to build in stone. Trading relations between Arabs and the local people contributed to the emergence of the Aksumites, who founded the kingdom of AKSUM in the Ethiopian highlands. Ethiopians also crossed the Red Sea into southern Arabia.

37

Arabs in Africa

By the 900s many peoples along the coast of SOMALIA and the interior lowlands had converted to Islam, and a number of Islamic states had been established. These states controlled trade in the region and posed a threat to the Christian communities that had developed in Ethiopia.

To the west of Ethiopia, NUBIA (in present-day SUDAN) consisted of a number of Christian kingdoms. By the 1300s these kingdoms had fallen to Muslims from Egypt. Their defeat increased the threat of a Muslim invasion of the Christian state of Ethiopia. Migrating Arabs intermarried with the people of Nubia and introduced the Arabic language and the practice of Islam, both of which spread rapidly throughout much of the southern Nile valley.

* **secession** formal withdrawal from an organization or country

In modern times, Arab Muslims have supported the secession* of ERITREA from Ethiopia. To counter the Muslim pressure, Ethiopia has sought other allies, including the nation of Israel. Meanwhile, Muslim groups in Sudan have tried to make the country entirely Muslim and Arab. This effort has led to periodic outbreaks of genocide* against the non-Muslims in southern Sudan by Arabs wishing to take their land and control its oil resources.

* **genocide** deliberate and systematic killing of a particular ethnic, religious, or national group

The Swahili Coast. Known to the ancient Arabs as the land of Zanj, the Swahili coast runs from present-day Somalia to MOZAMBIQUE. Easily reached by sea from southern Arabia, this region was an ideal location for trade between Africans and Arabs even before the rise of Islam. Later, Arab merchants settled in the area's growing city-states, such as Mombasa and Kilwa. By A.D. 900 the eastern African coast had emerged as a prosperous commercial center.

Islam became a major force along the Swahili coast. By adapting to local traditions, the religion gained new followers. Some people converted to Islam because it opened up opportunities for commerce and social advancement. The blending of Arab and African traditions in this region also led to the emergence in the 1000s and 1100s of the Swahili civilization. After reaching a peak in the 1200s and 1300s, this civilization declined when the region was colonized by people from Portugal and from Oman on the Arabian peninsula.

Western Africa. Trade, intermarriage, and shared religious beliefs shaped the relations between Arabs in North Africa and the peoples of western Africa. Although western Africa never experienced significant Arab migration, Islamic religion and culture took hold and spread in the region. Islamic traditions coexisted with local customs and beliefs. In many West African kingdoms, educated Muslims played key roles in administration and diplomacy*. The work of Islamic scholars from the Niger River region (in present-day MALI) became famous throughout the Muslim world.

* **diplomacy** practice of managing relations between nations without warfare

In the mid-1700s a strict Islamic religious movement swept through much of western Africa. When Europeans arrived in Africa, they were faced with this intense religious culture, and it influenced their policies during the colonial period. Arab influence is still very strong in parts of MAURITANIA, Mali, NIGER, and CHAD. In these lands, as well as in other parts of Africa, Arab culture is admired; as a result, many people claim to have Arab ancestors.

Colonial and Postcolonial Periods. Contact between Arabs and Africans south of the Sahara desert—including trade and migration—decreased during the colonial period. The policies of the European colonial governments altered the ties that had existed between Africa and the Arab world. The Europeans replaced Islamic learning with Western education, substituted the Roman alphabet for the Arabic one in the writing of many African languages, and stressed Arab involvement in the African SLAVE TRADE. Although the struggle against European colonialism brought Arab and African leaders closer together, the connection between them was based on nationalism* rather than on commerce or culture.

* **nationalism**   devotion to the interests and culture of one's country

In 1963 African and Arab resistance to colonialism led to the formation of the ORGANIZATION OF AFRICAN UNITY (OAU). The OAU played a significant role in strengthening relations between the two groups. Despite some suspicions and mistrust on both sides, African and Arab leaders managed to work together on matters of mutual interest, such as economic development. Numerous African nations, including Egypt, Libya, Sudan, Tunisia, Morocco, Algeria, Mauritania, Somalia, and DJIBOUTI also joined the Arab League, a regional organization of Arab states.

Muslim schools, such as this one in Fès, Morocco, educate young people through study of the Qur'an, the sacred text of Islam.

Arabs in Africa

* **sub-Saharan** referring to Africa south of the Sahara desert

In 1967 many of the nations of sub-Saharan* Africa supported Egypt in the Suez Canal war against Israel. However, some more recent conflicts in Africa—such as a civil war in Chad—have strained Afro-Arab relations by dividing Arabs and Arabic-speaking or Muslim Africans. Intervention in African affairs by Arab leaders such as Muammar al-QADDAFI of Libya has also frightened some African leaders and persuaded them to seek help from the West to counter Arab power.

* **Cold War** period of tense relations between the United States and the Soviet Union following World War II

Since the end of the Cold War*, some leaders in sub-Saharan Africa have become alarmed by the increasingly political role of Islam in North Africa and by attempts to make it a powerful force in other African nations with large Muslim communities. At the same time, however, a number of Muslim nations in North Africa have experienced internal disputes over territory and other matters. These unresolved issues restrain the relationship between Africa and the Arab world. (*See also* **Ethnic Groups and Identity, Islam in Africa, Languages, North Africa: Geography and Population, North Africa: History and Cultures, Sudanic Empires of Western Africa, Trade.**)

Archaeology and Prehistory

* **archaeological** referring to the study of past human cultures and societies, usually by excavating ruins

Africa's archaeological* heritage is both ancient and rich. Several million years ago, the first ancestors of humans emerged in Africa. About 100,000 years ago, the first modern people appeared there as well. Since that time, a pageant has unfolded across the continent's vast and varied landscapes. Multitudes of cultures have emerged, peoples have migrated, empires have risen and fallen, and Africans have interacted with traders and invaders from other parts of the world.

Because many African cultures did not use written language until the last century or two, historical records of Africa's past are rare. However, bricks and stones, broken pots and buried beads, and graves and bones may speak as clearly as words on a page to archaeologists, paleontologists*, and others trained to interpret them. Archaeology, the study of the physical traces left by people of the past, is the major source of information about how Africans have lived at various times in the course of their long history.

* **paleontologist** scientist who studies prehistoric life through fossils and other remains

The work of archaeologists is not limited to studying grand and well-known sites such as the PYRAMIDS of ancient EGYPT. As they discover prehistoric wall paintings in caves in the SAHARA DESERT, excavate ancient royal cities in western Africa, and unearth tools from centuries-old villages in central Africa, archaeologists are painting an increasingly complex and vivid picture of Africa's past.

INTRODUCTION TO AFRICAN ARCHAEOLOGY

African archaeology is as diverse as the continent's cultures and geographical regions. The objects it studies range from the simple stone tools used by ancient human ancestors to the ruins of great civilizations. African archaeology not only reveals something of the continent's most distant past, it also provides a background for understanding the traditions and roots of the many ethnic groups that live in Africa today.

Changing Views of the African Past. Ideas about the African past have changed since the mid-1900s. Before that time, Africa was sometimes called a "continent without a past." People outside Africa associated ancient Egypt with other great civilizations of the ancient world. They regarded North Africa and modern Egypt, which had been colonized and influenced by Arabs after the rise of the Islamic religion, as part of the Arab world. Most of the rest of Africa—sub-Saharan* black Africa—lacked written history, which led some people to think that it lacked archaeological history as well.

* **sub-Saharan** referring to Africa south of the Sahara desert

Politics and racism also shaped the attitudes of outsiders toward African archaeology. Europeans based much of the political and social structure of their colonies in Africa on the notion that black Africans were inferior to white people and "uncivilized." The controversy over the ruins of Great Zimbabwe shows how these attitudes affected African archaeology.

See color plate 1, vol. 3.

Great Zimbabwe is a collection of impressive stone ruins in the southern African country of Zimbabwe (formerly the British colony of Rhodesia). Some white archaeologists thought that Africans had built Great Zimbabwe. Many others, however, argued that the site's builders had been ancient voyagers from the Mediterranean region, Arabia, or even China—in their view, peoples from more highly developed civilizations than Africa. Since 1950 archaeologists using new scientific methods have shown beyond a doubt that the ancestors of the SHONA and other African groups built Great Zimbabwe and other stone structures as political and religious centers.

Archaeology is continually expanding Africans' knowledge of their history. Pointing out that archaeology had revealed unknown civilizations and cultures, Mali's national director of arts and culture urged sub-Saharan African nations to "make more use of archaeology to find the truth about their past." They must also take steps, he said, to protect Africa's archaeological heritage from destruction or misuse.

History and Prehistory. Archaeology can be divided into two basic categories. Historic archaeology deals with periods that have written records, produced either by local people or by outsiders. Prehistoric archaeology studies cultures or periods without written records.

Written history merely brushes the fringes of Africa's past. Although Egypt developed written language before 2000 B.C., ancient Egyptians recorded little about Africa outside the Nile Valley. A few ancient Greek and Roman scholars left written accounts of Egypt and North Africa, but their descriptions do not provide much accurate information about the indigenous* peoples of those regions. The civilization that arose in Ethiopia around A.D. 400 also kept written records. However, like the Egyptians, the ancient Ethiopians said little about lands beyond their own borders.

* **indigenous** native to a certain place

Much later, beginning in the A.D. 900s, Arabs documented their visits to the southern regions of the Sahara and to the East African coast. Europeans began exploring the African coastline in the 1400s, but their descriptions of local peoples and cultures are not always reliable. For much of the continent, recorded history is only a century or two old. As

Archaeology and Prehistory

* **evolution** changes in groups of organisms that occur over time

* **artifact** in archaeology, an ornament, tool, weapon, or other object made by humans

a result, prehistoric archaeology is the main key to unlocking Africa's past.

Archaeologists studying prehistoric Africa may use various research tools to fill in the picture of the past. Paleontology, which focuses on the physical remains of early humans, offers clues about the evolution* of prehistoric peoples. Another tool is oral history, a group's traditions, myths, and stories as passed down from generation to generation in spoken form. In some societies, oral history provides useful knowledge of the past century or two. Historical linguistics, another tool, concerns the relationships among languages and how they have changed over time. It may provide clues about the past migrations and relationships of ethnic groups. Ethnography, the study of present-day ethnic groups and their immediate ancestors, helps archaeologists trace connections between the past and the present. Geography and geology offer insights into the physical landscapes that earlier peoples inhabited. Of course, artifacts* are the most familiar objects of archaeological research. By studying tools and other material remains of past cultures, archaeologists can find clues about the way people lived long ago.

The Stone Age in Africa. Prehistoric archaeologists divide the past into different periods based on the kinds of tools people made. Several of these periods are grouped under the name the Stone Age.

Broadly speaking, the Early Stone Age in Africa began about 2.6 million years ago, when the ancestors of humans shaped the first large, handheld cutting tools of stone to carve the carcasses of animals. Scientists believe that these early beings hunted small game and looked for carcasses that had been killed by large animals. This way of life continued until around 200,000 years ago.

During the Middle Stone Age, from about 200,000 to 45,000 years ago, large stone tools were replaced by smaller tools made of sharp flakes struck from specially prepared rocks. As in the Early Stone Age, people lived off game killed by animals and gathering wild foods. Hunting probably played an increasing role during the Middle Stone Age. However, archaeologists differ as to whether people hunted large game animals, and if so, how and when they learned to do so.

Africa's climate became cooler and drier during the Middle Stone Age, producing environmental changes that challenged people to adapt to new conditions. Archaeologists who study the Middle Stone Age are trying to determine what the environment was like and how it affected human life.

The Late Stone Age, which began about 45,000 years ago, marked the appearance of very small stone blades and tools that people attached to handles of wood or bone. Late Stone Age people hunted and gathered a wide variety of plants and animals to eat, including seafood. They made beads, painted pictures on rock walls, and formally buried their dead. They also produced many artifacts of perishable organic materials such as wood, bone, leather, and shell, which have survived at a few sites. Among the oldest such artifacts are 10,000-year-old tools of wood, bark, and grass, found at Gwisho hot springs in Zambia.

* **domesticated** raised by humans as farm animals or pets

By 7000 B.C. people living in what is now the Sahara had domesticated* cattle. Between 6500 and 4000 B.C., climate changes caused these

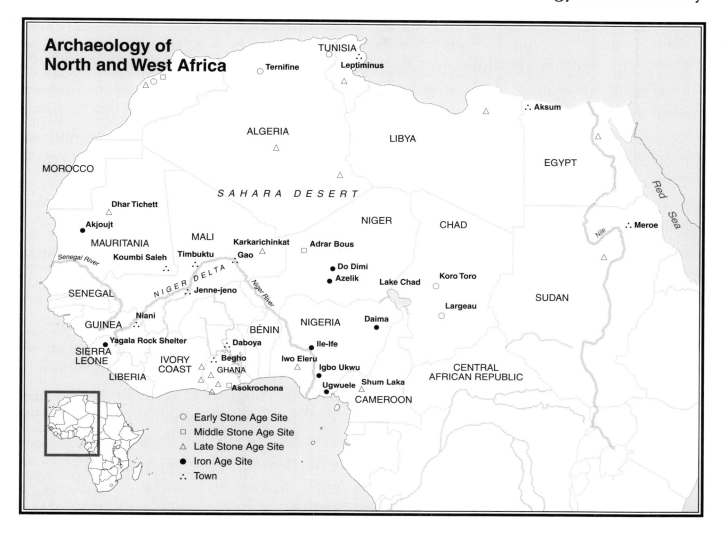

Archaeology of North and West Africa

○ Early Stone Age Site
□ Middle Stone Age Site
△ Late Stone Age Site
● Iron Age Site
∴ Town

cattle-herding societies to move southward, introducing domestic animals into sub-Saharan Africa. The development of economies based on livestock herding and farming marked the end of the Late Stone Age. At around the same time, ironworking technologies appeared in some regions, and new cultures began to develop.

Some of these new cultures were settled; others were nomadic. Some were based on agriculture, others on pastoralist* activities. In a few desert areas and within deep forests, small bands of hunter-gatherers continued to live much as their ancestors had done. Elsewhere, however, African societies grew more complex and began interacting with each other. Around the edges of the continent, they began to encounter people of other races and cultures. Each region of Africa followed its own route to the present, a route that can be retraced through archaeology.

NORTHERN AFRICA

Northern Africa includes Egypt, the northern half of Sudan, Libya, Tunisia, Algeria, and Morocco. The region's archaeological heritage ranges from the massive monuments of ancient Egypt to the faint traces

* **pastoralist** related to or dependent on livestock herding

43

Archaeology and Prehistory

* **savanna** tropical or subtropical grassland with scattered trees and drought-resistant undergrowth

The Romans, who conquered most of North Africa along the Mediterranean coast, constructed many temples and public buildings that still stand today. These ruins of a Roman bathhouse in Tunisia date from the A.D. 200s.

left by pastoral nomads thousands of years ago, when the Sahara was a wooded savanna* instead of the desert it is today.

Prehistory. One of the oldest archaeological sites in northern Africa is Ternifine, Algeria. There scientists have discovered both human fossils and stone axes mingled with the remains of animals that lived more than 500,000 years ago. Early Stone Age axes have been found throughout North Africa, from the Red Sea to the Atlantic Ocean and from the Mediterranean coast southward. In the Sahara they have often been unearthed near former springs and lakeshores that supported life during wetter eras in the region's past.

Archaeologists have studied Middle Stone Age settlement patterns at various places in the Egyptian Sahara. Some sites were quarries, where people obtained stone for their tools. Others, especially those on ancient lakeshores, served as workshops for the shaping of tools. In some places, people butchered their kills. Still other sites, back from the lakes, may have been where people slept, out of the way of large animals that hunted near the water at night. This pattern continued for thousands of years.

The Golden Mummies

In 1996 an Egyptian donkey led to a sensational discovery at Bahareya, an oasis southwest of Cairo. The donkey tripped in a hole that turned out to be a tomb containing dozens of mummies—preserved bodies of men, women, and children wrapped in cloth and wearing gold-painted masks. The mummies dated from the A.D. 100s, and their adornments reflected a blend of Egyptian and Roman traditions. One woman's mask combined a Roman hairstyle with an image of the ancient Egyptian goddess Isis. The tomb was part of a large cemetery that may contain thousands of mummies. Excavating the entire site is expected to take ten years or more.

Middle Stone Age sites in the Sahara and the MAGHREB (northwest Africa) show that people butchered rhinoceroses, giraffes, horses, antelopes, and gazelles. A few sites also contain stones that people may have used to grind wild plant foods to make them easier to eat. A location in the Nile River valley that has many fish bones, including some from very large deepwater fish, is among the oldest evidence in the world of fishing.

By the Late Stone Age, people in northern Africa had become very efficient hunters of large herd animals, such as wild cattle, gazelles, and sheep. Starting around 20,000 years ago, they began making a new kind of small stone blade that was often pointed. Sometimes they mounted several little blades together on a handle, a step toward more complex technology.

Archaeologists have studied many Late Stone Age sites in the highlands and mountains of northern Africa, but these may have been only seasonal hunting camps. Between 20,000 and 13,000 years ago, the sea level along the Mediterranean shore was much lower than today, and coastal regions that are now under water were probably the main centers of population. The Nile River, much smaller than it is today, supported a narrow ribbon of life surrounded on both sides by extreme deserts. The people who lived there probably had to compete for resources—many skeletons show evidence of violence, sometimes approaching the intensity of warfare.

Around 11,000 years ago, changes in rainfall patterns increased the flow of the Nile and also moistened the Sahara. Human population expanded into the Sahara, where some archaeological sites reveal fragments of early pottery and the bones of domesticated cattle. At first, people stayed in the Sahara only during rainy seasons. But by about 8,000 years ago they lived there year-round, digging wells and constructing round houses. They also set up large standing stones arranged in lines or circles, which perhaps had astronomical or religious meaning. Several thousand years later, the climate shifted again and much of the Sahara became too dry for humans to live in.

In the Nile Valley around 6,000 years ago, hunter-gatherers began herding, farming, and building villages. In some villages in northern Egypt, all houses were similar in size and had similar contents, suggesting that the inhabitants belonged to a society of equals with no class distinctions. In southern Egypt, however, burial sites reveal significant differences, and some graves had richer goods than others. This indicates that society was becoming more complex and social difference had emerged.

Archaeologists have not determined whether the growing complexity of the region's social structures and technology (such as pottery) reflects influences from Southwest Asia or from the eastern Sahara. Whatever the source, this development in the Nile Valley eventually led to the rise of a great civilization.

The Historic Period. By 3100 B.C. a nation-state ruled by kings known as pharaohs had emerged in Egypt. This ancient civilization has revealed itself to archaeologists through written records and also

Archaeology and Prehistory

The Mystery of Igbo Ukwu

Igbo Ukwu, in forested southern Nigeria, is an archaeological site that includes a burial mound from around A.D. 900. Among the objects uncovered there were more than 150,000 imported glass beads and many precious objects of ivory and metal. Rich and elaborate burials usually occur in highly developed societies, and graves similar to that at Igbo Ukwu generally contain kings. Yet around A.D. 900 that part of Nigeria had no large state. Who was buried at Igbo Ukwu remains a mystery—possibly the head of a religious brotherhood or a secret society. Such groups still have great influence in the region.

through monuments such as the pyramids, temples, graves, villages, palaces, and other structures.

South of ancient Egypt along the Nile was a land that the Egyptians called Kush and the Arabs later called NUBIA. Today the area is divided between Egypt and SUDAN. The home of a black African civilization, Kush grew into an empire that traded gold, ivory, slaves, and ostrich feathers to the Egyptians. Closely linked with Egyptian society, Kush even ruled Egypt from 760 to 656 B.C.

Like the Egyptians, the Kushites buried their rulers under pyramids. The Kushites actually built more pyramids than the Egyptians, though theirs were smaller. The largest Kushite pyramid, discovered at a site called Nuri in Sudan, measures about 95 feet (30 meters) a side. Archaeologists have focused their efforts on the northern part of Kush, studying as much as they could before a series of dams on the Nile flooded the area. Research in southern Kush has centered on the royal cities of Napata and MEROË.

The Egyptian civilization survived, passing through many phases, until A.D. 30. In that year Cleopatra, the last ruler descended from the pharaohs, died. By then Egypt had been under Greek and Roman influence, and sometimes political control, for several hundred years. Some important archaeological discoveries of recent times date from this Greco-Roman period. Among these are statues and buildings in the harbor of the city of Alexandria, drowned by waters that have risen since ancient times.

Greco-Roman ruins also dot the North African coast west of Egypt. The Tunisian site of Leptiminus, for example, was a Mediterranean port that came under Roman rule in the A.D. 100s. During the 1990s archaeologists excavated three Roman cemeteries there. One was located in an area that produced a distinctive type of pottery, a major trade item in the Mediterranean region for five centuries.

WESTERN AFRICA

Western Africa includes Mauritania, Mali, Niger, Nigeria, Chad, Cameroon, Benin, Burkina Faso, Togo, Ghana, Ivory Coast, Liberia, Sierra Leone, Guinea, Guinea-Bissau, Gambia, and Senegal. The region stretches into the Sahara desert in the north, but its coastal area consists primarily of tropical rain forest. Archaeologists believe that changes in climate—especially shifts between wetter and drier periods—played a key role in shaping the past societies of the region.

Prehistory. Although archaeologists think that parts of western Africa were inhabited more than 2 million years ago, they do not yet have a clear picture of the earliest settlements. In 1995 scientists found a fossil jaw and seven teeth at Koro Toro, Chad. The fossils came from an australopithecine, an early kind of human ancestor previously known only from sites in eastern and southern Africa.

Stone tools from both the Early Stone Age and the Middle Stone Age occur widely in western Africa, especially in the Sahara and northern Nigeria. At Asokrochona in Ghana and other sites in the southern part

See color plate 2, vol. 2.

See color plate 3, vol. 3.

of the region, archaeologists have found tools from the Middle Stone Age that may have been used in woodworking.

Relics of the Late Stone Age show how climate affected human life in the region. During a very dry period between 20,000 and 12,000 years ago, the Sahara desert extended farther than it does today, and no traces of human life from that time have been found in the northern part of the region. During the wetter years that followed, the Sahara was reoccupied, probably from the north. Rock paintings of elephants and wild buffalo in areas that are now extremely dry may date from this period.

Work at a number of Saharan sites has revealed harpoons and the remains of fish, crocodiles, and hippopotamuses, suggesting that people of this period had access to lakes and rivers. In 1998 archaeologists discovered a boat more than 25 feet long near the Yobe River in northeastern Nigeria. Known as the Dufuna canoe, it dates from around 6500 B.C. and is thought to be Africa's oldest boat.

Archaeological sites throughout western Africa highlight milestones in the region's prehistory. At a place called Iwo Eleru in the forested area of southwestern Nigeria, scientists have uncovered a rock shelter that was inhabited as early as 10,000 years ago. The shelter contained many small stone blades that may have been used as arrowheads or, attached to handles, as cutting tools. Pottery found in the Sahara dates from the same period. Cattle skeletons excavated at a site called Adrar Bous in Niger show that people were herding domestic cattle, sheep, and goats about 4,000 years ago. Other archaeological discoveries in Mali and Mauritania suggest that agriculture—specifically, the farming of millet, a cereal grain—began in the region between 4,000 and 3,000 years ago.

Beginning around 2000 B.C., agricultural production increased and settled communities developed in the forest and savanna regions in the southern part of western Africa. More than two dozen sites in Ghana and Ivory Coast have revealed houses in large settlements, complete with a variety of stone tools, remains of sheep and goats, and pottery vessels and figurines.

Around the same time, people in the area began to work metal. They may have learned techniques from cultures in Sudan and North Africa or developed them on their own. Discoveries in Niger show that people there worked copper as early as 2000 B.C. The earliest evidence of ironworking, also in Niger, dates from about 1000 B.C., although iron tools did not completely replace stone tools. A few centuries later, Nigeria, Mali, Ghana, Chad, and Senegal were also producing iron.

Historians used to think that western Africa developed large urban centers and complex social structures as a result of contact with Arabs from North Africa after the A.D. 600s. Growing archaeological evidence, however, reveals large, complex societies in western Africa long before that time. Some of the earliest such evidence comes from the Saharan Borderlands, where archaeologists excavated the city of Jenne-jeno in Mali. Established by 250 B.C., the town entered a period of rapid growth some 500 years later.

Elsewhere in western Africa large earthen mounds have been found. These contain burial chambers, human sacrifices, and various objects buried with the dead. Some archaeologists believe that such sites, together with evidence of expanding trade across the region, suggest the development of larger states and kingdoms. The trend toward centralization of power would eventually produce a number of great empires in western Africa.

The Historic Period. Oral tradition and a few written records, including accounts by Arab travelers, provide archaeologists with additional insights into western African states after A.D. 1000. Ancient Ghana, the subject of many of these reports, extended over much of present-day Mauritania, Mali, and Senegal. Arabic sources refer to Ghana as a flourishing kingdom. One description of a king's burial has shed light on the ritual purpose of burial mounds in the area. At Koumbi Saleh, a site in Mauritania thought to have been Ghana's capital, researchers have unearthed multistory stone buildings and graveyards.

As Ghana's influence faded, the kingdom of Mali became powerful in the region, reaching its peak in the 1200s and 1300s. Some archaeologists believe that Niani, a site in present-day Guinea, was the capital of Mali. Although the site has extensive ruins, excavations suggest that it was unoccupied during Mali's most powerful era. The exact location of the capital, as well as the true extent of ancient Mali, remain undetermined.

Arabic and European sources describe the rich and powerful kingdom of Benin in Nigeria, which reached its peak between the 1200s and 1600s. Archaeologists have added detail to these written accounts. Their research reveals that the inhabitants of Benin City, the capital, worked with copper and built massive earthen walls around important structures.

Archaeological sites along the coast of western Africa include forts and castles built by Europeans as they explored and traded in the area in the 1400s and later. Recent archaeological work has focused on indigenous towns and states near these European outposts, studying how local Africans responded to contact and trade with Europeans. One of the most fully studied sites is Elmina on the coast of Ghana, the location of the first and largest European trading post in sub-Saharan Africa. By the 1800s, the African town there had grown to 15,000 or 20,000 inhabitants. Excavations have revealed evidence of far-flung trade: European pottery, glass and beads, and fine ceramics from China.

See color plate 5, vol. 2.

EASTERN AFRICA

Eastern Africa includes Djibouti, Eritrea, Ethiopia, Kenya, Somalia, Tanzania, and Uganda. Organized archaeological research did not begin in this region until around 1960, though some earlier work was done by colonial officials who collected various artifacts.

Eastern Africa first became famous in the 1960s when dramatic fossil discoveries were made by members of the LEAKEY FAMILY. These findings cast new light on the earliest human origins in Africa. Other archaeological work has focused on more recent eras in the region's human history.

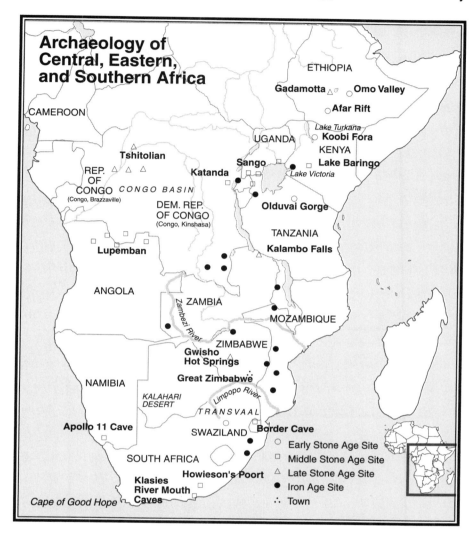

Archaeology of Central, Eastern, and Southern Africa

See color plate 1, vol. 2.

A key feature of current archaeology in the region is the growing participation of African scientists, students, universities, and museums. Interpretation of the region's history was once largely in the hands of Westerners, but now more local archaeologists and other scholars are studying their own past. In addition, eastern Africa has turned some archaeological sites into tourist attractions and has created local museums to educate schools and communities about their archaeological heritage.

Prehistory. Discoveries by the Leakeys and others have made sites in eastern Africa, such as the well-known Olduvai Gorge in Tanzania, centers of paleoarchaeological research. Paleoarchaeology concerns the study of very old traces of human existence and culture. One area of research is the evolution of the first humans several million years ago. Another is the emergence of the modern human species, *Homo sapiens.*

Theories that suggest an African origin for *Homo sapiens* have focused attention on the Middle Stone Age sites, such as Gadamotta near Lake

Archaeology and Prehistory

Zwai in Ethiopia. The inhabitants of Gadamotta used obsidian—glassy, volcanic rock that can hold a sharp edge—to manufacture tools more than 200,000 years ago. Other important sites in Tanzania contain stone tools more than 100,000 years old.

Archaeological remains from the Late Stone Age, including small stone tools and rock art, are found at many sites in eastern African. At Gamble's Cave and Nderit Drift, near Lake Nakuru in Kenya, archaeologists have found blades, scrapers, and other tools crafted from obsidian between 13,000 and 9,000 years ago. Sites on the shores of Lake Turkana in Kenya have revealed bone harpoons, stone scrapers, scrapers, grinding stones, and pottery. Hunter-gatherers there ate a wide variety of foods, including crocodile, hippopotamus, fish, and plants. In the vicinity of Lake Victoria, Africa's largest lake, archaeologists have located relics of a hunter-gatherer population they call the Oltome culture. Among its artifacts are pieces of highly decorated pottery with stamped decorations. The best-known Oltome site is Gogo Falls, which dates from between 4000 and 1000 B.C.

Archaeological evidence suggests that the herding of domestic livestock began in eastern Africa about 4,000 to 5,000 years ago, and many groups in the region still follow a pastoral way of life. The most common domesticated animals were cattle, sheep, and goats, though archaeologists have also uncovered bones of camels from sites in Ethiopia and northern Kenya. The earliest indications of farming in the region come from Lalibela Cave in the highlands of Ethiopia, which contained traces of beans, barley, and chickpeas. Evidence of domesticated wheat, grapes, and lentils has been found at other Ethiopian sites. Although grown in eastern Africa, all these food plants originated in the Near East and would have been introduced to the region.

An economy that combined farming and trading developed rapidly in the Ethiopian highlands starting about 2,500 years ago. Local African communities traded valuable raw materials, such as gold, skins, and ivory, across the Red Sea to the Arabian peninsula. Several hundred years later, Ethiopia became part of a trading network that also crossed the Indian Ocean. These farming communities of Ethiopia are known from archaeological excavations at Aksum, which eventually developed into a major state.

The first communities to use iron in eastern Africa arose along the shores of Lake Victoria between 2,500 and 1,700 years ago. Archaeologists have not yet identified the origins of these communities, and evidence remains scarce. By about A.D. 500, farmers using iron tools seem to have occupied areas of eastern Africa with wooded and wet environments, especially the coastal hills and plains.

Historic Era. Early evidence of complex African societies comes from the coast of eastern Africa, where urban communities based on Indian Ocean trading networks were developing by A.D. 800. Some communities built large structures of timber, coral, and limestone and minted their own coins. There is evidence of Islam, the religion that originated in Arabia. The inhabitants of these urban centers at Zanzibar and elsewhere along the coast were the ancestors of the Swahili coastal traders who now live in east African towns such as Mombasa.

> **Remember:** Words in small capital letters have separate entries, and the index at the end of this volume will guide you to more information on many topics.

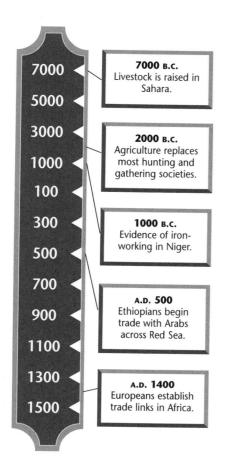

7000
5000
3000
1000
100
300
500
700
900
1100
1300
1500

7000 B.C.
Livestock is raised in Sahara.

2000 B.C.
Agriculture replaces most hunting and gathering societies.

1000 B.C.
Evidence of iron-working in Niger.

A.D. 500
Ethiopians begin trade with Arabs across Red Sea.

A.D. 1400
Europeans establish trade links in Africa.

Fierce debate has swirled around the origins of the Swahili coastal communities. Earlier generations claimed that Asian colonists had "brought civilization to Africa." However, Swahili is a native African language. Archaeologists now believe that the Swahili coastal culture originated in Africa but that colonists from southern Arabia influenced the culture.

The pattern of peoples and cultures in eastern Africa today is largely the result of events during the past thousand years. Chief among these events are migrations from the north, with waves of livestock-herding people settling in the area. The newcomers developed a dairy economy, keeping cattle for milk and sheep and goats for meat.

The past thousand years also saw the emergence of large population centers around the lakes of eastern Africa. One such center, Bigo, had earthen walls more than 6.2 miles long, with ditches up to 16 feet deep. Some states that appeared in the region later, such as Buganda and Bunyoro, have survived.

CENTRAL AND SOUTHERN AFRICA

Africa's central and southern regions include Angola, Botswana, Burundi, Central African Republic, Democratic Republic of Congo, Equatorial Guinea, Gabon, Lesotho, Malawi, Mozambique, Namibia, Republic of Congo, Rwanda, São Tomé and Principe, South Africa, Swaziland, Zambia, and Zimbabwe. Archaeological sites in these areas contain evidence for the origins and evolution of humans, as well as more recent remains of complex civilizations and trade networks. Research has been uneven, however, and many areas remain unexplored.

Prehistory. Archaeologists first uncovered fossils of humanlike australopithecines in South Africa in the 1920s and 1930s. The importance of these discoveries was not immediately recognized, but eventually paleontologists realized that australopithecines are the earliest human ancestors. Most likely they lived by gathering wild foods and scavenging carcasses killed by large animals. Some of the australopithecine fossils found in the region were individuals killed by animals, and the sites where they were found do not necessarily represent the places where they lived or made tools of stone and bone.

Some archaeological sites in southern Africa, such as Border Cave in Swaziland and Klasies River Mouth on the coast of South Africa, contain skeletons of *Homo sapiens* along with evidence of "modern" behavior such as the development of family groups, food sharing, and the planned use of resources. These sites may be more than 100,000 years old.

Archaeological evidence shows that, during the Late Stone Age, the peoples of central and southern Africa were largely nomadic, moving with the seasons between mountainous areas and low-lying lands. They trapped and hunted animals, gathered a wide variety of plant foods, and used marine resources such as shellfish. They also carefully buried their dead, sometimes placing various objects in the grave, and painted complex images on the walls of rock shelters—facts that lead archaeologists

Archaeology and Prehistory

Louis and Mary Leakey, shown here at work in Olduvai Gorge, Tanzania, made major contributions to scientific knowledge about human origins.

to believe that these Stone Age people had a strong sense of the spiritual world.

Around 2,000 years ago, the Stone Age way of life began to change in the region. In the drier western areas, domesticated sheep became an important part of the economy. Scientists debate the origins of this pastoralism, questioning whether local hunter-gatherers developed livestock herding on their own, or whether pastoral peoples arrived in the region from the north. Researchers agree, however, that the early pastoralists were the ancestors of the KHOISAN, the indigenous people of southern Africa.

In parts of central and southern Africa with fairly dependable summer rainfall, people adopted a system of mixed agriculture, combining grain farming with livestock raising. Excavation of many ancient villages has shown that this way of life was firmly established by A.D. 200. The villages were linked by the exchange of goods, such as food products, pottery, salt, and iron. They may also have interacted with hunter-gatherers who still followed the Stone Age way of life because stone tools have been found in some village sites.

Historic Era. The archaeological picture of central and southern Africa is clearer for the past thousand years or so. Domestic livestock, especially cattle, became very important throughout much of the region. Farming settlements spread into the highlands, where ruins of stone-built communities indicate the existence of large, thriving populations.

By the A.D. 1100s, complex states were emerging. Mapungabwe and other hilltop towns along the Limpopo River in Zimbabwe and Botswana were centers of such states. These societies were organized into different economic and social classes. Their rulers controlled both the local economy and connections with the outside world. These links occurred with traders from Arabia on the coast of the Indian Ocean, where African goods such as gold, ivory, and animal skins were exchanged for foreign items such as glass beads and cotton cloth.

The Mapungabwe state was followed by Great Zimbabwe, which flourished until the 1400s. At its peak Great Zimbabwe probably had a population of more than 10,000 people and included territory from eastern Botswana to near the Indian Ocean. The large stone walls in the center of the town reflected the high status of the ruling class; ordinary people lived in mud and thatch houses around the central stone buildings. More than 50 smaller regional centers, built in the same style, helped maintain the power of Great Zimbabwe.

The Arab traders who linked southern Africa to the Indian Ocean limited their settlements to the coast. European colonists, beginning with the Portuguese in the early 1500s, ventured into the interior. They were following rumors of vast wealth. Portuguese forts, Dutch trading posts, and British colonial buildings and settlements are the focus of archaeological research into the recent colonial past of southern and central Africa. Many parts of the region, however, are not well known archaeologically. Much work remains to be done, particularly in the great tropical rain forest that covers much of central Africa. Future research will

undoubtedly challenge and change present ideas about the past of central and southern Africa and of the continent as a whole. (*See also* **Africa, Study of; Animals, Domestic; Art; History of Africa; Hunting and Gathering; Humans, Early; Islam in Africa; Livestock Grazing; Roman Africa; Sudanic Empires of Western Africa.**)

Architecture

* indigenous   native to a certain place

See color plate 9, vol. 4.

From small mud huts to towering steel skyscrapers, African architecture is a mix of indigenous* and foreign, old and new. The continent's diverse architecture reflects its varied climates and environments as well as the many different cultures and traditions of African peoples. Outside influences have played a major role as well. European designs and building methods can be seen in countries throughout the continent, and Islam has shaped much of the architecture of North Africa. Nonetheless, African traditions continue to be the most important factor.

TRADITIONAL ARCHITECTURE

Indigenous architecture in Africa is closely connected to the lives of the people of an area. Their social systems, livelihood, and religion influence the type of structures they build and the way in which they lay out their communities. The climate and natural resources of a region also play a role in determining the forms and materials used in construction. Both culture and natural resources of an area affect the way people create and decorate their architecture.

Role of Culture.   People throughout Africa have developed styles of architecture that are central to the cultures of particular ethnic groups. In many rural societies, especially those based on agriculture, people live in compounds consisting of several separate buildings connected to or surrounded by a wall or fence. Such compounds typically house an extended network of family members. The individual dwellings of mud, wood, and thatch are round in some regions and rectangular in others.

Each building in a compound has a specific purpose. There are spaces for cooking, sleeping, storage, worship, domestic animals, and sometimes for burying the dead. The buildings and outer walls of a compound surround a central courtyard, which is usually the main working place for the family.

Many African towns and cities are patterned after the basic rural compound. Many cities were originally enclosed by walls made of wood, earth, or stone, depending on the available natural resources. Markets and palaces of rulers surrounded the large central square. In North Africa, towns with narrow twisting streets and tightly clustered homes were often protected by a massive outer wall and defensive fort called a Casbah.

In some cultures, belief in a spiritual life after death focused architectural efforts on creating elaborate monuments and tombs. Among the most famous structures on the African continent are the great temples and PYRAMIDS of ancient Egypt. Built for Egyptian rulers believed to be

Architecture

gods, these tombs were constructed of massive stones and designed to last forever. The ancient AKSUM culture in what is now Ethiopia and Eritrea once built monuments on a similar scale, including pillars carved in the shape of multistory buildings that towered over 100 feet high. These remain standing today.

In contrast to these monumental structures is the temporary housing of hunting-gathering societies and some pastoralists*. Their architecture often consists solely of tents and other shelters that can be assembled and taken apart quickly. Built of various lightweight materials, such as wood, grasses, and hides, these portable structures accommodate the nomadic lifestyle of their inhabitants.

Environment and Building Materials. The environments found in Africa range from harsh deserts to tropical rain forests to temperate savannas*. The architecture of each region is directly related to its environment and the building materials available.

In tropical regions of heavy rainfall, people typically build homes with sloping roofs that allow water to run off easily. Numerous openings in exterior and interior walls permit outside air to pass through a building and cool it. Because vegetation is often dense in such regions, common construction materials include wood and plant matter, such as leaves and vines. By contrast, in hot, dry regions where timber is scarce, dried mud or bricks are often used for buildings. Thick walls with few openings help keep out the daytime heat, allowing the interiors to remain relatively cool. In areas that have strong, regular winds from a certain direction, structures are placed to take advantage of the cooling effects of breezes and some walls may be reinforced to withstand storms.

The building materials used in traditional architecture depend largely on a region's resources. In North Africa and along the east African coast, many ancient cities and monuments were made of stone. The Egyptians constructed temples and pyramids of local limestone. The coastal-dwelling Swahili built with blocks of coral. Even today, some settled rural populations in East Africa use stone for houses, grain storage buildings, and the foundations of walls because stone lasts far longer than wood in tropical climates.

In the rainforest regions of Africa, people harvest hardwood for walls, ceilings, roofs, and doors. Some tropical hardwoods are brought to savanna areas, where trees and bushes are scarce. Other common rainforest building materials are bamboo and the flexible roots of trees. Palm fronds, grasses, and vines are woven into mats that are used for walls and roofs and for decoration.

In many parts of Africa, buildings are made of earth. Some people use mud to form cone-shaped or rectangular bricks that are dried or baked until hard. Others build with balls of wet mud. Clay pots and pottery may be employed as paving tiles, gutters, and wall linings.

African builders frequently work with combinations of stone, earth, timber, textiles, and other materials. They top earthen roofs with wooden planks, dry straw, or plant leaves. They reinforce earthen walls and arches with tree roots and bamboo sticks, and they make tents with branches, leather, and textiles.

* **artisan** skilled crafts worker

* **mosque** Muslim place of worship

* **rite** ceremony or formal procedure

* **bas-relief** type of sculpture in which figures are raised slightly from a flat surface

See color plate 13, vol. 3.

The Construction Process. Building in rural Africa has traditionally been a family or even community effort. Many people lend their skills to erect a building. The building process might involve blacksmiths, woodworkers, weavers, and potters. Specific tasks are often assigned according to gender. Usually, men cut and carve wood, mold and shape bricks, and construct the earthen walls of houses. Women may make architectural pottery such as tiles, gutters, and decorative features, carry water to the work site, and apply the finishing coats of plaster or mud on walls, floors, and other surfaces.

In Africa's Islamic cities, however, construction has generally been left to specialized groups of builders and artisans*. Deeply respected, these workers have held a high place in society. Many people have also feared them, believing them to have magical powers. Often Islamic political and military leaders designed the cities. They planned city walls, mosques*, and palaces based on religious principles and the decorations found in the Qur'an, the holy book of Islam.

The construction process in Africa often includes religious rites*. Many peoples perform sacrifices and other ceremonies before, during, and on completion of a building project. Such rites are believed to help ensure that the structure will remain strong and stable and that the life of its occupants will be peaceful and prosperous. Some nomadic groups build a house as part of their marriage ceremony.

Decoration in Architecture. For some African groups, decoration is an important part of a building's construction. The bricks or stones in a wall may be laid so that they form a particular design. The Rozwi people of southern Africa, for example, built intricately patterned stone walls during the 1600s and 1700s. Some groups arrange straw or other grasses in appealing patterns on roofs; others twist branches and plant materials into decorative features. Designs and colors may be woven into roof and wall mats, such as those made by the Kuba people in the Congo.

Decorative elements may also be added to structures after they are built. The most commonly applied surface decoration—used primarily on stone or earthen walls—is dried mud. The mud may be colored with vegetable dyes, carved in bas-relief*, or embedded with pieces of pottery, seashells, or other materials. Architectural decoration is found most frequently on doorways and entrances, around window openings, on exterior walls and interior courtyards, and on the tops of roofs. It may also be used to mark a significant place, such as a hearth or storeroom, or an important building in the community.

The patterns of surface design vary according to ethnic group, religion, and building function. The ancient Egyptians added paintings and carvings to their architecture to tell stories and communicate religious messages. In Islamic communities, buildings are usually adorned with geometric and scriptlike designs because the Muslim religion forbids making pictures of people and animals. In many cultures, certain colors or patterns may hold special symbolic meaning. The HAUSA of northern Nigeria decorate the outside of their homes with bas-relief or painted designs, sometimes including pictures of bicycles and cars to represent high social standing. The NDEBELE of South Africa decorate homes, churches, and other buildings with bold and colorful geometric patterns.

EARLY FOREIGN INFLUENCE

Travelers from Europe and Asia have long influenced Africa's architecture. The ancient Mediterranean civilizations of Phoenicia, Greece, and Rome built great cities in North Africa. Later Arabs introduced Islamic architecture to the people of Africa's northern coast. Christianity played a lesser role in the continent's early architecture, although it inspired some unique early churches in northeastern Africa.

Greek and Roman Influence. Settlers and invaders from the around the Mediterranean—particularly the ancient Greeks and Romans—brought their own styles of architecture to Africa. Around 800 B.C., the Phoenicians, a seafaring people from the eastern Mediterranean, built the thriving city of CARTHAGE in what is now Tunisia. The Romans destroyed the original buildings around 150 B.C. Later they rebuilt the city and made it the capital of their African province. The new city boasted an amphitheater, a forum, and miles of aqueducts that carried water to luxurious baths like those in Rome. After Carthage declined, later generations of Tunisian builders reused its stones in surrounding cities.

This enclosed village in Ghana combines shelter for family groups with a courtyard for activities such as weaving mats.

This fortress in central Morocco was built on a hillside overlooking the valley below. It includes square towers and an ornamental roofline, features common to many other North African buildings.

The Greeks constructed another of North Africa's great cities, ALEXANDRIA, in ancient Egypt. Founded in 332 B.C. by Alexander the Great, the city included palaces, parks, and temples in the Greek style. Among its most famous buildings were a vast library and a museum, which served as an institute for higher learning. A towering lighthouse with a fire at its peak guided ships into Alexandria's harbor and was considered one of the wonders of the ancient world.

Islamic and Christian Influence. By the 900s, Arabs were spreading Islamic culture and architecture along the coasts of northern and eastern Africa. Mosques are among the most striking forms of Islamic architecture in Africa. They are often decorated with elaborately carved stucco and wood and with detailed tile and glass mosaics. Built around a courtyard and a prayer hall, many mosques feature horseshoe-shaped archways, multiple domes, arched ceilings, and up to six minarets—tall, thin spires from which Muslims are called to prayer. North African mosques are particularly ornate.

Although mosques in Africa are distinctly Islamic in function and decoration, they include elements of indigenous architecture. In Cairo, mosque builders used an ancient Egyptian technique to carve finely detailed decorations directly into the surface of stone. In East Africa, Swahili palaces and mosques are constructed of coral blocks. Several early West African mosques, including one in TIMBUKTU in Mali, are made in the local fashion using mud strengthened with numerous wooden poles that poke out from the exterior walls. The ends of the poles serve as a scaffold for workers to climb up and repair the mud walls when they are damaged by heavy downpours during the rainy season.

Although Christianity spread to Africa in the first centuries A.D., it had little effect on African architecture until the late 1800s when European-style churches were introduced. One exception is the churches built in what is now Ethiopia and Eritrea. In the 1200s indigenous Christians of that area carved massive churches out of solid rock. The style of these churches owed something to the carved monuments of the earlier Aksum culture. Another uniquely African style of Christian architecture developed in the Gondar and Lake Tana regions of Ethiopia in the late 1500s. Churches built in this area were round and were surrounded by long walkways covered with arches and walls topped by towers.

COLONIAL ARCHITECTURE

When Europeans began to colonize Africa in the 1500s, a new style of African architecture was born—colonial architecture. From government and commercial buildings to the houses of wealthy Africans, colonial architecture reflected the political and economic relations between

Some ancient mosques in West Africa, like this one in Djenné, Mali, were built of hardened mud.

Europeans and Africans. It was primarily an expression of European power and authority.

European Influence. Although many European nations played a role in colonizing Africa, no clear distinction can be seen in the architecture of their colonies. Rather, these colonial powers produced a common style with variations that reflected local African building traditions, climate and natural resources, and political developments.

Some of the earliest colonial architecture appeared in West Africa. From the 1500s to the 1800s "Portuguese-style" houses were constructed along the West African coast. Rectangular in shape, these buildings had a whitewashed exterior and a veranda—a long, roofed porch. In Saint-Louis (in present-day Senegal), the first colonial capital of French West Africa, merchants built houses with interior courtyards and second-floor porches. During the mid-1800s, European missionaries in West Africa constructed two-story buildings with a porch and covered passageway.

During the late 1800s, Brazil, a former colony of Portugal, lent its own flavor to colonial architecture in West Africa. Wealthy middle-class residents of African and Brazilian ancestry built lavish dwellings with the ground floor devoted to business and the upper stories for living quarters. They featured highly decorated facades—building fronts—that proclaimed the wealth of their owners.

See color plate 11, vol. 3.

The Dutch and British had an influence on the colonial architecture of South and East Africa. Dutch colonial houses combined thatched, or straw-covered, roofs and white plastered walls with ornate gables. When the British took over the region in the early 1800s, they replaced these simple houses with a grander style of architecture that featured fancy facades. British colonial-style buildings were one or two stories tall with encircling porches. Some were made of prefabricated materials, and most had roofs covered with sheets of metal.

Common Characteristics. By the late 1800s a formal colonial style had developed in Africa. This style was also found in India, Southeast Asia, the West Indies, and other European colonial areas. The typical residential structure was a two-story building raised on pillars. Doors and windows were aligned to take full advantage of air currents, and a veranda surrounded the building on both levels. The veranda existed in West Africa before the arrival of Europeans, who readily adopted it for their own use because it created a shaded living area open to cooling breezes.

Government and administrative buildings, located in the capital cities of African colonies, had an important role in colonial architecture. Built to reflect colonial power and prestige, such buildings were large and impressive. They included various durable materials such as stone and hardwoods that were meant to last a long time.

MODERNIZATION

Since the colonial period, foreign design and technology have continued to influence architecture in Africa. Colonial policies, urban growth,

Architecture

migration, and Western technology encouraged the introduction of new building materials, systems of construction, and building functions. In many rural areas, however, the basic forms of traditional architecture have remained relatively unchanged. But now instead of using grasses and palm leaves for roofing, African builders often replace these natural materials with sheets of iron or aluminum. Instead of sun-dried brick, they may use concrete blocks.

The impact of foreign cultures and new materials is especially evident in cities. Many African nations have adopted the universal concrete and steel urban architecture, submerging much of the unique character of African architecture. However, some nations, such as Morocco, have taken steps to promote the use of local design and decoration in new buildings. The character of indigenous architecture also continues to change rapidly, as professionally trained architects become increasingly involved in developing new forms of architecture. (*See also* **Art, Cities and Urbanization, Crafts, Colonialism in Africa, Roman Africa.**)

ARMIES

See *Warfare.*

Art

Each of the hundreds of different cultures in Africa has its own artistic traditions and its own ideas of what is beautiful or important. Variations in the style and form of artworks, as well as in the materials used to produce them, reflect such factors as a region's geography and climate, its social customs, and the available technology. Of course, the skill and tastes of individual artists—and the purpose for which the work is created—also play a role in shaping the final product.

OVERVIEW OF AFRICAN ART

African art takes many forms, from sculpture and paintings to masks, textiles, baskets, jewelry, and utensils. Artistic style also covers a wide range, from lifelike representations of people or animals to abstract* geometric patterns. The YORUBA of Nigeria and the Bamileke of Cameroon, for example, believe that sculptures should resemble their subjects and must also show certain ideal qualities such as youth and beauty. The BAMBARA of Mali favor geometric shapes and idealized images over realistic portrayals of people or animals.

In sub-Saharan* Africa, many art objects are created to serve a particular purpose. These purposes include dealing with the problems of life, marking the passage from childhood to adulthood, communicating with spirits, and expressing basic beliefs. Artists carve figures to honor ancestors, rulers, and gods. They make masks for use in rituals* and funerals and for entertainment. They design jewelry and body painting that often function as a sign of wealth, power, and social position.

In North Africa, Islamic* beliefs restrict the creation of images of living things. As a result, artists have applied their skills to decorative arts such as carpet weaving and calligraphy, or ornamental writing.

* **abstract** in art, referring to designs or shapes that do not represent a recognizable object or person

* **sub-Saharan** referring to Africa south of the Sahara desert

* **ritual** religious ceremony that follows a set pattern

* **Islamic** relating to Islam, the religion based on the teachings of the prophet Muhammad; religious faith of Muslims

Twins in Life and Art

Among the Yoruba of Nigeria, small carved figures play a significant role in family life. When one child in a pair of twins dies in infancy, the mother asks an artist to make a figure representing the deceased child. Carved in wood, the figure has hair, often dyed a rich blue-black. The mother cares for the figure as if it were a real child, providing it with food, expensive clothing, and jewelry until the surviving twin is old enough to take care of it.

* **divination** practice that looks into the future, usually by supernatural means

Calligraphy can be seen on buildings, household items, sacred books, and other places.

Meaning in African Art. The subject of a work of art and the way in which it is made often have an influence on its meaning. In some cases, objects of great social and ritual significance have to be assembled according to certain procedures. Following the rules ensures that the piece will be filled with the appropriate "power." If the rules are broken, the artwork loses its power and becomes an ordinary object. In other cases, the power is given to the object after it is completed.

Some objects serve as a base for materials that add to their significance. For example, when a carver makes a mask, village elders may contribute medicines or herbs to give the mask power. The resulting piece is considered to have a personality of its own.

Design and decoration play a major role in the meaning of an object. An artist may make a mask large to indicate that it is important and add a prominent forehead to suggest that the mask is swollen with spiritual power. Certain patterns have particular significance, perhaps standing for water, the moon, the earth, or other ideas. Objects that represent spirits or spiritual powers are often abstract because the things they represent are abstract. Figures that represent living rulers tend to be more realistic to make it possible to recognize the individual's features. Some objects include symbols that represent powerful animals.

In one type of African art, forms that have known meanings are used in creating images of figures and ideas. The purpose is to portray rulers or ancestors as superhuman and, at the same time, to communicate a sense of permanence. Another category of art includes sculptures and masks that represent the visible world but refer as well to an unseen world behind them. These objects may be used in activities such as healing ceremonies and divination*.

A third type of African art consists of everyday objects, such as spoons, pots, doors, cloths, and so on. Some of these items have elaborate decorations, such as the intricate human faces carved into the handles of wooden ladles from Ivory Coast. Often reserved for the wealthy, these objects can also be markers of social position.

Collecting African Art. Europeans began collecting African artworks as early as the 1600s, and by the 1800s interest in these objects was high. However, the first African pieces brought to Europe were regarded as curiosities rather than works of art. While admiring the workmanship, some people considered African art to be "primitive" and without artistic value. Nevertheless, by the end of the 1800s many European museums had acquired African pieces for their collections, usually to show everyday life in their countries' colonies.

African works did not attract much attention as art until the 1920s, when interest focused mainly on sculptures in wood and bronze. Since the 1950s Western collectors, scholars, and museums have come to recognize more and more African objects as valuable works of art. Prices of these works have risen accordingly.

In the early years, European museums often displayed African objects with exhibits of animals, rather than with other works of art. Today,

Art

Power Figures

Carved figures or other objects thought to have magical power (sometimes called fetishes) are found in societies in many parts of Africa, including the Kongo and the Fang. The figures can take various forms, from representations of ancestors or other humans to images of real or imaginary animals. No matter what they represent, most of the figures contain special ritual substances to give them their "power." These substances—often blood, vegetable matter, minerals, or parts of animals—are placed in a cavity inside the figure or attached somewhere on its body.

* **motif** in art and music, repeated theme or design

See color plate 8, vol. 3.

* **savanna** tropical or subtropical grassland with scattered trees and drought-resistant undergrowth

museums present African pieces in their art collections. Furthermore, collectors now understand that, although individual works are not signed, many African artists are well known in the continent by name and reputation.

Art collecting has also changed in Africa. In the past, Africans sometimes threw objects away when they were thought to have lost their power. Without a specific function, the items had little value. Recently, however, more Africans have begun to collect works of art and a number of museums have been established on the continent with collections of African art.

Recent African Art. Over the centuries, African art has changed with the times. Not surprisingly, modern African society and culture are reflected in the recent work of African artists. Some of the religious rituals and other traditional activities for which African art was created no longer exist. Furthermore, new traditions, such as those connected to the practice of Christianity, have been introduced. Some artists have combined African ideas and Christian themes in their work. Others have produced pieces with African motifs* and designs that are not intended for use in rituals. Yet, though much of the current art reflects modern concerns and issues, traditional art forms continue to play a meaningful role in the lives of ordinary people.

Styles of art change as well. Traditional designs often appear in new ways, such as using body painting designs in paintings on canvas. Perhaps one of the most notable features of recent African art is its role in the modern marketplace. In many places, an art industry has developed to produce objects specifically for Western tourists and collectors. Such "tourist" art may include copies of older art forms as well as contemporary designs.

SCULPTURE

For sculpture, perhaps sub-Saharan Africa's greatest art form, the most commonly used materials are wood and clay and metals such as iron, bronze, and gold. Unfortunately, wood decomposes and is easily destroyed, so few pieces of early wooden sculpture have survived.

West Africa. Sculpture is one of the major art forms in West Africa. Scholars divide the artistic traditions of the region into two broad geographical areas: the western Sudan and the Guinea Coast. Although some common themes appear in the art of these areas, the most striking feature of West African sculpture is its diversity.

The western Sudan, a savanna* region that extends across West Africa, includes several well-defined sculptural traditions. Figures from this region often have elongated bodies, angular shapes, and facial features that represent an ideal rather than an individual. Many of the figures are used in religious rituals, and they often have dull surfaces encrusted with materials placed on them in ceremonial offerings.

The Mande-speaking peoples of the western Sudan create wooden figures with broad, flat surfaces. The body, arms, and legs are shaped like cylinders, while the nose may be a large vertical slab. Artists often burn

These beaded dolls made by the Ndebele people in South Africa include items worn by married Ndebele women and were originally fertility charms.

patterns of scars—a common type of body decoration—into the surface of figures with a hot blade. Scar patterns also consist of large geometric shapes. The Mande wooden figures are usually dark brown and black.

Another important sculptural tradition of this region is that of the Dogon people of Mali. Much Dogon sculpture is linked to ancestor worship. The Dogon carve figures meant to house the spirits of the dead, which they place on family shrines. Their designs feature raised geometric patterns, such as black-and-white checkerboards and groups of circles in red, white, and black.

The Guinea Coast extends along the Atlantic Ocean from Guinea-Bissau through central Nigeria and Cameroon. Sculptural figures of this region tend to be more realistic in design than those from other parts of West Africa. The arms, legs, and bodies of figures are curved and smooth. Detailed patterns representing body scars—also typical of this region—rise above the surrounding surface. Many figures are adorned with rings around the neck. A common form of body adornment, the rings are symbols of prosperity and well-being.

Two noteworthy sculptural traditions of the Guinea Coast are those of the ASANTE (Ashanti) and the Fon. The Asante carve dolls that represent their idea of feminine beauty. They also produce swords and staffs, covered in gold foil, for royal officials. The Fon people are known for their large copper and iron sculptures of Gun, the god of iron and war.

The artistic traditions of Nigeria are very old indeed. Among the earliest sculptures from northern Nigeria are realistic clay figures of animals made by the Nok culture as early as the 400s B.C. The human figures produced by the Nok, with their tube-shaped heads, bodies, arms, and legs, are less realistic. The ancient kingdom of Benin in Nigeria was renowned for its magnificent brass sculptures. Dating from about the A.D. 1400s, these include images of groups of animals, birds, and people.

Another important sculptural tradition is that of Ife, an ancient city of the Yoruba of southwestern Nigeria. Between A.D. 1100 and 1450, the people of Ife were creating realistic figures in brass and clay, and some of these probably represent royalty. Life-sized Yoruba brass heads from this time may have played a role in funeral ceremonies. Yoruba carvings typically portray human figures in a naturalistic style. The sculptural tra-

See color plate 6, vol. 3.

Art

* **cult** group bound together by devotion to a particular person, belief, or god

* **relics** pieces of bone, possessions, or other items belonging to a saint or sacred person

ditions of Ife are still followed, but individual cults* often have their own distinct styles.

Central Africa. Central Africa, a vast area of forest and savanna that stretches south from Cameroon to Angola and west to the Democratic Republic of Congo, contains a great diversity of cultures and arts. Yet, in most cases, the differences in artistic styles are so striking that experts have no trouble identifying the area where an object was produced.

A number of groups in Central Africa have ancient sculptural traditions, and some of the most impressive carving in Africa comes from this region. Pieces range from the wooden heads made by the Fang people to the royal figures carved by the Kuba to guard boxes of ancestral relics*. The Kuba figures are decorated with geometric patterns and objects symbolizing each king's accomplishments. The Kuta-Mahongwe work in a more abstract style to produce guardian figures covered with sheets of brass or copper.

The varied sculpture of Central Africa does have some characteristic features, such as heart-shaped faces that curve inward and patterns of circles and dots. Some groups prefer rounded, curved shapes, while others favor geometric, angular forms. Specific details are often highlighted. Particularly striking are the richly carved hairdos and headdresses, intricate scar patterns and tattoos, and necklaces and bracelets. Although wood is the primary material used in carving, the people of this region also create figures from ivory, bone, stone, clay, and metal.

Eastern Africa. Although sculpture is not a major art form in eastern Africa, a variety of sculptural traditions can be found in the region. An unusual sculptural form in some parts of eastern Africa is the pole, which is carved in human shape and decorated. Usually associated with death, pole sculptures are placed next to graves or at the entrances to villages. Among the Konso of Ethiopia, for example, the grave of a wealthy, important man may be marked by a group of carved wooden figures representing the deceased, his wives, and the people or animals he killed during his lifetime.

Sculpture is mainly associated with the dead in parts of Madagascar as well. Figures are often placed on tombs or in shrines dedicated to ancestors. The tombs of prominent Mahafaly individuals may be covered with as many as 30 wooden sculptures. Carved from a single piece of wood, each sculpture stands about 6 1/2 feet high. The lower parts are often decorated with geometric forms, while the tops are carved with figures of animals, people, and various objects.

Southern Africa. Sculpture does not have a particularly strong tradition in southern Africa. The oldest known clay figures from South Africa, dating from between A.D. 400 and 600, have cylindrical heads, some with human features and some with a combination of human and animal features.

Among the more notable carved objects found in southern Africa are wooden headrests in various styles from geometric designs to more realistic carvings of animal figures. Some headrests were buried with their owners, and some were handed down from one generation to the next.

MASKS

Masks are one of the most important and widespread art forms in sub-Saharan Africa. They may be used in initiation ceremonies, such as that marking the passage from childhood to adulthood. Masks also serve as symbols of power to enforce the laws of society.

See color plate 2, vol. 1.

Masks are usually worn as disguises in ceremonies and rituals, along with a costume of leaves, cloth, feathers, and other materials. Although masks may represent either male or female spirits, they are almost always worn by men. The person wearing the mask in the ceremony is no longer treated as himself or herself but as the spirit that the mask represents.

In addition to face masks (which just cover the face), there are helmet masks (which cover all or most of the head) and crest masks (worn on top of the head like a headdress). Made of wood, clay, metal, leather, fabric, or other materials, masks may be painted and decorated with such things as animal skins, feathers, beads, and shells.

West Africa. Many different forms and styles of masks can be found in West Africa. The Bambara people of Mali have specific masks for their various male societies. Many of these masks represent animals that stand for mythical characters. The masks are decorated with real antelope horns, porcupine quills, bird skulls, and other objects. The characteristics of several animals are combined in masks of the Senufo people of Ivory Coast.

Masks play a role in rituals and ceremonies related to death or ancestors. Once a year, in elaborate performances honoring their ancestors, the Yoruba of Nigeria put on masks made of colorful fabrics and small carved wooden heads. In other parts of Nigeria, masks representing both human and animal characters are worn at the funerals of important elders as a way of honoring the deceased.

The IGBO people of Nigeria have two types of masks to mark the transition from childhood to adulthood. Dark masks represent "male qualities" such as power and strength, prosperity, and impurity, while delicate white masks symbolize "female qualities" of beauty, gentleness, and purity. Among the Mende people of Sierra Leone, elaborate black helmet masks representing the Mende ideals of feminine beauty are used in rituals initiating young girls into womanhood. This is the only case of women wearing masks in Africa.

Central and Eastern Africa. Many Central African masks signify rank and social position, representing the authority and privilege of kings, chiefs, and other individuals. Some also function as symbols of identity for specific groups. While certain masks are considered the property of individuals, others are owned collectively by the group. Used in a variety of situations, masks may inspire fear, fight witchcraft, or entertain. As elsewhere in Africa, many masks are linked with initiation and funeral rituals.

Among the most notable masks of Central Africa are large helmet masks with figures of humans, animals, and scenes on top. Too heavy to be carried or worn, they are displayed during important ceremonies. The

Art

The wooden mask shown here was carved by the Yaure of the Ivory Coast. The Yaure often use fine patterns of lines to indicate beards, hairlines, jewelry, and scars.

* **amulet** small object thought to have supernatural or magical powers

masks of the Pende people of Angola and Congo (Kinshasa) are among the most dramatic works of art in Africa. These large helmet masks have faces with angular patterns and heavy triangular eyelids. Topped by plant fibers that represent hair, they are thought to possess mysterious powers. The Pende make smaller versions of these masks in ivory or wood for use as amulets*. In nearby Zambia, various materials are used to create ceremonial masks. The Mbundu work in wood, and the Luvale and Chokwe attach pieces of painted bark cloth to a wicker frame.

Masks do not play an important role in the art of eastern Africa. However, the Makonde of Mozambique and southeastern Tanzania create distinctive face masks and body masks.

PAINTING

Painting on canvas is a recent development in Africa. Although Africans have always painted, they have done so primarily on rock surfaces or on the walls of houses and other buildings. Africans also apply paint to sculpted figures, masks, and their own bodies.

The earliest known African paintings are on rocks in southern Africa. Made by the KHOISAN people about 20,000 years ago, these rock paintings portray human and animal figures, often in hunting scenes. The paintings may have had ritual or social significance, though no one knows for sure. Other ancient rock paintings have been found in the Sahara desert in North Africa. Dating from as early as the 4000s B.C., these paintings also portray animals and human figures. The strongest traditions of rock painting are found in eastern and southern Africa.

Eastern Africa. The people of eastern Africa have traditionally painted and marked their bodies in various ways. Such decoration has been considered a sign of beauty as well as a form of artistic expression. Some of it is temporary, as in the case of body painting with various natural pigments and other coloring agents. The patterns and designs used often signify group identity, social status, and passage through important stages in life.

Other forms of painting can be found in Ethiopia. Christian influence has been strong in Ethiopia for centuries, and around the A.D. 1100s Ethiopian artists began painting religious scenes on the walls of churches. Since the 1600s, Ethiopians have also produced religious pictures on canvas, wood panels, and parchment.

Traditions of painting are found in several other areas of eastern Africa as well. The Dinka and Nuer people of southern Sudan, for example, paint pictures of cattle and people on the walls of huts. Members of the secret snake charmer society of the Sukuma people in Tanzania decorate the interior walls of their meetinghouses with images of humans, snakes, and mythological figures. The LUO of western Kenya paint geometric designs on fishing boats, and the Mahafaly of Madagascar paint scenes on the sides of tombs.

Southern Africa. Wall painting on the interiors or exteriors of buildings is an important art form in southern Africa. Some very striking examples can be found in this region. Among the best known are those of the NDEBELE of South Africa and Zimbabwe. Almost exclusively the work of women, these paintings were traditionally done in natural earth colors using bold geometric shapes and symmetrical patterns. In recent years, Ndebele women have also used commercial paints, and their designs have become more varied, incorporating lettering and objects such as lightbulbs, as well as abstract designs.

DECORATIVE ARTS

The decorative arts include such items as textiles, jewelry, pottery, and basketry. While viewed as crafts in some Western cultures, these objects

See color plate 2, vol. 2.

See color plate 3, vol. 3.

See color plate 15, vol. 3.

See color plate 8, vol. 4.

North African artists use calligraphy to decorate buildings and a variety of household items.

See color plate 12, vol. 3.

See color plate 9, vol. 3.

* **raffia** type of palm used for weaving and basketry

can also be seen as works of art because of the care and level of skill that goes into their creation.

Many useful objects are carved from wood or other hard materials and then decorated. The SWAHILI of eastern Africa used ivory and ebony (a hard wood) to build elaborate "chairs of power" with footrests and removable backs. In West Africa, some Nigerian artisans make musical instruments and food containers from round fruits known as gourds. The outer surfaces of the gourds are covered with delicately carved and painted geometric designs.

African artists create jewelry for adornment, as symbols of social position, and even to bring good health and luck. They use materials such as gold, silver, and various types of beads to make necklaces, bracelets, crowns, rings, and anklets. In the KALAHARI DESERT in southern Africa, artisans fashioned ornaments with beads made from glass or ostrich eggshell. In West Africa the Asante are famous for their gold jewelry and gold-handled swords.

The Asante are also skilled weavers, known for their kente cloth—richly colored cotton or silk fabrics. Many groups of people in western and central Africa have developed their own weaving traditions, using particular types of looms and decorative techniques such as embroidery, patchwork, painting, stenciling, or tie-dyeing. Weavers use cotton, wool, wild silk, raffia*, or synthetic threads to create their designs. In Niger, the Zerma weave large cotton covers in vivid red and black patterns. The Mandjak of Senegal produce magnificently colorful cloth of synthetic silk, rayon, or lurex fibers.

In North Africa, one of the most important decorative art forms is calligraphy. Calligraphy has special significance for Muslims because they consider the written word a sacred symbol of Islamic beliefs. In addi-

See color plate 13, vol. 3.

tion, because of the restrictions on creating images of human beings, artists turn to calligraphy to decorate their work. Calligraphy is found on buildings throughout North Africa and on many objects used in daily life. Carved in wood and stone, painted on walls and pottery, burned into leather, woven into cloth, or shaped into jewelry, calligraphy appears in a wide variety of materials and styles. Geometric designs or flowing patterns of lines and curves resembling flowers, leaves, vines, and even animals often accompany the calligraphy. These designs are always highly stylized, not realistic in form.

Rugs are another major art form in North Africa. The production of intricate hand-knotted rugs began to flourish in Egypt in the 1400s under the Muslim Mamluk rulers. Early rugs featuring a central design surrounded by border elements sometimes contained as many as six colors. Woven carpets are produced in many areas of North Africa, including Sudan and Morocco, often by groups of BERBERS. (*See also* **Architecture, Body Adornment and Clothing, Crafts, Ethnic Groups and Identity, Festivals and Carnivals, Houses and Housing, Initiation Rites, Masks and Masquerades, Religion and Ritual, Rock Art, Spirit Possession, Witchcraft and Sorcery.**)

Asante

The Asante (Ashanti) are the largest and most powerful of a cluster of AKAN chiefdoms of southern GHANA and IVORY COAST. Originating around Lake Bosumtwi, the Asante migrated to the area around the town of Tafo in the early 1600s. Around 1700, Chief Osei Tutu made alliances with several surrounding kingdoms to form the Asante Union. Included in the union were the Mampong, Bekwai, Kokofu, Dwaben, and Nsuta people. It is legend that Osei Tutu, aided by Okomfu Anokye, established the Golden Stool as the traditional symbol of Asante unity, to be held by the Asante ruler. The stool is kept at the capital city of Kumasi.

By the early 1800s the Asante had expanded toward the Atlantic coast, threatening British control over trade there. Conflicts occurred with British troops, who burned Kumasi in 1874 and sent several important Asante into exile. In 1902 the British made the Asante state part of their colonial empire. Although they allowed the re-creation of the Asante Union in 1935, it became part of the Gold Coast, as Ghana was then called.

See color plate 9, vol. 1.

There are about three million Asante, most of whom make their living from agriculture. Their main products are gold, cocoa, palm oil, timber, bauxite, and rubber. Many Asante are highly educated and hold important positions in Ghana's government, businesses, and religious institutions. The Asante practice various religions, including Christianity, Islam, and traditional religions; most combine different forms of belief and worship. Of the approximately 150,000 Asante who are Muslim, the majority follow the Sunni school of the Maliki tradition, while a minority believe in the Shafi'i rite. Family inheritance is determined by matrilineal descent. (*See also* **Christianity in Africa, Islam in Africa.**)

Asantewa, Yaa

Asantewa, Yaa

ca. 1832–1921
Asante queen

* **siege** attempt to conquer a fortress or town by surrounding it with troops and cutting it off from supplies

Yaa Asantewa was queen of the ASANTE town of Edweso, located in present-day GHANA. In 1900 she led a three-month siege* against British troops in the Asante capital of Kumasi. The British had seized Kumasi four years earlier in an attempt to extend their control of the country, then known as the Gold Coast. They forced a group of Asante chiefs and elders, including Asantewa's grandson, to leave their land.

During this conflict, the Asante hid the Golden Stool, the sacred symbol of Asante kingship. When British governor Sir Frederick Hodgson arrived in Kumasi in 1900, he demanded payment from the Asante as well as surrender of the Golden Stool. These demands led to an uprising and siege by Asantewa and leaders of the surrounding Asante towns. The British eventually broke the siege and exiled Asantewa to the SEYCHELLES, where she died 21 years later. (*See also* **Colonialism in Africa.**)

ASHANTI

See *Asante.*

Askiya Muhammad I

(?)–1528
Ruler of the Songhai Empire

* **pilgrimage** journey to a shrine or sacred place

Askiya Muhammad I was a statesman and military leader who ruled the Songhai Empire of West Africa for more than 30 years. During his reign Muhammad not only expanded the empire, he also reorganized it and transformed it into a Muslim kingdom. He is said to have been a nephew of the Songhai emperor Sunni Ali Ber. Soon after Sunni Ali's death, Muhammad attacked and defeated the new emperor, Sunni Baru. He then gave himself the title Askiya. Two years later Muhammad made a pilgrimage* to Mecca, and when he returned in 1497 he made Islam the official religion of the Songhai Empire.

Muhammad conquered a wide area of northwestern Africa, and his empire's influence extended even farther. However, his main achievements were organizational. He divided the empire into provinces administered by governors and appointed separate ministers to direct financial affairs, justice, agriculture, and other areas of importance to the state. He also established a permanent army and a fleet of war canoes and placed them under the command of a general and an admiral. The well-run empire became a model for surrounding states.

Muhammad's children brought an end to his successful rule. They fought bitterly over the riches of his empire. In 1528 his eldest son killed Muhammad's new general in chief and exiled Muhammad to an island in the NIGER RIVER. When another son took power in 1537, he called his father back to the capital at Gao, where Muhammad died the following year. His tomb, an earthen pyramid topped by wooden spikes, still stands. It is considered one of the holiest Islamic sites in West Africa. (*See also* **Islam in Africa, Sudanic Empires of Western Africa, Sunni Ali.**)

Asma'u, Nana

1793–1864
Islamic poet and teacher

* **jihad** Muslim holy war

* **caliphate** state in the Muslim empire

* **Sufi** member of a Muslim movement characterized by mysticism and dedication to poverty and prayer

Nana Asma'u, an Islamic teacher in what is now northern Nigeria, was known for her writings and for her work in educating Muslim women. Fluent in Arabic and several African languages, she memorized the entire Muslim holy book, the Qur'an. Her father, UTHMAN DAN FODIO, was an Islamic ruler who led a jihad* in 1804 in Hausaland. Nana Asma'u later wrote extensively about this jihad.

After her father's death, Nana Asma'u became part of a team that organized a new Muslim community in the Sokoto Caliphate*. She also assisted her brother, Caliph Muhammed Bello, in translating and adapting a work on Sufi* women in verse form. Through her poetry Nana Asma'u reminded the new leaders of the caliphate of their responsibilities to the people. Some of her writings provide a glimpse into the workings of the Muslim community. She is perhaps most fondly remembered for creating an educational network for rural Muslim women that instructed students in their native languages. This network still exists today. (*See also* **Literature, Sufism.**)

AXUM

See *Aksum.*

Atlas Mountains

* **indigenous** native to a certain place

The Atlas Mountains are the principal geographic feature of the North African countries of MOROCCO, ALGERIA, and TUNISIA. They are made up of six mountain ranges—the Anti-Atlas, the High Atlas, the Middle Atlas, the Saharan Atlas, the Tell Atlas, and the Aurés—with high plateaus and plains between them. The mountains run northeast from the Atlantic coast of Morocco to the Mediterranean coast of Tunisia for approximately 1,250 miles.

The Atlas Mountains have had a profound effect on North Africa's climate, economic resources, and human history. Separating the coastal lowlands from the SAHARA DESERT in the interior, the ranges prevent the desert heat from reaching the coast. They also trap moist winter storms that blow in from the Atlantic Ocean and Mediterranean Sea, which causes rainfall along the coast and prevents rain from reaching the interior. In addition, snowfall in the mountains feeds rivers and streams that water the northern parts of Morocco, Algeria, and Tunisia. For these reasons, the northern districts are greener and better suited to agriculture than the flat desert lands found elsewhere in North Africa, and over the centuries people have chosen to settle in these more fertile areas.

The Atlas Mountains are home to several tribes of BERBERS, indigenous* North African people. Because of their isolation in the Atlas Mountains, the Berbers have been able to maintain their languages and customs. Many of them support themselves by farming and raising livestock.

The mountains' name comes from the Greek mythical figure Atlas, who bore the world on his shoulders. The ancient Greeks believed that Atlas lived among the North African peaks. The Arabs who later settled

Atlas Mountains

The Atlas Mountains act as a barrier between the coastal lowlands of western North Africa and the Sahara desert. The mountains trap moisture along the fertile coast and shield the region from the heat of the desert.

in the region called the mountains Jazirat al-Maghrib, "island of the west," because of their contrast to the surrounding desert. Today Morocco, Algeria, and Tunisia are sometimes called the MAGHREB or Maghrib.

Azikiwe, Benjamin Nnamdi

1904–1996
President of Nigeria

Benjamin Nnamdi Azikiwe was the first president of the Federal Republic of NIGERIA, after the country won its independence from Britain in 1960. As a young man, Azikiwe left Nigeria to study in the United States. He earned master's degrees in both political science and anthropology. After his studies, he worked for three years as editor of the newspaper *African Morning Post* in Accra, GHANA. Then Azikiwe returned to Nigeria and started the newspaper *West African Pilot*.

Azikiwe launched his political career in 1944, when he joined forces with Herbert MACAULAY, the founder of Nigeria's first political party, the

Nigerian National Democratic Party. Together they organized the National Council of Nigeria and the Cameroons. Azikiwe became leader of the party (renamed the National Convention of Nigerian Citizens) two years later.

Azikiwe served as premier of Eastern Nigeria under British rule from 1954 to 1959. After Nigeria achieved independence, he served as governor general from 1960 to 1963 and became the nation's first president in 1963. However, Azikiwe was deposed* three years later when the military seized control of Nigeria and banned political parties. After the ban was lifted in 1978, Azikiwe returned to political life as a member of the Nigerian People's Party. By the time he retired from politics in 1986, he had gained wide respect as a political strategist. He was also known as a Nigerian patriot and a champion of human rights. He wrote several books on African politics.

* **depose**   to remove from office

Bambara

With a population estimated at 3 million, the Bambara are the largest ethnic group in MALI. Large numbers of them live in northern IVORY COAST as well. They are sometimes called Bamana, the name of the Mande language they speak.

In the 1700s two Bambara kingdoms arose in the region, but they fell to Muslim forces during the 1800s. When the French moved into the area, they destroyed the remaining Bambara armies. By the early 1900s some Bambara had converted to Islam, the religion of their longtime Muslim enemies, as a way of resisting French rule. The process of conversion increased rapidly after World War II, and since the 1980s more than 70 percent of the Bambara have been Muslims.

Many of the Bambara who live in cities hold important positions in politics, business, and professions such as law and medicine. The Bambara of rural areas are mainly farmers, growing staple crops and several cash crops* including peanuts, rice, and cotton. They are renowned as artists and weavers of cloth that is exported around the world. In recent years many Bambara have moved from rural to urban areas to find work as laborers. (*See also* **Islam in Africa.**)

* **cash crop**   crop grown primarily for sale rather than for local consumption

Banda, Ngwazi Hastings Kamuzu

1906–
President of Malawi

Dr. Hastings Kamuzu Banda served as president of MALAWI from 1966 to 1994. His presidency was a time of one-party rule. Born in the British colony of Nyasaland (present-day Malawi), Banda left home at age 17 to study in SOUTH AFRICA. Later he traveled to the United States, where he attended college and medical school.

While practicing medicine in London and GHANA, Banda became involved in his country's politics. He joined the Nyasaland Congress and protested Britain's decision to create a federation linking Nyasaland with the neighboring colonies of Northern and Southern Rhodesia. In 1958 the Congress asked him to come back home.

Banda soon formed his own political party, the Malawi Congress Party (MCP). He was a lively and appealing public figure, and when

Banda, Ngwazi Hastings Kamuzu

Nyasaland won independence as Malawi in 1964, Banda became the country's prime minister. Three years later he was chosen president. In 1971 he changed his title to President for Life and made the MCP the only legal political party in the country. Banda's political opponents were driven into exile, imprisoned, or killed. His foreign policy favored Western governments. At home he sought to modernize Malawi's agriculture and public works, while enforcing a strict moral code on the people. Banda regulated everything from the length of women's skirts to the books people could read.

Despite his harsh rule, Banda was widely respected in Malawi and was nicknamed Ngwazi—meaning savior or conqueror—by the local media. However, he upset many African leaders by supporting South Africa's apartheid* government and by backing guerrilla* rebels in MOZAMBIQUE. In 1991 various groups spoke out against Banda's human rights abuses, further weakening his power. In 1994 Banda reluctantly allowed the first multiparty elections in nearly 30 years and resigned the presidency.

* **apartheid** policy of racial segregation in South Africa intended to maintain white control over the country's blacks, Asians, and people of mixed ancestry

* **guerrilla** type of warfare involving sudden raids by small groups of warriors

BANKING

See *Development, Economic and Social; Money and Banking.*

Bantu Peoples

The Bantu, a large group of related peoples, originated along what is now the border between NIGERIA and CAMEROON and spread throughout central and southern Africa. The term *Bantu* is sometimes used to describe all Africans and African culture in general. But this use of the term is inaccurate; Bantu peoples make up only about a third of Africa's population. Bantu is also the name of the family of related LANGUAGES spoken by these people. Over time, the many Bantu-speaking peoples have become very different from one another.

Bantu Origins. All Bantu languages arose from a single language known as proto-Bantu. About 4000 B.C. the people who spoke this language developed a culture based on the farming of root crops, foraging*, and fishing on the West African coast. Over the years, Bantu became more widely spoken than the languages of the nomadic peoples who lived in the same area. Its spread was probably aided by the unique social organization of the early Bantu, based on a system of cooperation between villages. Every village consisted of several "Houses," and each House formed working relationships with Houses from other villages. This strong but flexible social network may have helped the Bantu migrate across the continent.

* **forage** to hunt or search for food

According to archaeological* evidence, the Bantu migration began sometime after 3000 B.C. One group of Bantu moved southward, reaching southern Cameroon by about 1500 B.C. Within a thousand years the migrants also settled the coast of Congo and the Congo Basin in what is now the Democratic Republic of Congo (CONGO (KINSHASA)). These West Bantu people developed new skills such as ironworking and the

* **archaeological** referring to the study of past human cultures and societies, usually by excavating ruins

These Zulu women of South Africa speak one of the nearly 600 Bantu languages found on the continent.

* **interlacustrine**   between lakes

making of ceramics. They continued to live side-by-side with other peoples, but apparently shared little in the way of culture or technology.

The Interlacustrine Bantu. Long after the West Bantu migration, a second Bantu migration began—this one toward the east. Sometime before 1000 B.C. Bantu groups arrived in the northwestern Great Lakes area in what is now UGANDA. Known as the Interlacustrine* Bantu, these peoples learned new farming methods from neighbors in eastern Africa who spoke Cushitic and Sudanic languages. They raised livestock—particularly cattle—and practiced agriculture, growing grain crops such as sorghum. Bantu women eventually married Sudanic and Cushitic men and raised their children to speak the Bantu language. Between about 500 B.C. and A.D. 800, the Bantu language spread throughout the Great Lakes region.

Two specific developments brought steady prosperity to this region after A.D. 1000. The first was the emergence of plantain farming. The second was pastoralism—a way of life in which cattle were driven from place to place in search of new grazing land. Both plantains (a banana-like fruit) and cattle produced a reliable year-round supply of food, enabling communities to grow in size and complexity. The Bantu founded new settlements, created a new style of pottery, and developed new social and political ties.

Bantu Peoples

* **medium** person called upon to communicate with the spirit world

Bantu communities that practiced pastoralism were particularly influential in the area. Their cattle were a source of moveable wealth. People who owned cattle gained political power by loaning the cattle to neighbors, who were obligated to provide support and assistance to the lender in return. In this way, loaning cattle forged new political relationships and incorporated outsiders in existing political and social groups.

Bantu herding communities also spread their religion as they traveled, introducing new spirits and beliefs into the communities they visited. Their mediums* established new centers of spiritual and political power that competed with and often replaced the worship of local spirits. Between 1000 and 1500 the new forms of economic, political, religious, and social life that arose under Bantu influence completely transformed Africa's Great Lakes region.

Later Bantu Cultures. The Interlacustrine Bantu eventually spread east to modern-day KENYA and TANZANIA and south into the present-day countries of ZIMBABWE, BOTSWANA, MOZAMBIQUE, and parts of SOUTH AFRICA. This movement was very rapid and most likely occurred before 200 B.C. As in the west, Bantu languages scattered widely throughout eastern Africa. After the first eastern expansion ended, East Bantu speakers in southeastern Congo (Kinshasa) and ZAMBIA moved westward and joined with West Bantu speakers. The languages in this area show a mixture of East and West Bantu influences.

The most extensive archeological evidence of Bantu culture in eastern and southern Africa dates from about A.D. 400. By this time, cattle were so important in southern Bantu society that villages were erected around a central pen. In Kenya the first towns built by the SWAHILI—another Bantu people—appeared around 750. Swahili settlements soon dotted the Indian Ocean coast as far south as Mozambique. Around the same time, systems of farming and herding arose in Uganda and RWANDA. These regions featured Bantu settlements with fortified central areas that eventually grew into kingdoms after about 1500.

By A.D. 1000, settlements along the Limpopo River had developed into a town called Mapungabwe—the capital of a Bantu kingdom that controlled much of the surrounding territory. After Mapungabwe declined, it was replaced around 1250 by the kingdom of Great Zimbabwe. This powerful empire flourished for almost 200 years by supplying gold and ivory to Swahili traders from the North. Bantu civilizations continued to dominate south and east Africa politically until European colonial governments displaced them in the 1800s.

Today, the Bantu peoples are as diverse as the land they inhabit. Hundreds of societies in central and southern Africa trace their roots to the Bantu, and about 150 million Africans speak one of nearly 600 Bantu languages. Yet regional differences in environment, livelihood, and history have made each Bantu society and tongue unique. The Bantu languages are so distinct that people who speak one language usually cannot understand their neighbors who speak another. Bantu patterns of social organization, forms of government, and ways of tracing KINSHIP vary widely. (*See also* **Colonialism in Africa, Ethnic Groups and Identity, Livestock Grazing.**)

Barghash ibn Sa'id

**1833(?)–1888
Sultan of Zanzibar**

Sultan Barghash ibn Sa'id ruled ZANZIBAR from 1870 until his death in 1888. He was a reformer who tried to eliminate corruption and to improve the economy of Zanzibar.

Barghash rebuilt the clove economy after it was destroyed by a hurricane in 1872. Later he established a fleet of steamships that boosted the country's trade and revenues. The sultan used this new wealth to build a number of palaces and introduce public improvements such as electricity and piped water to the town of Zanzibar.

However, the sultanate soon came under the shadow of European colonial ambitions. In 1890 Germany and Britain signed two treaties that forced Barghash to accept reductions in the size of Zanzibar. Germany took Tanganyika (part of present-day Tanzania), leaving Zanzibar with only a narrow strip of coastal land in Kenya. The two offshore islands of Zanzibar and Pemba fell under British control. Barghash did not survive the breakup of his sultanate. (*See also* **Colonialism in Africa**.)

Barth, Heinrich

**1821–1865
German traveler and explorer**

* caliphate   state in the Muslim empire

Heinrich Barth was a German-born scholar who made two long trips to Africa that he recorded in a book called *Travels and Discoveries in North and Central Africa*. Barth's extensive knowledge of the peoples and places described in his book made it a standard reference for scholars of Africa.

Barth was educated in Berlin, where he earned a doctorate in 1844. Although he already spoke five languages, he went to London to perfect his Arabic before traveling in North Africa from 1845 to 1847. Shortly after his return to Germany, he accepted an invitation to join a British expedition to central Africa. The expedition began in 1850 but within a year its leader, James Richardson, died. Barth took over the expedition, which continued exploring as far south as the present-day countries of CHAD, CAMEROON, MALI, NIGER, and NIGERIA. Before returning to Europe in 1855, Barth visited the Arab leaders of the Sokoto Caliphate* as well as their rivals in the cities of Kukawa and TIMBUKTU.

After leaving Africa, Barth settled in London. There he wrote an account of his travels, but it received little attention. Furthermore, the proud Barth quarreled with the Royal Geographic Society and the British government. He went home to Germany in 1859 but had no success there either. He failed to win political posts he sought, and he was denied full membership in the Royal Academy of Sciences. The University of Berlin also refused to name him to succeed his mentor Karl Ritter as professor of geography. In 1862 he published an important book, the *Collection of Vocabularies of Central African Languages*. He died three years later without achieving recognition for his accomplishments. That recognition came years after his death. (*See also* **Travel and Exploration**.)

| BASUTOLAND | See *Lesotho.* |

| BECHUANALAND | See *Botswana.* |

| BELGIAN COLONIES | See *Colonialism in Africa.* |

Bello, Ahmadu

1910–1966
Premier of Northern Nigeria

Ahmadu Bello, a Nigerian leader, served as the first premier of Northern NIGERIA in 1954, when the country was under British rule. He was active in the Northern People's Congress (NPC), a cultural organization that he helped transform into a political party in the early 1950s. Under Bello's leadership, Northern Nigeria and the NPC dominated Nigeria's politics at the time of its independence in 1960.

Bello was a direct descendant of the founder of the FULANI empire of Sokoto, a state in Northern Nigeria. He hoped to become the *surdauna* of Sokoto, the spiritual leader of Northern Nigeria's Muslim population. This position would have given him both political power and religious authority. Bello's ambitions, however, were cut short when he was murdered by the military during an uprising in January 1966. (*See also* **Colonialism in Africa, Independence Movements.**)

Ben Bella, Ahmed

1918(?)–
First president of Algeria

A leading figure in Algeria's struggle for independence from France, Ahmed Ben Bella served as the country's first president from 1963 to 1965. Educated at a French primary school near Oran, ALGERIA, he became involved with the independence movement while pursuing further studies in the nearby city of Tlemcen. During World War II he served in the French army, receiving the prestigious Croix de Guerre in 1940.

After the war Ben Bella returned home and helped found an underground political movement devoted to armed struggle against French colonial rule. In 1950, to gain money for the independence effort, he robbed a post office. He was captured and served two years in jail. After escaping to EGYPT, he met followers of the Egyptian revolutionary leader Gamal Abdel NASSER.

In 1954 Ben Bella and other Algerian leaders living in Egypt formed the National Liberation Front (FLN). The organization called for the overthrow of French rule in Algeria, and launched a civil war. French

authorities arrested Ben Bella in 1956, and he remained in prison until Algeria won its independence six years later. With the support of Colonel Houari BOUMÉDIENNE, head of the National Liberation Army, Ben Bella became prime minister. He was elected president in 1963.

As president Ben Bella reestablished order in war-torn Algeria and instituted reforms in education and agriculture. However, his policies were often poorly planned. In 1965 Boumédienne overthrew Ben Bella, who remained under house arrest until after Boumédienne's death. Freed in 1980, Ben Bella spent the next ten years in exile, eventually returning to Algeria in 1990. (*See also* **Agriculture, Colonialism in Africa, Education, Independence Movements.**)

Bénin

T he Republic of Bénin is located in West Africa along the Gulf of Guinea. It is bordered by NIGERIA on the east, TOGO on the west, and by BURKINA FASO and NIGER on the north. Bénin's present-day borders were shaped by the kingdom of Dahomey, which extended through the region in the mid-1800s, and by European countries trying to establish empires in Africa.

GEOGRAPHY

Although Bénin lies entirely within the tropics, it has considerable variety in both its geography and climate. Southern Bénin was once covered with rainforests, but most of the land has been cleared for agriculture. The destruction of rainforests has led to a decrease in precipitation during the two rainy seasons the south experiences each year. Forests cover central Bénin, savanna* dominates in the northeast, and the Atakora Mountains rise in the northwest. Northern Bénin has only one rainy season per year, which makes the region less suitable for raising crops.

* **savanna** tropical or subtropical grassland with scattered trees and drought-resistant undergrowth

Most of Bénin's population is concentrated in the south, where the land is better suited to farming. Both Bénin's capital, Porto Novo, and its largest city, Cotonou, are located in this region.

ECONOMY

Bénin's economy is based on agriculture, informal trade (smuggling), and foreign aid. Due to a lack of infrastructure*—such as roads, railroads, and power generation—industry and trade have developed slowly in the country.

* **infrastructure** basic framework of a society and its economy, which includes roads, bridges, port facilities, airports, and other public works

* **gross domestic product (GDP)** total value of goods and services produced and consumed within a country

More than half of the people in Bénin make a living in agriculture, which accounts for about one third of the country's gross domestic product (GDP)*. However, most of the soil is of poor quality. Despite this disadvantage and a doubling of the population between 1962 and 1995, Bénin has been able to produce enough food to feed itself. It also exports food to Nigeria. Rice, corn, peanuts, and cotton are some of Bénin's main crops. Palm oil and palm kernel oil are also major agricultural exports.

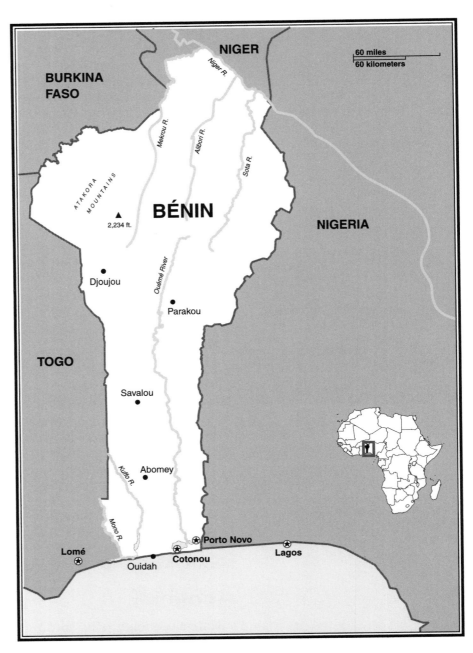

Bénin has a long history of people smuggling goods across its border with Nigeria. The goods move in both directions. Most of the cocoa crop that Bénin exports is smuggled in from Nigeria. Illegal drugs from South America also enter Bénin before being shipped to Europe.

Regular trade with countries outside of Africa accounts for more than one third of GDP. Trade with African countries is much smaller because of internal problems such as lack of transport, customs barriers, and officials who charge "tariffs" that they keep for themselves. These help drive up the cost of transporting goods.

Industrial development in Bénin, based on international financing, has not had much success. Bénin has reduced the amount of oil it

Modern Witch-Hunt

In the 1970s President Kérékou's government sought to replace Bénin's local leaders with people loyal to the president. Some of the old leaders were Vodun (voodoo) priests, and the program to replace them led to a campaign to detect sorcerers and witches, who were considered dangerous. The first people accused of witchcraft held positions of power, but later the accused were mostly women and the elderly. Torture was frequently employed to obtain confessions. Many people opposed the witch-hunt, but others were glad that a government finally addressed the fear of sorcerers shared by large numbers of people. Although the campaign split communities and families, it did allow the government to replace old leaders.

* **federation**   organization of separate states with a central government

See map in Archaeology and Prehistory (vol. 1).

* **coup**   sudden, often violent overthrow of a ruler or government

imports by producing oil using offshore resources. A large percent of Bénin's electricity is generated in GHANA.

Foreign countries and international institutions provide more than $250 million of economic assistance to Bénin per year. Much of this aid has been misspent on projects such as trying to introduce plow agriculture in the south. A great deal of the funds also goes to pay government salaries, which take up a large portion of the national budget.

HISTORY AND GOVERNMENT

The history of Bénin involves the history of several African kingdoms. Although Benin was the name of an ancient kingdom in what is now Nigeria, that kingdom is not related to present-day Bénin. This state is a twentieth-century invention, created by French colonial officials who combined areas that had few ties.

Precolonial Bénin.   Before the 1800s the peoples of north Bénin were closely connected to the other lands of West Africa. South Bénin was ruled by a series of kingdoms controlled by the Fon and the Adja, who were related to peoples from Togo and Ghana. The most powerful of these kingdoms was that of Dahomey, which occupied southern Bénin as well as parts of present-day Togo and Nigeria. Dahomey built its power and wealth from trading slaves captured in raids on northern lands. The kingdom also produced palm oil and sold it to the French. Thus when the transatlantic SLAVE TRADE ended in 1851, Dahomey had a product available to replace slaves.

Colonial Bénin.   The French hoped to build an empire in Africa and attempted to acquire territory on the West African coast. King Ghezo, who ruled from 1818 to 1856, gave France control over a portion of the coast that later became the city of Cotonou. However, the French wanted more territory, and in 1890 they mounted an attack on Dahomey with the help of the southern kingdom of Gun. The attack failed, but the French were successful two years later, and Dahomey became part of the federation* of FRENCH WEST AFRICA.

The French established an administration partially based on institutions from the kingdom of Dahomey. Colonial authorities relied on powerful local individuals to carry out policies in the villages and countryside. Overseeing this colonial structure were district officers who had the power to raise and collect taxes, recruit labor by force, and draft individuals into the military. However, French rule in Dahomey was quite unstable, and the colony produced little revenue.

In the early 1900s, Dahomey experienced a series of brief uprisings among several local peoples. Calls for independence grew louder after World War II. In 1960 France finally granted independence to Dahomey. Fifteen years later, Dahomey changed its name to Bénin.

Postcolonial Bénin.   Between 1960 and 1972 Bénin had 12 separate governments, 5 of which were overthrown in coups*. During this time, French "technical advisers" actually controlled the workings of government, and France paid Bénin's national debt. In 1972 military leader

Bénin

Mathieu Kérékou seized power and embarked on a communist* program of economic and social development. He took over large private plantations and turned them into cooperative* farms and nationalized* many businesses. The state also replaced local leaders who were not easily controlled by the central government.

In the early 1980s, Bénin suffered an economic crisis. Over the next several years, its state-owned banks began to fail and the salaries of government employees were paid irregularly. In 1989 the government cut its spending, and President Kérékou abandoned his communist political program and accepted a democratic constitution for Bénin.

In 1991 Nicéphore Soglo was elected president in free elections. Three years later, Bénin suffered an economic crisis when its currency was reduced in value by 50 percent, but the situation became more stable within a couple of years. In 1996 Kérékou defeated Soglo and returned as the country's president.

Government. Bénin's government is a democracy headed by a president elected by the people. The president nominates cabinet ministers and the governors of Bénin's six provinces. Bénin's parliament has the power to make laws and decisions about the budget. In some ways, modern Bénin still operates like the colonial government. Local author-

Bénin's waterways serve as vital transportation routes. The residents of this village construct their houses directly over the water on tall stilts.

 Republic of Bénin

POPULATION:
6,395,919 (2000 estimated population)

AREA:
43,483 sq. mi. (112,620 sq. km)

LANGUAGES:
French (official); Fon, Yoruba, Adja, Banba

NATIONAL CURRENCY:
CFA franc

PRINCIPAL RELIGIONS:
traditional 70%, Christian 15%, Muslim 15%

CITIES:
Porto Novo (capital), 330,000 (1999 est.); Cotonou, Abomey, Ouidah, Parakou, Natitingu

ANNUAL RAINFALL:
Varies from 58 in. (1,500 mm) in the southeast to 30 in. (770 mm) in the extreme north

ECONOMY:
GDP per capita: U.S. $1,300

PRINCIPAL PRODUCTS AND EXPORTS:
Agricultural: palm oil, cotton, coffee, cocoa, cassava, yams, corn, livestock, peanuts, timber
Manufacturing: vegetable oil processing, cement, textiles, palm products
Mining: offshore oil deposits, limestone, marble, iron ore

GOVERNMENT:
Independence from France, 1960. President elected by universal suffrage. Governing bodies: Assemblée Nationale elected by universal suffrage.

HEADS OF STATE SINCE 1980:
1972–1991 Major (later Lieutenant General) Mathieu Kérékou
1991–1996 President Nicéphore Soglo
1996– President Mathieu Kérékou

ARMED FORCES:
4,800 (1998 est.)

EDUCATION:
Compulsory for ages 6–12; literacy rate 37%

ities have a great deal of influence, and the central government relies on them to carry out policies. The laws of the state often have limited control over the workings of the local government, and the opportunities for corruption at the local level are great. Bénin does have a powerful constitutional court that requires that the government accounts for its actions. This has helped ensure that laws passed by the government follow the country's constitution.

PEOPLE AND CULTURES

The colonial government classified the people of Bénin by language, although that was only one of many ways by which they identify themselves. Some groups identify themselves through ancestry, and some through associations with other peoples. In reality the history of the people in the region has led to a pattern of settlement that is very mixed.

The largest single Béninese group is the Fon, whose language Fongbe is the dominant tongue in southern Bénin. Before the colonial period, Fon society was based on slave raiding, and many slaves became Fon when they were brought into Fon households. The Fon did not absorb members of every group they ruled over, however. The Ayizo, who had to send people to serve in the Fon army and who speak a dialect of Fongbe, resisted alliances or identification with the Fon. Bénin is home to several other former slave raiding peoples, such as the Wasangari and the YORUBA.

Gur speakers of the north, called Berba, identify themselves through a common initiation ritual. The Baseda and other groups living near the border with Togo belong to a cultural association based on mutual defense.

Bénin

The Béninese people belong to several different religious groups. Although one third of the people practice either Christianity or Islam, the majority follow traditional African beliefs. Many practice VODUN, or voodoo, a religion that originated in Bénin and that involves the worship of many gods. (*See also* **Colonialism in Africa, Ethnic Groups and Identity, History of Africa, Land Ownership, Slavery, Witchcraft and Sorcery.**)

Benin City

L ocated in the Bendel State of southern NIGERIA, Benin City is famous for the work of its numerous artisans. Despite its name, the city is not related to the nation of BÉNIN, which lies west of Nigeria.

Around A.D. 1000 a center of regional importance arose on the site of the present Benin City. This early town, also known as Benin, served as the seat of government for the ancient kingdom of Benin. In the mid-1200s Oba (king) Ewedo built an elaborate palace in the heart of the city. Destroyed by a revolt in about 1480, the capital was rebuilt by the victorious leader, Oba Ewuare. From that time on, the city became a center for the production of works of art in brass, ivory, and wood.

In 1897 the British sacked Benin City, seizing most of the palace's ornaments as well as items symbolizing the king's power. The city remains an important hub of regional trade today, receiving most of its income from the export of palm oil, rubber, and wood.

Berbers

T he Berbers are a cluster of peoples who live in North Africa and in the northern parts of the Saharan countries of MALI, NIGER, and MAURITANIA. The Berbers have their own languages, which belong to the Hamitic or Afro-Asiatic language family, and they write in their own scripts.

The native people of the region, the Berbers resisted the Arab conquest of North Africa in the A.D. 600s. Eventually, though, they accepted Islam, the religion of the Arabs. During the 700s the Berbers took part in the Arab conquest of Spain. A few centuries later, they established the Almoravids and the Almohads, two of the Islamic empires that ruled North Africa and Spain. During the 1800s the Berbers fought against French colonization in Africa.

With a estimated population of more than 12 million, the Berbers consist of at least 200 groups or tribes. The Kabyle, Rif, and Shluh are the largest of the Berber groups. The desert-dwelling TUAREG are among the best known.

Traditionally the Berber economy depended on the herding of livestock, especially camels, and the farming of grain. Some mountain-dwelling Berbers on the fringe of the Sahara desert continue to graze livestock, moving seasonally to provide their herds with water and pasture. Most Berbers, however, live in rural settlements or small towns. Their livelihood is based partly on family farms and partly on the labor

The Tuareg, a Berber group of the northern Sahel, are skilled camel herders. In this photo, a Tuareg rider presses forward in a camel race.

of the men, who spend time working in North African or European cities and sending money home. Regarded as inferior by some urban Arabs and ruling parties, many Berbers live in poor and unproductive districts. (*See also* **North Africa: History and Cultures.**)

Beti, Mongo

1932–
Cameroonian novelist

Mongo Beti is Cameroon's most celebrated novelist. His early novels usually explore the conflict between traditional African values and those of European colonialists. His best-known works, published in the 1950s, feature characters who come to understand the injustice of colonial rule and to realize they must help end it.

Beti's most famous novel, *Le Pauvre Christ de Bomba,* tells the story of a well-meaning missionary sent to convert a small village. He eventually realizes that the villagers come to him only to learn about Western technology, and they neither want nor need European religious guidance.

Beti's later writing, starting with the 1972 work *Main basse sur le Cameroon: Autopsie d'une décolonisation,* deals mainly with the abuses of dictatorship in post-colonial Africa. This book, which condemned the postindependence regime of CAMEROON, was banned in France for five

years. Beti's other novels are also strongly political, and many of them are still banned in his native land. (*See also* **Literature**.)

BIAFRA, REPUBLIC OF

See *Nigeria*.

Biko, Steve

1946–1977
South African social activist

* **apartheid** policy of racial segregation in South Africa intended to maintain white control over the country's blacks, Asians, and people of mixed ancestry

Steve Biko, an outspoken opponent of apartheid*, earned fame as a leader of the black consciousness movement in the 1960s and 1970s. The movement was based on the belief that the divisions between whites and blacks in South Africa were so great that blacks could not count on whites to end apartheid. Biko also insisted that blacks had to form their own political structures and to develop a new sense of pride in their own culture, religion, and ethical system.

Born in the eastern Cape Province of SOUTH AFRICA, Biko studied medicine at the University of Natal. While in college he became politically active and established a number of all-black associations. His activities led the South African government in 1973 to restrict his movements and to forbid him to speak or write publicly. Four years later Biko was arrested and held without trial for violating his travel restrictions. He died in prison after being tortured by the police. His death served to rally opponents of apartheid, and Biko has been remembered worldwide in song, drama, and film. (*See also* **Apartheid**.)

Blyden, Edward Wilmot

1832–1912
Pioneer of Pan-African Unity

Edward Blyden was a teacher and author who promoted the idea of black African pride. He stressed the importance of African languages and culture but also explored the possibility of combining African and Western cultures. The inventor of the phrase "African personality," Blyden laid the groundwork in his writings for the NEGRITUDE movement of the mid-1900s.

Of African descent, Blyden was born on the Caribbean island of St. Thomas. In 1850 he went to the United States to study at a theological college. However, the school refused to accept Blyden because of his color. The following year Blyden emigrated to LIBERIA, where he worked as a minister, teacher, and newspaper editor. He also served as Liberian ambassador to Great Britain and president of Liberia College. Blyden later moved to FREETOWN, the capital of SIERRA LEONE. There he became increasingly interested in Islam and held the post of director of Muslim education. Blyden died in Freetown in 1912, but his ideas had enormous influence in the twentieth century among African and African American leaders and intellectuals. (*See also* **Independence Movements**.)

Body Adornment and Clothing

People communicate information about themselves by the clothes they wear and the way that they adorn their bodies. In Africa body decoration and dress may offer clues to a person's age, ethnic group, region, social position, and even political opinions. As Western-style attire becomes more common in Africa, some traditional types of adornment and dress are fading from everyday use—especially in the cities. However, many Africans still wear traditional clothing and decoration for special occasions or as a form of self-expression.

Body Adornment. Africans have been decorating themselves with paint or pigment since at least 4000 B.C., when people in SUDAN used ocher* as a cosmetic. Ancient Egyptians used cosmetics as well, enhancing their lips and cheeks with red coloring. Men, women, and children in EGYPT wore eye paint, or kohl, on both their upper and lower eyelids. In addition to being considered beautiful, kohl helped protect the eyes from insects and the glare of the sun.

Body paint also functions as a sign of social status and ethnic background and as part of many African rituals*. Turkana men in KENYA cake their hair with clay and red coloring to celebrate a successful hunt or the end of planting. In many parts of the continent, decorating the body with white clay represents spirituality. Ceremonies marking a new stage in life often involve body painting. Young Dan women from IVORY COAST, for example, paint themselves with bold geometric patterns during rituals that mark the passage from girlhood to womanhood.

For many years, people throughout Africa have created permanent body decorations by scarification, or making small cuts in the skin. As they heal, these minor wounds form scars. The procedure is usually performed during childhood, and the patterns and designs of the scarification are often similar to those used in a group's pottery and sculpture. Both men and women bear these scars, usually on the face, torso, thigh, or upper arm.

Some types of scarification carry special meanings. Certain scars on the foreheads of men in the IGBO region of Nigeria, for example, indicate high social rank. In some cultures, scarification is believed to make a person more beautiful or to provide magical or protective benefits. Because various peoples have developed distinctive styles of scarification, scars may also identify the wearer as a member of a particular ethnic group.

Other types of body decoration practiced in Africa are also permanent. In North Africa, some Bedouin and BERBER tribes mark their faces with tattoos. Berber tattoos often indicate membership in a particular group and are modeled after ancient Libyan script. Some East African peoples beautify themselves by extracting certain teeth or by filing or chipping their teeth into sharp points. Other groups pierce holes in their lips and earlobes and then gradually stretch them by inserting larger and larger plugs or plates.

Clothing. Long ago Africans dressed in skins, woven grass and raffia*, leaves, and cloth made of tree bark. Today such items are used only in a few places or during certain ceremonies. The Kuba people of CONGO

* **ocher** red or yellow earth containing iron ore, used to color paints and textiles

* **ritual** religious ceremony that follows a set pattern

* **raffia** type of palm used for weaving and basketry

Body Adornment and Clothing

The Ancient Art of Beadwork

Since prehistoric times Africans have made beads of stone, shell, ivory, metal, and glass. People of western and central Africa cover garments with complex pictures or patterns of tiny beads. Some fine beadwork was traditionally reserved for officials, such as the kings of Benin and Yoruba. Women in Nigeria and Mali work beads into elaborate hairstyles. In eastern Africa both men and women may wear beaded ornaments indicating their clan, village, wealth, age, and marital state. African beadwork is more than simply beautiful. It is a powerful expression of personal identity and style.

* **amulet**   small object thought to have supernatural or magical powers

See color plate 15, vol. 1.

See color plate 12, vol. 3.

(KINSHASA) still produce the embroidered raffia shirts with geometric patterns that both men and women used to wear for rituals and public events. However, today the main function of these shirts is to dress the dead at funerals.

Most Africans wear garments of woven cotton cloth. Men appear in a wide variety of smocks and robes. Rural men in Egypt and Sudan may wear the *jellaba,* an ankle-length robe with sleeves and side pockets, made to be worn over a shirt. A similar long, loose robe is the *dishdasha,* used by both men and women in ALGERIA.

A number of African garments consist of a single piece of cloth. Women frequently wear wrappers—large rectangles of cloth they wrap around their bodies. Often a woman dresses at home in a single wrapper tucked and twisted under her arms, and she adds additional items when appearing in public. The typical outfit of YORUBA women consists of a wrapper tied at the waist, a smaller cloth worn over the first wrapper or over the left shoulder, and a long-sleeved blouse. Nomadic men in Mali wear patterned wool blankets during the cold nights of the dry season. In parts of GHANA and Ivory Coast, men wrap themselves in a large, rectangular piece of cloth that is draped over the left shoulder.

Some African attire has special significance. A man's social position may be proclaimed by the size and shape of his smock or by the decoration of his robe. Among the BAMBARA people of MALI, hunters display their skill by wearing white smocks adorned with leather-covered amulets* and hunting trophies. An expert hunter's shirt may be almost invisible under the horns, claws, and bits of fur or hide the wearer has attached to it. Sometimes a particular pattern of cloth has a name that refers to a proverb, local event, or political issue. People wear these cloths because of the messages communicated by the patterns.

Accessories and Hairstyles. Jewelry and other accessories may express even more about their wearer than clothing does. Various styles of brass, stone, bone, or iron bracelets and armlets may declare an African's success, gender, or religion. In some cases, much of a person's wealth is worn in the form of gold jewelry. Belts, caps, and jewelry may be decorated with beadwork in designs that represent a certain idea or message.

Accessories often indicate a person's authority. In some societies, only leaders or members of special groups may wear items made of precious materials, such as ivory or gold. The pharaohs who ruled ancient Egypt wore a type of beaded necklace reserved only for gods. In ancient Benin, the traditional costume of the king consisted of a coral-beaded crown and smock, and jewelry of ivory and coral. The red of the coral represented power, while the white of the ivory stood for spiritual purity. Among the ZULU of SOUTH AFRICA, the king wears a necklace of leopard claws, while lesser chiefs wear ornaments of bone carved in the shape of leopard claws. Fly whisks—animal hair attached to handles and used to wave away flies—are symbols of leadership used by men throughout Africa. Both traditional and modern rulers often carry them during public appearances.

In North Africa the head covering is perhaps the most common

Africans use a wide range of items to decorate themselves and their clothing. These Gikuyu dancers in Kenya paint their faces and wear beaded belts and bracelets.

accessory. Some men wear the traditional Arab head cloth, or *kafiyya*, held in place with a coil of cord. Others may wear the fez, a cylinder-shaped hat that originated in the region. Among the TUAREG people of the Sahara region, men cover their heads and faces with long veils dyed blue with indigo, while women wear headcloths. Women in Muslim countries or communities have traditionally covered their heads and faces with a veil.

Hairstyles are also used in parts of Africa to express symbolic meaning as well as personal style. Common styling techniques include shaving, braiding, stringing beads on the hair, interweaving fibers with the hair, and shaping the hair with mud or clay. Some peoples use hairstyles to mark stages in life. Young men of the MAASAI shave their heads when they become adult warriors. Then they let their hair grow long, spending hours styling each other's hair into elaborate arrangements of many twisted strands coated with red mud. (*See also* **Art**, **Crafts**, **Initiation Rites**.)

BOER WAR

See *Afrikaner Republics; South Africa; Southern Africa, History.*

Bokassa, Jean-Bédel

1921–1996
President of the Central African Republic

* **coup** sudden, often violent overthrow of a ruler or government

* **embezzlement** illegal taking of money entrusted into one's care for personal use

Military leader Jean-Bédel Bokassa became the president of the CENTRAL AFRICAN REPUBLIC after a coup* in 1966. Eleven years later, he had himself declared emperor and renamed the country the Central African Empire.

The son of a village chief, Bokassa began his military career in the French army in 1939. He fought in Indochina and achieved the rank of captain in 1961. By that time, the Central African Republic had gained its independence from France, and David Dacko was the new country's president. Bokassa returned home and was appointed chief of staff of the armed forces in 1964. He overthrew Dacko's government two years later, and in 1977 Bokassa declared himself emperor of the Central African Republic.

After more than 12 years as president and emperor, Bokassa's downfall began in 1979 when he ordered the army to shoot protesters. About 400 people died. Strikes by teachers and students led to the arrest, torture, and killing of children. Bokassa was overthrown and went to live abroad. When he returned the Central African Republic in 1986, he was arrested and charged with embezzlement*, murder, and cannibalism. He was sentenced to death in 1987. Freed six years later, Bokassa remained in the Central African Republic until his death.

Bornu

* **dynasty** succession of rulers from the same family or group

The empire of Bornu existed in north central Africa from about 1400 to 1900, when it became part of Britain's colonial empire. Bornu had its origins in an earlier state named Kanem that arose around 1200 in what is now southwestern CHAD.

The leaders of Kanem were divided into two competing dynasties*: the Duguwa and the Sayfuwu. Driven out of Kanem in the mid-1200s, the Sayfuwu founded the state of Bornu on the southwestern shore of Lake Chad. They increased their power by defeating the local Sao people in the early 1300s. However, dynastic feuds troubled Bornu until the ruler Ali Gaji took power in the mid-1400s. Under his rule, Bornu extended its influence as far as the HAUSA states (now northwestern NIGERIA).

Bornu invaded Kanem in the early 1500s and again in the late 1500s, forcing its rulers to flee to the southeastern part of the kingdom. Under King Idris Alauma, Bornu conquered territory north into present-day LIBYA and drove the Sao onto islands in Lake Chad.

Attacked by the FULANI people in the early 1800s, Bornu managed to defeat the invaders in the 1820s. In the late 1800s the Arab warrior Rabih Zubayr conquered Bornu. Rabih died in 1900, and two years later the British moved into Bornu and made it part of their colony of

Nigeria. The kingdom of Kanuri still exists and is possibly the oldest state in Africa. (*See also* **Sudanic Empires of Western Africa**.)

Botswana

See map in Minerals and Mining (vol. 3).

he country of Botswana is located in the center of southern Africa, surrounded by ZIMBABWE, ZAMBIA, NAMIBIA, and SOUTH AFRICA. Since gaining independence from Great Britain in 1966, Botswana has emerged as one of the most successful new nations in Africa.

Geography and Economy. Botswana is a dry land dominated by the KALAHARI DESERT, which occupies the western two-thirds of the country. Drought is a permanent feature of the climate. Almost all of Botswana's surface water lies in the rivers of the Okavango Delta in the northwest. Most of the vegetation consists of dry grasses, which are used for grazing cattle. Gaborone, the capital, is located in the southeast near the border with South Africa.

Before the discovery of diamonds in the 1970s, Botswana's economy was based on livestock and money sent home by migrant laborers. Revenue from diamonds, however, has made Botswana the world's fastest-growing economy. The country has managed its wealth well,

Botswana

* **infrastructure** basic framework of a society and its economy, which includes roads, bridges, port facilities, airports, and other public works

* **socialism** economic or political system based on the idea that the government or groups of workers should own and run the means of production and distribution of goods

* **apartheid** policy of racial segregation in South Africa intended to maintain white control over the country's Blacks, Asians, and people of mixed ancestry

* **sanction** measure adopted by one or more nations to force another nation to change its policies or conduct

avoiding the cycles of boom and bust common to many mineral-based economies. It has a small but well-functioning infrastructure*, and the government has actively promoted the growth of industry and commerce. As a result, average income is much higher than in most developing countries.

Most of the people of Botswana, who are known as Batswana, still live in rural areas and make their living by farming and raising livestock. The country relies heavily on South Africa for industrial goods, and the gap between the rich and the poor is among the highest in the world. Despite these difficulties, Botswana's economy is considered a model of success for developing countries.

History and Government. The people of the area now known as Botswana had little or no contact with Europeans until the late 1800s. At that time fighting broke out with Afrikaners (or Boers), Dutch settlers from what is now South Africa. In 1885 KHAMA III, chief of the Tswana people, asked Britain for help against the Afrikaners, and the region (then known as Bechuanaland) came under British protection.

After World War II, Bechuanaland, like many other African territories, sought independence from colonial rule. The independence movement gained momentum in the 1950s under the leadership of SERETSE KHAMA, a descendant of Khama III. By 1960 the people of Bechuanaland had gained the right to form independent political parties.

The most influential of the early political parties was the Bechuanaland People's Party (BPP). Supported by urban migrant workers, the BPP called for immediate independence and a socialist form of government. Seretse Khama, who felt that the BPP was too extreme, formed the rival Bechuanaland Democratic Party (BDP). The BDP's followers were mostly rural, and its leadership consisted mainly of cattle owners who had inherited their wealth. Like the BPP, the party sought independence, but it was not interested in socialism*. The BDP overwhelmingly won the first multiparty national elections in 1965. The following year, Bechuanaland achieved independence and renamed itself the Republic of Botswana.

Following independence, Botswana opposed South Africa's apartheid* government. However, it did not support UNITED NATIONS sanctions* against South Africa because it was dependent on trade with that country. During the 1970s Botswana had a tense relationship with the racist state of Rhodesia (now Zimbabwe), and it offered a haven to Rhodesian refugees. Rhodesia occasionally raided Botswana in pursuit of these refugees. During the 1980s South Africa accused Botswana of protecting anti-apartheid terrorists, and South African forces attacked Botswana in 1985. Since that time the conflict between Botswana and South Africa has calmed down, and the two countries have established diplomatic relations.

Political power in Botswana is shared by a directly elected National Assembly and a president chosen by the assembly. Elected councils oversee affairs at the district, town, and city level, but all these councils depend on the national government for funding. A body called the House of Chiefs, made up of the hereditary leaders of the main Tswana

Republic of Botswana

POPULATION:
1,576,470 (2000 estimated population)

AREA:
231,804 sq. mi. (600,372 sq. km)

LANGUAGES:
English, Setswana (both are official)

NATIONAL CURRENCY:
Pula

PRINCIPAL RELIGIONS:
Christian 50%, traditional 50%

CITIES:
Gaborone (capital), 134,000 (1999 est.); Serowe, Francistown, Lobatse, Selibi-Phikwe, Kanye, Maun, Molepolole, Ramotswa, Mochudi, Ghanzi

ANNUAL RAINFALL:
Varies from 18–25 in. (460–625 mm) in the extreme north-west to less than 5 in. (125 mm) in the extreme southwest

ECONOMY:
GDP per capita: U.S. $3,600

PRINCIPAL PRODUCTS AND EXPORTS:
Agricultural: livestock, sorghum, maize, millet, pulses, peanuts, beans, cowpeas, sunflower seeds
Manufacturing: meat processing, diamond processing, soda ash
Mining: diamonds, nickel, copper, coal, salt, potash

GOVERNMENT:
Independence from Great Britain, 1966. President elected by National Assembly. Governing bodies: National Assembly, elected by universal adult suffrage, and House of Chiefs.

HEADS OF STATE SINCE INDEPENDENCE:
1966–1980 President Seretse Khama
1980–1998 President Quett Ketumile Joni Masire
1998– President Festus Mogae

ARMED FORCES:
8,500

EDUCATION:
Compulsory for 7 years; literacy rate 70%

tribes, advises the assembly and carries out local political and judicial functions.

The political situation in Botswana has been remarkably stable since independence, with free and open elections. This has been made possible largely by the fact that the BDP has little effective opposition. The strength of Botswana's diamond-based economy has also helped the party maintain political power. The Botswana National Front (BNF) has been the main opposition party since independence. Although the party achieved some success in local elections, it has not gained much power nationally.

See color plate 2, vol. 4.

Peoples and Cultures. The main language groups in Botswana are Bantu and KHOISAN. Among the Bantu speakers, the Tswana are the most numerous as well as the largest single group in Botswana. The Tswana are divided into smaller local groups, each with its own chief.

Tswana families often have three homes: one in a village near schools and shops, one near a water hole where they keep their cattle, and one near their farmland. In the village, the Tswana practice a democratic form of leadership based on discussions in the *kgotla,* a central meeting place. Women usually work the land where crops are planted, and men generally tend the herds at the cattle post. The Tswana place a high value on cattle, which are often used as a form of payment. Other Bantu-speaking groups include the Herero and Mbanderu, who also raise cattle, and the Mbukushu, whose livelihood is based on fishing and farming.

The Khoisan peoples of Botswana can be divided into northern, southern, and central language groups. Many of them work herding cattle for Tswana landowners. The northern Khoisan are known as the

!Kung, and the main southern group is the !Xo. Cattle and goat herding people called the Khoikhoi also live in the south near the border with Namibia. The central Khoisan group includes a great number of peoples who have adopted Tswana customs, including the herding of cattle. In addition, Botswana contains a substantial white population, many of whom are ranchers living near the South African border or in the central-western Kalahari. (*See also* **Apartheid, Bantu Peoples, Climate, Colonialism in Africa, Deserts and Drought, Livestock Grazing, Refugees**.)

Boumédienne, Houari

ca. 1927–1978
President of Algeria

* **coup** sudden, often violent overthrow of a ruler or government

Houari Boumédienne was the first vice president of ALGERIA after it won independence from France in 1962. Three years later, he led a coup* against President Ahmed BEN BELLA. Boumédienne became Algeria's president and remained in that position until his death.

In his youth, Boumédienne was involved in the movement for Algerian independence. He rose to prominence as a military leader in the National Liberation Army during the Algerian War of Independence (1954–1962). Although he and Ben Bella supported each other in the early years, political differences arose between them over governing the newly independent country.

After Boumédienne staged his coup and took over the government, he kept control of the economy because he believed that it was better for economic decisions to be made by a central authority. He is credited with helping to improve the Algerian economy, but it had begun to suffer a decline by the time of his death. (*See also* **Independence Movements**.)

Boundaries in Africa

* **indigenous** native to a certain place

Before the arrival of European colonists, African boundaries were very loosely defined. Borders reflected the territories inhabited and controlled by different ethnic groups, and they often changed over time—generally as a result of migration or conquest. Moreover, these boundaries did not define all the available space in Africa. Some areas remained unclaimed or served as neutral zones between indigenous* ethnic groups.

European nations began to redraw African territorial lines in the late 1800s, when their interest turned from establishing coastal trading posts to developing the continent's rich inland resources. By the 1880s European explorers such as Sir Richard BURTON, David LIVINGSTONE, Henry Morton STANLEY, and John Speke were staking national claims to larger and larger portions of African territory. Many explorers arranged treaties with African chiefs, claiming the land for European rulers. Although much of Africa remained unknown and unexplored, European competition for territory increased with the desire to gain control of mineral resources and other riches from the African interior.

During this "Scramble for Africa," European countries tried to aquire as much territory as possible. The amount of territory that each nation actually colonized depended largely on its power in Europe. Britain, France, Germany, and Italy, which were strong and rising European forces, ultimately controlled more land in Africa than weaker countries such as Spain and Portugal.

As a result of the "Scramble," the map of Africa changed from a collection of loosely defined ethnic territories into a series of fixed colonial states. European colonists set boundaries according to their territorial claims, with no regard for the traditional borders of indigenous peoples. In some cases, these new territorial lines divided ethnic groups between different colonial powers. In other cases, they placed groups with a history of hostility toward each other together in one colony.

The Europeans set boundaries by geography—or sometimes merely by drawing a straight line on a map. Natural features, particularly rivers and lakes, often became the borders of European colonies. For the most part such lines remained fixed, except when they were redrawn as a result of the changing fortunes of the colonial powers. For example, Germany lost its African territories after suffering defeat in World War I, and these territories were incorporated into the colonies of other nations.

African nations began to gain their independence in the 1950s, but the colonial boundaries remained basically unchanged. At first some African leaders called for creating a type of United States of Africa, with relatively open borders between nations. That idea never took hold. In some regions, border disputes—such as that between SOMALIA and ETHIOPIA—have contributed to ongoing or recurring conflicts.

Today, the boundaries that separate and define Africa's many nations are still based largely on the lines drawn by Europeans. National borders often divide members of ethnic groups or force historical enemies to live together. In such areas, people's allegiance to the state is often challenged by tribal and ethnic loyalties, and political unrest is common. (*See also* **Colonialism in Africa, Ethnic Groups and Identity, Nationalism.**)

Bourguiba, Habib

1903–2000
President of Tunisia

* **nationalist** devoted to the interests and culture of one's country

* **socialism** economic or political system based on the idea that the government or groups of workers should own and run the means of production and distribution of goods

Habib Bourguiba, son of a former Tunisian army officer, grew up under French colonial rule in TUNISIA. He was a leader in his country's independence movement and became its first president in 1957.

After receiving a good education in Tunisia, young Bourguiba studied law in Paris. There he met other North Africans who were committed to independence from France. Bourguiba's interest in politics developed at this time, and on his return home he became active in the nationalist* movement. In the 1930s he established the Neo-Destour party. Over the years he transformed the nationalist movement into a mass movement. He also spent some time in prison for his political activities against French colonial rule.

Faced with broad support for independence across the country, the French decided to negotiate. They agreed to self-rule for Tunisia in 1955 and full independence in 1956.

The new President Bourguiba soon embraced socialism*, declaring his own Neo-Destour political party as the only one in the country. His gov-

* **cooperative farm** large plot of land worked by many farmers

ernment took over Tunisia's trade and industry and established cooperative farms*. When his policies proved unpopular, he changed course somewhat. Bourguiba's calls for a settlement in the heated Arab-Israeli dispute did not win him friends among the Arab nations. In addition, his policy of discouraging traditional Muslim religious practices made him unpopular with many in his own country.

By the late 1970s, Bourguiba's government was under attack for failing to make political changes. Moreover, his poor health led to extended bouts of unexplained behavior. In 1987 his appointed successor, General Zayn al-Abidine Ben Ali, had doctors declare Bourguiba unfit to rule. The ousted president retired to live in a palace in his home village along the Tunisian coast. (*See also* **Colonialism in Africa, Independence Movements**.)

Braide, Garrick Sokari

ca. 1882–1918
Nigerian religious leader

* **cult** group bound together by devotion to a particular person, belief, or god

* **Anglican** Church of England

* **sedition** resistance or rebellion against a lawful authority

Garrick Sokari Braide, a Nigerian missionary and prophet, was largely responsible for the spread of Christianity in the Niger Delta region of Africa in the early 1900s. His preaching and methods combined traditional African elements with Christianity and stressed prayer and faith healing.

Braide was born in the village of Obonoma, the center of a cult* to a god called Ogu. Some accounts of Braide's life say that he practiced Ogunism as a youth. After becoming a Christian, Braide campaigned against the use of African religion symbols. But elements of Ogunism remained in his practice of Christianity.

In the late 1880s Braide probably attended the open-air Christian meetings that took place in his village. He became involved with the Anglican* Church and took instruction in Christianity for many years. He completed his studies and was baptized at the age of 28.

Braide went on to become a preacher and missionary and a prominent leader in the Niger Delta Pastorate Church. He was known for his gifts of prayer, prophecy, and healing. His reputation for performing miracles and magic, such as causing rain and storms, gained him wide recognition.

Braide preached against the use of alcohol, because drunkenness was a problem in the Niger Delta villages. His anti-alcohol movement caused conflicts with the British, who ruled Nigeria at the time and profited greatly from the sale of alcohol in their colonies. Uneasy about Braide's emergence as a public figure with a large following, the British arrested him in 1916 for sedition*. Braide was found guilty and jailed, but he was released several months before his death.

Braide left Africa with two legacies—the first was the spread of Christianity in Nigeria. The number of baptized Christians in the Niger Delta increased by almost 11,000 during the years he was preaching. Second, Braide showed Nigerians that they had the potential to become independent. As a leader who took a position against the colonial government and broke with the traditional church, he demonstrated that Africans could rise up and take control. (*See also* **Christianity in Africa, Religion and Ritual**.)

Brazzaville

The city of Brazzaville is the capital of the Republic of Congo and one of the country's main industrial centers. It sits on the west bank of the Malebo Pool at the beginning of the navigable portion of the Upper CONGO RIVER, a place known as "the gateway to the heart of Africa." Founded by the French in 1883, the city takes its name from explorer Pierre de Brazza, who signed a treaty with a local king that gave France control of key parts of the region. Because of its location, Brazzaville became an important base in France's colonial empire in West Africa. During World War II it was the center in Africa of the French resistance to Germany and its allies.

Today Brazzaville is one of the industrial centers in the Congo (the others are Pointe-Noire on the Atlantic Coast and N'kayi, which lies between Brazzaville and Pointe-Noire). The leading industries in Brazzaville are textiles, food processing, and leather goods. Many goods are shipped between Brazzaville and Pointe-Noire, both by train and, in recent years, by motor vehicle and by air. Brazzaville is home to one of the Congo's two international airports.

Brazzaville has served as capital of the Congo since the country gained its independence in 1960. The city has about 1 million inhabitants, almost one third of the country's population. It is a main port on the Congo River and serves as the headquarters for many important African organizations. These include the World Health Organization's African headquarters, the Pan African Union of Science and Technology, and the African Petroleum Producer's Association. Brazzaville is also home to many educational, scientific, and technical institutions. (*See also* **Congo (Brazzaville)**.)

Brink, André

1935–
South African novelist

* **apartheid** policy of racial segregation in South Africa intended to maintain white control over the country's blacks, Asians, and people of mixed ancestry

André Phillipus Brink is a South African novelist who writes in both Afrikaans and English. He became known as known one of the "Sixtyers," writers of the 1960s who wanted to revolutionize South African fiction by addressing social, moral, and political issues.

Born in SOUTH AFRICA, Brink was educated both there and in France. His early books were not political in nature, but his later ones examined the human cost of the government's policy of apartheid*. His novel *An Instant in the Wind* (1975) deals with the destructive nature of racism by exploring the relationship between a black man and a white woman. In *The Chain of Voices* (1982), Brink looks at an 1825 slave revolt through the eyes of characters on both sides of the conflict. Though praised outside of South Africa, Brink's novels have often been unpopular in his homeland, and some were banned by the South African government. (*See also* **Apartheid, Literature**.)

BRITISH COLONIES

See *Colonialism in Africa.*

Burkina Faso

Burkina Faso

Burkina Faso, formerly known as Upper Volta, is a landlocked nation in western Africa. It is one of many states formed after the breakup of the French colonial empire. Although the nation went through periods of unrest after gaining independence in 1960, it has become a relatively stable country. The name *Burkina Faso* means "Land of the Honorable People" or "Homeland of the Proud People."

GEOGRAPHY AND ECONOMY

* **savanna** tropical or subtropical grassland with scattered trees and drought-resistant undergrowth

Burkina Faso is a fairly flat country dominated by forests and savannas*. Towering mounds of red termites dot the grasslands. The northern region is quite dry, as is the country's southern edge, averaging only about 5 inches of rain per year. The central and southern regions of the country are generally much wetter, receiving 2 to 3 feet of rain annually. In all areas, the rains tend to fall in brief, heavy storms that can wash away crops and topsoil.

Most of the population makes a living from agriculture, raising livestock, cotton, and food crops. Livestock and related products such as meat and leather contribute about one-third of Burkina Faso's export revenues. Another important export is labor. About a million Burkinabé live in neighboring IVORY COAST and send money home to relatives. Many more residents leave the country to find work on a temporary or seasonal basis.

* **infrastructure** basic framework of a society and its economy, which includes roads, bridges, port facilities, airports, and other public works

The small amount of industry in Burkina Faso is mainly concentrated in towns such as its capital, Ouagadougou. For years most industries were owned by the state, but since 1991 many have been transferred to private ownership. The nation's gold mining industry has grown in importance since the 1980s. However, a lack of funding and infrastructure*, such as roads and railroads, has hindered the mining of other minerals.

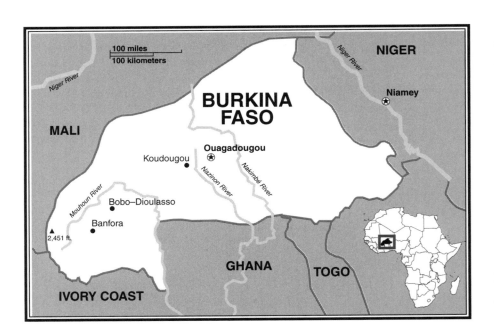

98

Burkina Faso

HISTORY AND GOVERNMENT

Unlike much of western Africa, Burkina Faso was untouched by European influence until the late 1890s. Then the French gained control of the area and ruled it from 1904 to 1960.

Precolonial and Colonial History. Before the arrival of Europeans, many small household- and village-based societies occupied the western portion of what is now Burkina Faso. Mossi people from the south invaded the central and eastern areas of the region during the 1400s. According to tradition, the Mossi were descended from Naaba Wedraogo, the son of a princess of a town in northern Ghana. For many years, the Mossi moved throughout the region conquering new areas. In the late 1400s and early 1500s they established several kingdoms, the most important of which were Ouagadougou and Yatenga. The kingdoms featured complex political and religious systems.

The French arrived in the region in the 1870s. Over the next decades, they formed alliances with African societies that lived around the Mossi. In 1896 and 1897 the French defeated the Mossi and other independent peoples nearby. Naming the region Upper Volta, the French declared it a military zone in 1899. A few years later, they incorporated the area into the colony of Upper Volta-Senegal-Niger. The French colonial government introduced taxes and a military draft and forced the Africans to work for little or no pay. This treatment led to several rebellions—especially among the western peoples. The French crushed these uprisings and destroyed all traces of African rule.

Upper Volta became a separate colony in 1919. However, the French soon found that its only economic value was as a source of laborers for other colonies. Within 13 years, they divided Upper Volta's territory between the colonies of Ivory Coast, Niger, and Soudan (now Mali). After World War II, France granted new political rights to its African colonies. In response to pressure from Mossi leaders, it made Upper Volta a separate colony again in 1947.

In 1958, when France allowed each of its African colonies to vote for independence, Upper Volta chose to remain a largely self-governing French colony. Maurice Yaméogo, the head of Upper Volta's main political party, the Rassemblement Démocratique Africain (RDA), was elected president of the Council of Ministers. In 1960 he banned the main opposition party. Later that year Upper Volta requested and received independence from France. With no organized opposition, Yaméogo was chosen president, and the RDA became the dominant political force in the country.

The Early Republics. Yaméogo was reelected in 1965 with nearly 100 percent of the vote. He then tried to place tight restrictions on government spending. Trade unions protested the restrictions by calling a general strike in January of the following year. Amid the unrest, the army overthrew Yaméogo's government, and Colonel Sangoulé Lamizana took over the presidency. Lamizana ended Yaméogo's ban on political activity. However, when violence erupted between competing political

Film Festival

For more than 30 years Burkina Faso has been a major center of African film. Every other year the nation's capital hosts the largest film festival in Africa, Festival Panafricain du Cinéma et de la Télévision de Ouagadougou (FESPACO). The event features a competition of African films from the whole continent.

Soon after film enthusiasts started the festival in 1969, FESPACO became a government-sponsored institution. Today FESPACO acts as a market for African film and television professionals, publishes works about African cinema, and maintains a African film library. It also strives to promote African cinema in other international festivals.

Traditional and modern cultures mingle in this urban market in Burkina Faso, where handcrafted items are sold alongside factory-produced household equipment.

* **coup**   sudden, often violent overthrow of a ruler or government

groups, Lamizana re-imposed the ban. He announced military rule but promised to restore civilian government after four years.

Free elections were held in 1970, and a new constitution created Upper Volta's Second Republic. The constitution provided for Lamizana to continue as president for four years, and it called for the military to participate in all political institutions. A new crisis arose in 1974, when Prime Minister Gérard Ouédraogo lost support in parliament but refused to resign. Lamizana again proclaimed military rule and banned political parties. When he tried to establish a single political party for the nation the following year, the trade unions responded angrily with another general strike. Lamizana backed down, and in January 1976 he appointed a new government consisting mostly of civilians.

In 1977 another constitution established the Third Republic. It limited the number of political parties to the top three vote-winners in the national elections that followed. Lamizana was reelected president. However, no single political party won control of a majority of the seats in the assembly. The result was a weak government that once again ran into difficulty with the trade unions. A strike in late 1980 was followed by a military coup* led by Colonel Saye Zerbo. However, friction grew between leaders of the military government, and Zerbo himself was overthrown in late 1982.

Burkina Faso

POPULATION:
11,946,065 (2000 estimated population)

AREA:
105,869 sq. mi. (274,200 sq. km)

LANGUAGES:
French (official); Mossi, Dyula, many local languages

NATIONAL CURRENCY:
CFA Franc

PRINCIPAL RELIGIONS:
Muslim 50%, traditional 40%, Christian 10%

CITIES:
Ouagadougou (capital), 1,100,000 (2000 est.); Bobo-Dioulasso, Koudougou, Ouahigouya, Kaya, Banfora

ANNUAL RAINFALL:
Varies from 40 in. (1,000 mm) in the south to less than 10 in. (250 mm) in the north

ECONOMY:
GDP per capita: U.S. $1,000

PRINCIPAL PRODUCTS AND EXPORTS:
Agricultural: peanuts, livestock, cotton, sesame, sorghum, millet, maize, rice, shea nuts
Manufacturing: cotton tint, food and beverage processing, soap, agricultural processing, cigarettes, textiles
Mining: gold, manganese, limestone, marble, antimony, copper, nickel, bauxite, lead, phosphate, zinc, silver

GOVERNMENT:
Independence from France, 1960. President elected by universal suffrage. Governing bodies: Bicameral national legislature—Assemblée des Députés Populaires and Chambre des Représentants.

HEADS OF STATE:
1980–1982 Colonel Saye Zerbo
1982–1983 Surgeon-Major Jean-Baptiste Ouédraogo
1983–1987 Captain Thomas Sankara
1987– President Captain Blaise Compaoré

ARMED FORCES:
5,800 (1998 est.) Compulsory 18-month service.

EDUCATION:
Compulsory for ages 7–13; literacy rate 19%

* **communist** relating to communism, a system in which land, goods, and the means of production are owned by the state or community rather than by individuals

* **totalitarian** referring to a government that exercises complete control over individuals, often by force

Communist Rule and The Fourth Republic. The leaders of the coup created a ruling body called the Council for the People's Salvation (CSP). The CSP named Surgeon-Major Jean-Baptiste Ouédraogo president and Captain Thomas Sankara prime minister. Sankara quickly abandoned the nation's allies in the West and established ties with developing countries such as Libya, Cuba, and North Korea. Critics within the government arrested Sankara in May 1983, but Captain Blaise Compaoré freed him in August and overthrew the CSP.

Backed by communist* groups, Sankara adopted a foreign policy that rejected Western governments. To symbolize the country's break with its colonial, pro-Western past, Sankara changed Upper Volta's name to Burkina Faso in 1984. He established "revolutionary councils" at all levels of society to try to establish a totalitarian* system with himself at its head. However, as Sankara began using force to maintain power, opposition to his rule increased. He eventually lost the support of his own people, and in October 1987 Captain Compaoré ordered his troops to kill Sankara.

Compaoré reversed many of Sankara's policies and rejected the previous government's communist ties. In 1991 a new constitution was approved reestablishing multiparty politics and direct election of the president and National Assembly (Assemblée des Députés Populaires). Later that year Compaoré was elected as the first president of the Fourth Republic. However, the opposing parties refused to participate in the election because they felt the government was not protecting their rights. In response, Compaoré ended persecution of his political opponents and called new elections in April 1992. He was again elected and

Burkina Faso

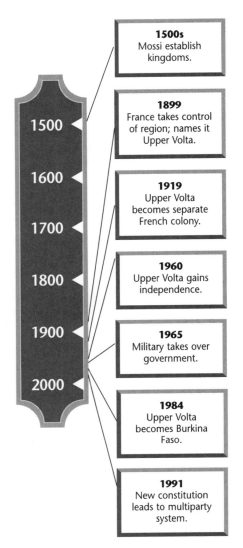

1500s
Mossi establish kingdoms.

1899
France takes control of region; names it Upper Volta.

1919
Upper Volta becomes separate French colony.

1960
Upper Volta gains independence.

1965
Military takes over government.

1984
Upper Volta becomes Burkina Faso.

1991
New constitution leads to multiparty system.

* **tribute**   payment made by a smaller or weaker party to a more powerful one, often under the threat of force

continues to serve as president of the country. However, his government has not always responded well to criticism, and in 1995 an opposition leader was jailed for insulting Compaoré.

PEOPLES AND CULTURES

Burkina Faso is home to many different ethnic groups. The largest of these, the Mossi, make up nearly half of the population. Other major groups include the FULANI, the Gulmanceba, and the Gurunsi. The social organization of most of these peoples is based upon the lineage—a kind of extended family. Each lineage traces its origins back to a common, often mythical, ancestor and forms a group that usually lives in a particular village neighborhood. Most lineages trace descent through male family members.

Older members of society are treated with great respect. In many places the oldest male member of the family makes all of the important decisions for his family. The oldest male in a lineage is in charge of dealing with local gods. In many cases, he also has responsibility for enforcing laws and serves as a peacemaker. Although women hold few leadership posts or religious offices, they do exercise informal influence.

A male political leader, a *naaba*, holds a sacred position among the Mossi, the Gulmanceba, and the Gurunsi. In addition to his special spiritual powers, the *naaba* owns the land and its inhabitants. At one time he could require subjects to serve him as warriors and laborers and to pay tribute*. The *naaba* protected his power by granting distant villages and lands to certain princes and to descendants of the founder of the empire.

The peoples of Burkina Faso share a rich religious heritage. In traditional agricultural religions, the spirit of the earth and the spirits of ancestors are particularly important. These spirits ensure that people follow custom and tradition, and they provide the community with rain, fertility, and health. The spirit of heaven is also prominent in local religions. Heaven, which made the world, is responsible for rain, fate, and children's souls.

Bush spirits rule the land outside the villages. Besides controlling the abundance of game and the fortune of hunters, they also punish wrongdoers. These spirits appear in the form of animals—most often reptiles—who serve the lineage elders. Lineage members must not kill or eat these animals because they may help elders find water or lead them to victory over enemies. The spirits inhabit prominent places in nature such as hills, rocks, lakes, and caves.

Fortune-tellers play an important part in traditional beliefs. They give people advice on what actions to take in everyday life, and they teach them to use nature's powers for their own purposes. However, WITCHCRAFT or other types of magic that cause damage or trouble are generally avoided. Although many people still follow traditional religious beliefs and practices, some of Burkina Faso's people have adopted Christianity, and about half the nation's population is Muslim. (*See also* **Colonialism in Africa, Unions and Trade Associations.**)

Burton, Sir Richard Francis

1821–1890
British explorer

* **diplomatic** involved with conducting relations with other nations

Sir Richard Francis Burton made four journeys in Africa in the mid-1800s. Although he failed in his mission to locate the source of a branch of the Nile River, he contributed greatly to European knowledge of African geography.

Born in Torquay, England, and raised in France and Italy, Burton served in the British army in India. He mastered many languages, including Arabic, and became famous for disguising himself as a Muslim and entering the holy city of Mecca in Arabia. In 1854–1855, an expedition with fellow explorer John Hanning Speke into eastern ETHIOPIA and what is now SOMALIA ended in disaster when Somalis wounded both men. In 1857 the two explorers again moved westward from the East African coast, seeking the source of the White Nile. Their friendship ended in disagreement over whether the river originated in Lake Victoria. Burton, who claimed that it did not, was later proven wrong.

Burton's later career included three years of diplomatic* service in West Africa, during which he studied local customs. His books about West African life, along with the popular narratives of his earlier explorations, formed the popular image of Africa. Burton died in Trieste, in northeastern Italy. (*See also* **Travel and Exploration**.)

Burundi

* **escarpment** long, clifflike ridge of land or rock

* **savanna** tropical or subtropical grassland with scattered trees and drought-resistant undergrowth

* **cash crop** crop grown primarily for sale rather than for local consumption

* **subsistence farming** raising only enough food to live on

* **cassava** starchy root plant; source of tapioca

* **sorghum** family of tropical grasses used for food

A small, densely populated country located in the heart of east central Africa, Burundi is one of the poorest nations in the world. It also has experienced some of the most serious and violent conflicts on the African continent. These conflicts are rooted in a struggle for control between the country's two main ethnic groups, the Tutsi and the Hutu.

GEOGRAPHY AND ECONOMY

Located just south of the equator, Burundi is a land of rolling hills and lakes. There are spectacular escarpments* in the northeast and savannas* in the southwest. Bujumbura, the capital, sits along the shore of Lake Tanganyika, which forms the country's southwestern border.

Much of Burundi's original forest has been cut down, with woodlands remaining mostly on upper mountain slopes. Burundi's wildlife includes antelopes, baboons, and warthogs, but poaching—illegal hunting—has taken a toll on many species, including the elephant.

Although Burundi lies near the equator, its high elevation keeps the climate mild year-round. Rainfall is fairly evenly distributed throughout the year except for a dry season from May to August. Although soil erosion is a serious problem in hilly areas, the rich soil in the larger river valleys provides good conditions for farming.

Burundi's economy is based primarily on agriculture. The main commercial crops are coffee, cotton, and tea. Coffee, the leading cash crop*, accounts for the majority of the nation's export earnings. Most agriculture, however, consists of subsistence farming* of food crops such as beans, corn, cassava*, and sorghum*. Raising livestock such as cattle, sheep, and goats, is also important.

Burundi has very little industry or mining, and its poor transportation system limits industrial growth. Concentrated in Bujumbura, the country's few industries consist of consumer goods manufacturing and food processing. In addition, political instability has damaged the economy in recent years, causing Burundi to rely heavily on foreign aid to meet its basic needs.

PEOPLES AND CULTURE

The people of Burundi belong to three main ethnic groups—the Hutu, the Tutsi, and the Twa. The majority of the people are Hutu, and the

Tutsi Culture

The Tutsi, one of the two main ethnic groups in Burundi, possess a rich artistic heritage. Traditional Tutsi ceremonies included graceful dances accompanied by pulsing rhythmic music. Dancers wore elaborate costumes ornamented with animal skins and hair. The Tutsi were also noted for their singing, often used to tell a story. One Tutsi song identifies warriors on their way into battle; another describes the actions of hunting dogs tracking game.

* **hierarchy** organization of a group into higher and lower levels

* **clan** group of people descended from a common ancestor

* **League of Nations** organization formed to promote international peace and security; it functioned from 1920 to 1946

* **coup** sudden, often violent overthrow of a ruler or government

* **insurrection** violent uprising against authority; rebellion

Tutsi make up about 20 percent of the population. The Twa, a Pygmy people and the original inhabitants of the region, represent less than 1 percent of the population today.

The people of Burundi speak three major languages: Rundi, French, and Swahili. Rundi, the most widely spoken, is a Bantu language. People involved in trade often use Swahili. A large percentage of the population is Christian, mostly Roman Catholic. However, many people—including some Christians—also practice traditional African religions.

Although Burundi has one of the highest population densities—the number of people who inhabit each square mile—in Africa, few people live in urban areas or even in villages. Most live in small family compounds scattered around the countryside. In these isolated settlements, family members build clusters of beehive-shaped huts.

Burundi's society is made up of a hierarchy* of rankings based on ethnic or clan* identity. Traditionally, the Twa have occupied the lowest level. The highest social rank has consisted of princely Tutsi families, who are descended from the rulers of ancient kingdoms that occupied the region.

Traditionally, the Hutu have been farmers, while the mostly tall Tutsi have raised cattle. A long history of mistrust and fear between the Hutu and Tutsi has led to periodic struggles between the two groups. In the 1970s the ethnic conflict between the Hutu and Tutsi erupted in civil war, resulting in the deaths of hundreds of thousands of people.

HISTORY AND GOVERNMENT

The Hutu began migrating into Burundi around A.D. 1000; the Tutsi arrived about 400 years later. Although outnumbered by the Hutu, the Tutsi eventually gained dominance in the area and founded a number of kingdoms. By the 1800s the entire region was ruled by a Tutsi king.

In 1890 Burundi and its neighbor RWANDA became part of the colony of German East Africa. In 1919, after Germany's defeat in World War I, the League of Nations* placed the region under Belgian rule. Belgian control of the territory—later known as Ruanda-Urundi—continued until 1962, when the region became the two independent nations of Rwanda and Burundi.

Ethnic Conflict. After independence on July 1, 1962, Burundi became a constitutional monarchy ruled by the Tutsi *mwami,* or king. Hostilities between Hutu and Tutsi began to increase over the next several years, and fighting broke out a number of times. In October 1965, a group of Hutu army officers tried to overthrow the monarchy. The attempt failed, and the Tutsi retaliated by executing many Hutu—political leaders, intellectuals, and ordinary citizens.

A military coup* in November 1966 ended the monarchy and led to the establishment of a republic. Michel Micombero, a Tutsi, became president of the new government. At this point, Burundi politics tended to revolve around internal struggles within the Tutsi minority. In the background, however, there loomed the threat of insurrection* by the Hutu majority.

105

Burundi

Since independence ethnic conflict between Burundi's Hutu and Tutsi has periodically erupted in episodes of violence. In this photo a group of Hutu return to their homes after a Tutsi attack.

In 1972 a wave of violence erupted in Burundi as the Hutu rebelled against Tutsi oppression. The uprising triggered massive attacks by the Tutsi against the Hutu. At least 100,000 Hutu were killed between April and September. The killings and repression intensified the hatred between the two groups. The attack marked an important point in the Hutu–Tutsi conflict, as it truly brought the Hutu people together because they were suffering at the hands of the Tutsis.

Conflicts within the Tutsi led to the overthrow of Michel Micombero by a military coup in 1976 and the rise to power of Jean-Baptiste Bagaza, another Tutsi. Bagaza was overthrown in 1987 by another military coup led by Pierre Buyoya. Under Buyoya, Burundi was ruled by a military

* **junta**   group that runs a government, usually after seizing power by force

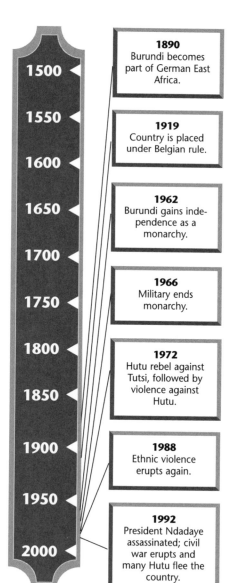

1890
Burundi becomes part of German East Africa.

1919
Country is placed under Belgian rule.

1962
Burundi gains independence as a monarchy.

1966
Military ends monarchy.

1972
Hutu rebel against Tutsi, followed by violence against Hutu.

1988
Ethnic violence erupts again.

1992
President Ndadaye assassinated; civil war erupts and many Hutu flee the country.

junta*. Ethnic hostilities between Hutu and Tutsi erupted again in 1988, causing many Hutu to flee the country.

Attempts at Reform. Attempts by President Buyoya to reform the government and lessen ethnic divisions led to the adoption of a new constitution in 1992. The document prohibited political organizations based on ethnic identity and required political parties to include representatives from both the Hutu and Tutsi. Under this new constitution, Burundi held its first free democratic election in 1993. Hutu leader Melchior Ndadaye won the presidency in a landslide, ending nearly 30 years of Tutsi control.

Ndadaye freed many political prisoners and set up an administration that was two-thirds Hutu and one-third Tutsi. However, this attempt at two-party government came to a dramatic end in October 1993, when Ndadaye was assassinated in a Tutsi-led military coup. News of Ndadaye's assassination outraged the Hutu, who responded by killing tens of thousands of innocent Tutsi civilians.

The wave of violence in 1993 was followed by attacks against the Hutu led by the largely Tutsi army, causing nearly 800,000 Hutu to flee to neighboring countries. An uneasy calm returned to Burundi when moderate leader Cyprien Ntaryamira became president in January 1994. However, his term of office came to an abrupt end the following April when the plane in which he and Rwandan president Juvenal Habyarimana were traveling crashed in suspicious circumstances.

The announcement of Ntaryamira's death had little effect in Burundi. In Rwanda, however, the death of President Habyarimana had a dramatic impact. Like Burundi, Rwanda also has a population of Hutu and Tutsi divided by ethnic rivalries. Suspicion for the crash and the death of President Habyarimana fell on Tutsi groups, setting off a wave of violence against Rwandan Tutsi.

Outlook for the Future. Events in Rwanda increased ethnic tension in Burundi. Tens of thousands of Hutu and Tutsi refugees fled Rwanda and sought safety in Burundi. The presence of these refugees carried the seeds of further conflict.

After the death of President Ntaryamira, the Hutu leader Sylvestre Ntibantuganya became acting president of Burundi. Days later Tutsi soldiers began attacking Hutu, and a group of Tutsi tried to stage a military coup. The coup failed and outbreaks of violence continued.

Growing international concern about Burundi prompted the United Nations to send advisers to study the situation in 1995. By 1996 UN reports of civil war in various parts of Burundi led the United States and many European nations to suspend their foreign aid to the country.

The threat of violence remains high in Burundi, and the country faces continuing political and economic problems. A military coup in 1996 returned president Pierre Buyoya to power, and he has struggled to resolve the many problems facing his country. Meanwhile, fighting has continued in many parts of Burundi. It remains to be seen whether the nation will be able to resolve its problems in the near future. (*See also*

Burundi

Republic of Burundi

POPULATION:
6,054,714 (2000 estimated population)

AREA:
10,747 sq. mi. (27,834 sq. km)

LANGUAGES:
Rundi, French (both official); Swahili

NATIONAL CURRENCY:
Burundi franc

PRINCIPAL RELIGIONS:
Christian 67%, traditional 32%, Muslim 1%

CITIES:
Bujumbura (capital), 300,000 (1994 est.); Gitega, Ngozi, Kayanza, Mwaro

ANNUAL RAINFALL:
Ranges from 1,194 mm (47 in.) on the plateaus to 762 mm (30 in.) in lower areas

ECONOMY:
GDP per capita: U.S. $740

PRINCIPAL PRODUCTS AND EXPORTS:
Agricultural: coffee, cotton, tea, cassava, sorghum, maize, livestock, hides
Manufacturing: light consumer goods, food processing
Mining: nickel, uranium, vanadium, phosphates

GOVERNMENT:
Independence from Belgium, 1962. Transitional regime. President elected by universal suffrage. Legislature: Assemblée Nationale (elected by universal suffage)

HEADS OF STATE SINCE 1976:
1976–1987 President Jean-Baptiste Bagaza
1987–1993 President Pierre Buyoya
1993 President Melchior Ndadaye
1993–1994 Interim government; President Cyprien Ntaryamira
1994–1996 President Sylvestre Ntibantuganya
1996– President Major Pierre Buyoya

ARMED FORCES:
40,000

EDUCATION:
Compulsory for ages 7–13; literacy rate 35%

Agriculture, Bantu Peoples, Class Structure and Caste, Colonialism in Africa, Ethnic Groups and Identity, Genocide and Violence, Refugees, Tribalism, United Nations in Africa.)

BUSHMEN

See *Khoisan.*

Busia, Kofi A.

**1913–1978
Prime minister of Ghana**

Born into African royalty, Kofi A. Busia was elected prime minister of GHANA in 1969 and led his country for a brief period. In addition to politics, Busia focused on philosophy and economics. He earned a doctoral degree from Oxford University in England and wrote many books, including *Africa in Search of Democracy* (1967).

In 1942 Busia was appointed one of the first African district commissioners under British colonial rule. He continued his political activities as a member of the colonial legislative assembly in 1951. As Ghana neared independence in 1956, Busia became the leader of the National Liberation Movement (NLM). The party was formed to oppose the government of Prime Minister Kwame NKRUMAH. After Nkrumah moved against political opponents, Busia fled Africa fearing arrest. He spent the next years in the Netherlands and Britain.

In 1966 military leaders overthrew Nkrumah, and Busia returned to Ghana as an adviser to the new government. Three years later he became prime minister. His government was marred by conflicts with workers and the military, a sagging economy, and the exile of non-Ghanaian Africans from the country. Overthrown by the military in 1972, Prime Minister Busia again left Ghana and spent the rest of his life in Britain.

Cabinda

Cabinda, a province of the country of ANGOLA, is separated from Angola by a narrow strip of land belonging to the CONGO (KINSHASA). Though small in size (about 2,800 sq. miles), Cabinda has figured prominently in the economics and politics of the region for many years—particularly because of its valuable oil fields.

Europeans visited the region in the 1500s to trade for copper, ivory, and slaves. When European powers carved Africa up into colonial empires, the Portuguese gained control of Cabinda. To keep a close watch on separatist groups within the local population, Portugal made the port city of Cabinda a district capital of northern Angola. Portuguese companies exported the riches of Cabinda, including timber, cocoa, palm products, and other resources.

In the 1960s oil was discovered offshore, making Cabinda one of Angola's key resources. When Angola won independence in 1975, a civil war began between the Popular Movement for the Liberation of Angola (MPLA) and the National Union for the Total Independence of Angola (UNITA). Both groups hoped to control Angola eventually, and neither wanted to lose the valuable Cabinda. While the rest of Angola's economy suffered during the war, government forces protected Cabinda's oil operations and oil production continued.

At the same time, the Front for the Liberation of the Enclave of Cabinda (FLEC), formed in the 1960s, waged a guerrilla* war for Cabindan independence. It sometimes fought from bases in neighboring countries. Both the MPLA and the UNITA attacked FLEC at one time or another. In the mid-1990s, the MPLA and the UNITA officially ended their conflict, but FLEC continues its battle. Although many Cabindans support independence, FLEC is too divided by internal rivalries to accomplish this goal. However, it seems likely that a majority of the population would vote for some type of independence if a free vote was held. It is also hard to determine the size of the Cabinda population due to the area's instability in the late twentieth century and the coming and going of refugees. It has been variously estimated at 100,000 and 200,000.

Meanwhile, Cabinda's rich resources continue to make the region of vital importance to Angola. The Cabinda Gulf Oil Company, run by the American firm Chevron, produces over half of Angola's oil. Natural gas deposits have also been found in the area. (*See also* **Colonialism in Africa.**)

* **guerrilla** type of warfare involving sudden raids by small groups of warriors

Cabral, Amílcar Lopes

Cabral, Amílcar Lopes

1924–1973
Political and revolutionary activist

* **oppression**   unjust or cruel exercise of authority

Born in the Portuguese colony of GUINEA (later, GUINEA-BISSAU), Amílcar Lopes Cabral went to Portugal to study. After graduating from the University of Lisbon, he returned home a revolutionary leader, and he brought about Guinea-Bissau's independence.

Cabral believed that people who opposed oppression* should take action and commit themselves to social reform. He won respect at home and abroad for his political convictions. In 1956 he formed and led an underground movement against Portuguese rule. In time the movement achieved military and political victories, but Cabral himself was assassinated by Portuguese agents in 1973. The following year Guinea-Bissau gained independence, and Cabral's brother became the first president of the new country.

Cairo

* **medieval**   referring to the Middle Ages in western Europe, generally considered to be from the A.D. 500s to the 1500s

* **sect**   religious group

* **mosque**   Muslim place of worship

Cairo is the capital of EGYPT and the largest city in Africa. The city's strategic location on the NILE RIVER has made it a defensive stronghold for Egypt for nearly 1,500 years. In medieval* times, Cairo was one of the busiest centers of trade and education in the Mediterranean and Middle East. Today the city remains a vibrant hub of Islamic culture and politics.

History. Before the founding of Cairo, other great cities had risen and faded in the area. Just to the southwest was Memphis, the first capital of ancient Egypt, built by the pharaohs around 3000 B.C. To the northeast stood Heliopolis, an important religious center around 2500 B.C. It later housed Greek schools where Plato and other famous philosophers studied.

Modern Cairo began as a military camp. It was established in A.D. 640 by Amr ibn al-As, an Arab leader who brought ISLAM to Egypt. Over the next 300 years Arab rulers added to and improved the city, known as al-Fustat, which developed into a major river port.

In 969 the Fatimids, an Islamic sect*, invaded the region and built the city of al-Qahirah (meaning "The Victorious") northeast of al-Fustat. *Cairo* is the Westernized version of al-Qahirah. The Fatimids expanded the city and built the mosque* and university called al-Azhar, one of the greatest centers of learning in the medieval world. The university still exists today. Al-Fustat remained the region's commercial center for nearly 200 years. In 1168, however, it was burned by the Muslims to keep it from falling into the hands of Christian invaders. The Muslim leader, Saladin, went on to establish a large empire with Cairo as its capital.

During the Middle Ages, Cairo occupied an important place in the spice trade between Europe and Asia. By the 1340s its population had reached half a million. But beginning with an outbreak of the Black Death in 1348, Cairo was struck by a series of plagues and other misfortunes. A sea voyage that occurred just before 1500 changed the country's fortunes. The Portuguese explorer Vasco da Gama reached Asia by sailing around the southern tip of Africa, opening a new route to the countries that grew spices and eliminating Cairo's key role in that trade. Then, after the Turks conquered Egypt in 1517, Cairo lost its place as the

Islam has been a large part of the culture of Cairo since the 600s. Minarets rising from the city's many mosques dot the skyline.

capital of a major empire. The city fell into decline. By 1800 its population had shrunk by nearly half.

In the mid-1800s the construction of the nearby SUEZ CANAL and a railroad between Cairo and ALEXANDRIA brought immigration and new growth to Cairo. After 1850 the city developed along European lines inspired by improvements made in Paris. Large boulevards were added to handle motorized vehicle traffic, new bridges were built, and utilities such as gas, electricity, water, and telephone were provided. New public transportation services enabled suburbs to multiply outside Cairo, and by the end of World War II the city was home to more than 2 million people. Since then, Cairo has grown enormously, with new suburbs spilling out into the surrounding desert and Nile delta.

Modern Cairo. Today Cairo's population approaches 12 million people, which means that about one in every five Egyptians lives in the city. Cairo's rapid growth, however, has caused serious problems of pollution and unemployment in the area. Although predominantly Muslim, the

See color plate 14, vol. 4.

city contains the largest concentration of Coptic Christians in the world.

Cairo is the center of Egyptian government, industry, finance, and culture. It contains most of Egypt's banks and businesses and a good part of its recreational and entertainment facilities. Cairo's lively film and music industry attracts the most popular entertainers of the Arab world. The city also offers more than 20 museums, various performing arts organizations, and several noted universities that draw students from many Arab nations. (*See also* **Cities and Urbanization, Copts.**)

Calendars and Time

In African cities, many people use the Western system of clocks and calendars for official and business purposes. They divide the day into 24 hours and the year into 12 months based on the earth's movement around the sun. As in the West, a general system of dating is used to create a common framework for past events from many locations.

Traditionally, however, African societies have not used formal, structured methods to measure, count, or keep track of hours and months. Instead, they marked time by the rhythms of daily life and by the events of a community's or people's shared history. This approach still shapes the idea of time in rural and traditional African cultures.

Months, Seasons, and Years. People in North Africa, where Islam is the dominant religion, use the Muslim calendar, which has 12 months in a year. Unlike the Western calendar, however, Muslim months are based on the 29.5-day cycle of the moon's phases. Each month begins on or near the date of the new moon and contains either 29 or 30 days.

The Muslim year has a total of either 354 or 355 days—10 or 11 days shorter than the Western year, which is based on the solar cycle. This difference means that the Muslim months do not occur in the same season every year. Over a period of 32.5 Western years, each Muslim month moves through the cycle of seasons.

* **sub-Saharan** referring to Africa south of the Sahara desert

In sub-Saharan* Africa, some groups do not identify and name months. People in these cultures are aware of the phases of the moon and the yearly cycle of seasons. But instead of using a calendar to schedule their work, they carry out their activities—hunting, farming, rituals*—in accordance with regular events they observe in nature. Such events include the positions of the stars and the sun, the flowering of plants, the rise and fall of rivers, and seasonal changes in temperature, rainfall, and wind.

* **ritual** religious ceremony that follows a set pattern

* **indigenous** native to a certain place

Other indigenous* groups—especially those centered on agriculture—do have systems of named months, with calendars based on the lunar cycle. Like the months of the Muslim calendar, the months of a traditional African lunar calendar do not occur in the same season each year. For this reason, the timing of agricultural activities cannot be based on a lunar calendar. Even in calendar-keeping societies, farming is thought of not in terms of months or dates but as a succession of

tasks, such as tilling, planting, weeding, scaring away birds, and harvesting. Each task is performed when certain conditions occur.

A few groups correct the imbalance between the lunar calendar and the solar cycle by adding an extra month to the calendar or by repeating a month when the calendar falls significantly out of line with the solar year. In most cases, however, traditional African calendars are used mainly for timing social and ritual activities. Even when a calendar of months exists, the year does not necessarily begin in one specific month. A group may observe separate agricultural, ritual, and legal years that begin in different months. The year usually starts in whatever season is most important to a particular society, such as the rainy season.

The people of sub-Saharan Africa did not develop systems of dates applied across large areas and based on historical events. However, some states in West Africa and East Africa have maintained royal genealogies, or lists of their kings. Scholars and historians once believed that such lists provided an accurate chronology* for these societies. But in recent times, they have realized that many factors make the king lists inaccurate. The list-makers sometimes added early names to make their societies appear more ancient. They also dropped the names of rulers who were later overthrown or adjusted the lists to support the current ruler's claim to the throne. Though valuable as cultural documents, king lists are not reliable as chronologies.

Hours and Days. Some traditional African societies divide each month into halves—before and after the full moon—and count days within each half. More important than the counting of days, however, is organizing them into weeks. Most groups define a week according to the cycle of local market days. The week is as long as the interval between the beginning of one market cycle and the next, usually around five days.

The African day begins at dawn or sunrise, not in the middle of the night as in the Western system. Indigenous groups do not divide the day into fixed hours, minutes, or seconds. Instead, they organize the day by the changing position of the sun and the social activities associated with it. A typical daily sequence might be: first light, sunrise, breakfast, going to the fields, noon, cattle returning, sunset, supper, and sleep, followed again by first light. The night is not usually subdivided into any periods, and a 24-hour period may be called a "day," a "night," or a "sleep."

* **chronology**   order of events

Camara Laye

1928–1980
Guinean author

Camara Laye is one of Africa's best-known and most respected francophone (French-speaking) authors. His first novel, *L'enfant noir* (*The Black Infant*) is also one of his most popular. Written in 1953, the book tells of Camara's childhood in the town of Kouroussa, GUINEA. On the one hand, it is a personal account of the author's Mande culture, including a description of secret initiation rites. On the other, it is the story of an African exiled to France who remembers the culture he was forced to abandon.

Camara Laye

Dramouss, another work based on Camara's personal experiences, is about his disappointment with the political regime of President Sékou Touré. The Guinean ruler's cruelty forced Camara into exile in SENEGAL. Camara's last book, *Le mâitre de la parole,* is a retelling of the Mande epic* about the medieval* Emperor Sunjata. Camara wrote down and translated the tale from the performance of a traditional storyteller.

Another novel that appeared under Camara's name was *Le regard du roi (The Radiance of the King).* Some people doubted that Camara was actually the author of the book, and shortly before his death he confirmed that the novel was written by someone else. Camara Laye died in Senegal in 1980. (*See also* **Literature**.)

Cameroon

The West African country of Cameroon extends from the shores of the Atlantic Ocean to Lake Chad in the interior. As one of the most culturally diverse nations in Africa, Cameroon includes hundreds of different ethnic groups. Long a crossroads for merchants from the Middle East and Europe, it was controlled by various European powers before gaining independence in the 1960s.

GEOGRAPHY AND ECONOMY

Cameroon's Atlantic coast is swampy and densely forested. Mount Cameroon, an active volcano and the highest peak in western Africa, towers above the rest of the coastline. Farther inland, the country divides into two main regions: the western highlands and the southern plateau.

Landforms. The mountains of Cameroon's western highlands serve as a natural boundary with NIGERIA. The mountains contain various mineral deposits and are covered with rich volcanic soil. The western highlands merge into the southern plateau, also known as the Bamileke Grassfields. This area of gently rolling hills stretches eastward into the CENTRAL AFRICAN REPUBLIC. Cameroon's capital city, Yaoundé, is located in the center of the southern region.

Northern Cameroon features the Benue Depression, a low-lying district around the Kebi River valley that is enclosed on three sides by mountains. Beyond the mountains the Chad Plain gradually slopes down to the shores of Lake Chad. Cameroon's many rivers, noted for their rapids and waterfalls, are used for transportation and the production of hydroelectric power.

Climate and Vegetation. Cameroon's climate and vegetation vary with the terrain. Southern Cameroon has a warm and rainy equatorial* climate. Mangrove* swamps along the southern coast eventually give way to thick rain forests, particularly in the southeast.

The coast has a wet season that runs from May through October, followed by a dry season from November to April. The coast receives more rainfall than the interior, where the rainy season lasts only two or three months. Farther north the climate is hotter and drier, and the vegetation changes from rain forest to wooded grasslands. The far north experiences desertlike conditions. Grass and shrubs grow during the wet season, but the region has little vegetation during the rest of the year.

Two Traditions

The colonial powers of France and Britain left widely different legacies in Cameroon—in such areas as language, educational institutions, and political systems. When Cameroon achieved independence, these different traditions became the source of conflict. In an effort to smooth out some of the differences between English- and French-speakers, Cameroon declared itself bilingual, making both languages official. In 1984, to symbolize the unity of the country, its name was changed from the Federal Republic of Cameroon—suggesting a federation of separate parts—to the Republic of Cameroon.

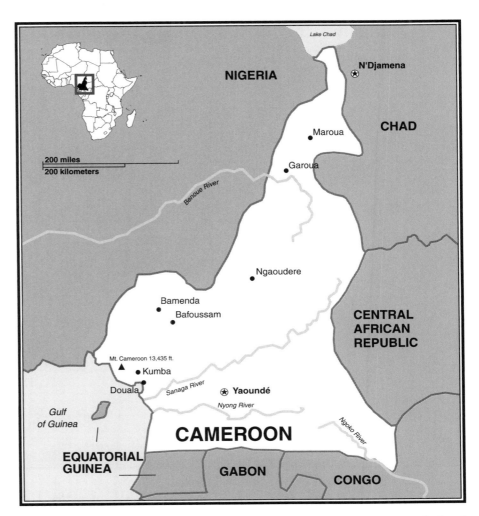

Economy. Cameroon's strong agricultural base produces enough food for its growing population as well as a surplus for export. The main agricultural exports are cocoa, coffee, and timber. Cameroonian industries produce both oil and tin, and the country also contains deposits of uranium and iron ore. In addition, the peoples of the southern plateau produce items such as wood carvings for sale to outside markets.

The transportation infrastructure* is relatively well developed, with good roads connecting most towns and cities to the surrounding areas. These roads allow many people of the densely populated southern plateau to leave the area to work and send money home to family members. However, despite its natural resources, Cameroon's economy was in crisis in the 1990s due to political instability and poor investment of the profits from agriculture and industry.

HISTORY AND GOVERNMENT

Several powerful kingdoms existed in Cameroon before the arrival of Europeans in the late 1400s. During the colonial era, which began in the late 1800s, the region was controlled by three different European powers: Germany, Britain, and France. Modern Cameroon reflects the legacy of these various political influences.

* **infrastructure** basic framework of a society and its economy, which includes roads, bridges, port facilities, airports, and other public works

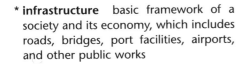

See map in Archaeology and Prehistory (vol. 1).

Northern Cameroon has long been a stronghold of Fulani culture. These Fulani riders and their festively decorated horses parade through the northern town of Rey Bouba.

Precolonial and Colonial History. People of Cameroon's early societies crossed the Sahara desert to trade with Egypt and other civilizations along the Mediterranean Sea. Gradually, separate kingdoms arose around Lake Chad and in the eastern grasslands. Trade, migration, and expansion brought the kingdoms of the region into contact with one another. In the 1400s the Bamileke and Bamum kingdoms joined together to form a confederation. Another early kingdom, Mandara, was conquered by the BORNU empire in the 1500s.

Many of the first Europeans in Cameroon were merchants. They began exporting ivory and slaves from the area. By the late 1800s several European powers had set their sights on Cameroon. In 1884 the Germans established the Kamerun Protectorate in the region, but during World War I the British and French took over the colony. After the war, Britain and France divided the colony and ruled it under the supervision of the League of Nations, an organization formed to promote international security.

Britain controlled the northwestern portion of the country, known as British Cameroons and incorporated it into the colony of Nigeria. However, Britain did little to develop the area. In fact, British rule is seen as a time of neglect, and many Cameroonians were angry with both the British colonial leaders and the Nigerians. France invested much more

 Republic of Cameroon

POPULATION:
15,421,937 (2000 estimated population)

AREA:
183,568 sq. mi. (475,400 sq. km)

LANGUAGES:
French, English (official); Bantu dialects (24)

NATIONAL CURRENCY:
CFA franc

PRINCIPAL RELIGIONS:
Traditional 51%, Christian 33%, Muslim 16%

CITIES:
Yaoundé (capital) 1,119,000 (1999 est.); Douala, Nkongsamba, Maroua, Bafoussam, Foumban, Garoua, Limbe, Bamenda, Kumba

ANNUAL RAINFALL:
Varies by region from 23 in. (600 mm) in the extreme north to 390 in. (10,000 mm) along the coast

ECONOMY:
GDP per capita: U.S. $2,000

PRINCIPAL PRODUCTS AND EXPORTS:
Agricultural: coffee, cocoa, cotton, rubber, bananas, livestock, timber
Manufacturing: textiles, lumber, food and beverage processing
Mining: petroleum, bauxite, iron ore

GOVERNMENT:
German colony until 1916, then divided by League of Nations between France and England. In 1960 French portion declared independence. In 1961 English portion voted to split, with part joining Nigeria, remainder joining Cameroon. Multiparty democracy; president and Assemblée Nationale elected by universal suffrage.

HEADS OF STATE SINCE INDEPENDENCE:
1960–1982 President Ahmadou Ahidjo
1982– President Paul Biya

ARMED FORCES:
13,100 (1998 est.)

EDUCATION:
Compulsory for ages 6–11; literacy rate 63%

time and money in French Cameroun, and a large number of French citizens settled there. By the time of independence, this part of the country was wealthier, more educated, and had a much stronger infrastructure than the British section.

In 1958 pressure for greater political freedom caused France to declare Cameroun a republic with limited self-government. Two years later the republic became independent. In 1961 the northern section of British Cameroons voted to join Nigeria; the southern section became part of the Federal Republic of Cameroon.

From Colony to Dictatorship. The first president of the new republic, Ahmadou Ahidjo, promised to maintain close relations with France and to build an economy based on capitalism*. One of Ahidjo's main goals was to unite the English- and French-speaking parts of the country. He hoped to get Cameroonians to identify with the nation rather than their own ethnic groups. To achieve his goals, Ahidjo combined the nation's political parties into a single party, the Cameroon National Union (CNU). The president ruled as an absolute dictator, with power concentrated in his hands and exercised through the CNU.

Problems soon arose in stabilizing the country's economy. During the early years of independence, Cameroon was heavily dependent on foreign trade and produced few goods for its own population. With the discovery of oil in 1976, petroleum became Cameroon's main source of income. However, much of this money was spent on poorly planned projects.

In 1982 Ahidjo resigned and his prime minister, Paul Biya, took over the presidency. However, Ahidjo tried to maintain control of the gov-

* **capitalism** economic system in which businesses are privately owned and operated and where free markets coordinate most economic activity

Cameroon

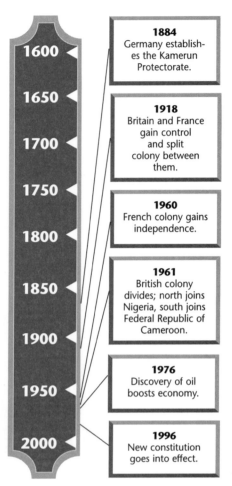

1600
1650
1700
1750
1800
1850
1900
1950
2000

1884
Germany establishes the Kamerun Protectorate.

1918
Britain and France gain control and split colony between them.

1960
French colony gains independence.

1961
British colony divides; north joins Nigeria, south joins Federal Republic of Cameroon.

1976
Discovery of oil boosts economy.

1996
New constitution goes into effect.

* **authoritarian** relating to strong leadership with unquestioned powers

ernment from behind the scenes, and this led to a confrontation between the two men. Forces loyal to Ahidjo staged an uprising in 1984, but Biya defeated them and exiled Ahidjo. Up to this time Biya had been trying to make the country more democratic, but the uprising caused him to adopt more authoritarian* measures.

The people of Cameroon, who wanted more political freedom, opposed Biya's policies. They pressed the government for democratic reforms and staged demonstrations in 1990. New political parties emerged and multiparty elections were held in 1992. Still, Biya and his party managed to maintain their majority. Biya then arrested the leader of the main opposition party, leading to clashes between the government and its opponents. A new constitution, drafted the following year, gave the president and the central government very strong powers. Although parliamentary elections were held again in 1997, Biya's party was able to control the process under the new constitution. Many observers considered the elections unfair.

Government. The president of Cameroon is elected directly by the people for a seven-year term and may serve a maximum of two terms. The president appoints the prime minister, the official head of the government. The legislature consists of the Assemblée Nationale, whose members are directly elected, and the Senate. The people elect regional and local councils, but the president may suspend or dissolve these councils. In general, the president holds enormous political power and progress toward democracy has been slow.

PEOPLES AND CULTURES

Cameroon is home to over 250 ethnic groups and more than 300 different languages. The ethnic groups correspond to the various geographical regions of the country. The southern coast and inland forests are inhabited by a wide variety of agricultural and fishing societies as well as nomadic Pygmy groups. Most people in the inland forests live in small villages headed by a chief or a council of elders. Christianity and formal education are more widespread near the coast, where contact with Europeans occurred earlier than in the inland villages.

The Bamileke, a group of tightly organized chiefdoms, live in Cameroon's grassy plateaus. These communities vary in size from a few people to tens of thousands. Although most of the Bamileke practice Christianity, the ruling families of one group, the Bamum, converted to Islam in the 1800s.

Northern Cameroon has been heavily influenced by a Muslim people known as the FULANI. Several dozen Fulani states were established in northern Cameroon during the 1800s and absorbed much of the non-Muslim population. As a result, Islam is widespread in the region. With the migration of many rural people to the cities of northern Cameroon, the influence of Fulani culture has continued to spread. (*See also* **Climate, Colonialism in Africa, Islam in Africa, Pygmies, Slave Trade.**)

Canary Islands

The Canaries are a group of seven volcanic islands that lie off the northwestern coast of Africa. The westernmost islands are actually the peaks of mountains that rise from the ocean floor to heights several thousand feet above sea level. The eastern Canaries are much flatter. Gran Canaria and Tenerife are the two most important islands.

The Canaries have a fairly consistent subtropical climate year-round with temperatures ranging between 64°F and 79°F and little rainfall. Vegetation varies by altitude. Plants suited to hot, dry conditions grow at lower elevations, while fruits and vegetables are raised at elevations above about 1,400 feet. Bananas are the most important export crop, along with potatoes, tomatoes, oranges, and grapes. Since the 1960s, however, tourism has been the mainstay of the economy, and some 80 percent of the island's inhabitants are connected in some way with the tourism. Aside from a large petroleum refinery in Santa Cruz that processes crude oil, there is little industry on the islands.

The Canaries were originally inhabited by a North African Berber people known as the Guanche. The king of MAURITANIA visited the islands in about 40 B.C., a journey that was noted by the ancient Romans. The name of the islands probably comes from the Latin word *canis,* meaning dog, because of the many large dogs found there. European sailors first arrived in the 1200s, and Spanish settlers took over the islands during the 1400s. For hundreds of years the Canaries served as an important port on Spain's transatlantic route to the Americas. Christopher Columbus stopped in the islands for supplies on each of his westward voyages across the Atlantic.

The Canaries were a Spanish province until 1927, when rivalry between the main islands of Gran Canaria and Tenerife caused Spain to split them into two separate provinces. In 1982 the entire island group became a self-governing community, electing its own representatives to the Spanish parliament and senate. Most of the islands' approximately 1.5 million inhabitants are descended from the original inhabitants and the Spanish conquerors. The two major cities are Las Palmas and Santa Cruz. Canarians speak Spanish and the local culture is largely Catholic. (*See also* **Colonialism in Africa**.)

Cape Coloured People

* **apartheid** policy of racial segregation in South Africa intended to maintain white control over the country's blacks, Asians, and people of mixed ancestry

Cape Coloured People are the mixed race population of various towns in Cape Province, SOUTH AFRICA. They are descendants of Dutch, British, and Kxoe people (various non–Bantu-speaking groups of southern Africa), as well as of slaves brought from MADAGASCAR and East Asia. Until the late 1950s, when apartheid* policies were adopted in South Africa, most of the Cape Coloured lived in cities such as CAPE TOWN or Port Elizabeth. During the 1970s, they were sent to undeveloped areas outside the towns and their homes were given to white families.

Most of their 2 million members belong to Dutch Protestant churches, but a small minority is Muslim. The Cape Coloured People speak a form of Dutch called Afrikaans, but they maintain a cultural identity separate from both whites and blacks. Politically, they have tended to support the white-led National Party rather than the black-led African National Congress. (*See also* **Apartheid**.)

119

Cape Town

Cape Town

See color
plate 15,
vol. 4.

* **shantytown** poor, run-down section of a city, often inhabited by immigrants

Located about 30 miles north of the Cape of Good Hope, Cape Town is the oldest city in SOUTH AFRICA. With its many gardens, parks, beaches, historical buildings, and mountains, it is considered one of the most beautiful cities in the world.

Cape Town (known as Kaapstad in Afrikaans) was founded in 1652 as a supply station for Dutch ships sailing between Europe and Asia. The Dutch brought in slaves from Asia and MADAGASCAR. French and Dutch colonists settled there later. The British took the city in 1806 and abolished slavery, causing many Dutch settlers to leave Cape Town. These settlers trekked north in the 1830s and eventually founded the AFRIKANER REPUBLICS.

In the late 1800s the discovery of diamonds and gold in the northern Transvaal led to the founding of JOHANNESBURG. The new town soon replaced Cape Town as the leading city in southern Africa. However, Cape Town remained the region's principal port until the 1980s. It still boasts one of the world's largest dry docks and offers offshore services for large tankers.

Cape Town has long been known for its diverse ethnic population. Before South Africa introduced its policy of APARTHEID in 1948, the city was largely integrated. Afterwards, thousands of CAPE COLOURED PEOPLE—mixed-race descendants of European,

KHOISAN, and Asian ancestors—were expelled from Cape Town and forced to settle in undeveloped areas outside the city. As a result, many thousands of black people from elsewhere in South Africa were brought in to replace them as laborers. One of the worst of these areas, Crossroads, grew to a shantytown* of 70,000 people. Since the end of apartheid in the 1990s, Cape Town has once again became an extremely diverse city. (*See also* **Colonialism in Africa**.)

Cape Verde

* **arable** suitable for producing crops

* **coup** sudden, often violent overthrow of a ruler or government

The nation of Cape Verde (also known as Cabo Verde) consists of 15 islands about 400 miles off the coast of SENEGAL. Although the name means "Green Cape," the islands actually have a hot, dry climate and very little arable* land. The capital city of Praia is on the island of Santiago

Before its discovery by the Portuguese in 1460, Cape Verde was uninhabited. Portugal used the islands as a supply base for slave ships making the voyage from Africa to America. The islands eventually became home to descendants of African slaves and European settlers from Portugal and the Mediterranean. The Portuguese often chose Cape Verdeans to administer their other African colonies; many served overseas.

During the late 1950s, Cape Verde joined GUINEA-BISSAU in seeking independence from Portugal. By 1975 both colonies had won their independence, and for the next five years one political party, the PAIGC, governed both countries. Aristides Pereira became the first president of Cape Verde. The nation planned to unite with Guinea-Bissau, but a 1980 coup* in Guinea-Bissau altered the course of events. The

Cape Verde PAIGC changed its name to the PAICV and declared itself the country's only legal party.

Cape Verde's government has been remarkably stable since independence, with only a single unsuccessful coup attempt in 1977. In 1990 opposition political groups formed the Movement for Democracy (MPD) and pressured the government to end single-party rule. Multiparty elections were held in 1991, and António Mascarenhas Monteiro of the MPD was elected president.

The population of Cape Verde, about 400,000, is ethnically homogenous*. Almost all the people are Catholic and speak Crioulu, a Portuguese-African language. In culture, Cape Verdeans are closer to the Portuguese than to West Africans.

With little rainfall, the islands produce only enough food to supply about 10 percent of the needs of the people. Drought and famine are common occurrences. Nevertheless, the majority of the people work in agriculture. Much of the land is held by landlords who hire laborers to work their fields. Most farms are very small, typically less than three acres in size.

For many years, a large number of men have emigrated to find work overseas. Many have worked in the cod fishing industry in the north

* homogenous   similar in nature

Cape Verde contains ruins of many Portuguese forts, like this one on the island of São Vicente. The Portuguese held Cape Verde for more than 500 years and had a lasting influence on the islands' culture.

Atlantic ocean and have settled in southeastern New England. In fact, twice as many Cape Verdeans live outside the country as live on the islands. These emigrants send millions of dollars home each year, contributing a large percentage of the country's foreign earnings. Because so many men have left the islands, the adult population is about 55 percent female, and women head almost 40 percent of all households. (*See also* **Colonialism in Africa, Slave Trade**.)

CARNIVALS

See *Festivals and Carnivals.*

Carthage

Carthage, a rich and powerful city of the ancient world, once dominated the coast of North Africa. It stood on a peninsula in what is now TUNISIA, with a good harbor on each side. At one time the city controlled an empire that included North Africa, southern Spain, the Mediterranean islands of Sardinia and Corsica, and part of Sicily.

The Phoenicians, a trading and seafaring people of the eastern Mediterranean, founded Carthage sometime before 814 B.C. The city grew wealthy as a result of mining silver in North Africa and Spain. After gaining independence from Phoenicia around 600 B.C., Carthage had several conflicts with the Greeks and then began enlarging its territory about 410 B.C. At the time Rome was a rising power, and the Carthaginians and Romans eventually clashed over control of Sicily. Between 264 and 146 B.C. the two powers engaged in a series of struggles that the Romans called the Punic (meaning Phoenician) Wars. Rome finally defeated Carthage and burned it to the ground.

Roman rulers later sent its citizens to colonize Carthage, and for several centuries after 29 B.C. the rebuilt city was a major center of Roman administration in North Africa. About A.D. 700, Carthage was captured by the Arabs as part of their conquest of North Africa. Many Roman structures were destroyed, and the city was absorbed into the Arab town of Tunis. (*See also* **North Africa: History and Cultures**.)

CATHOLICISM

See *Christianity in Africa.*

Central African Federation

The Central African Federation was created in 1953 by the union of the British colonies of Northern and Southern Rhodesia and Nyasaland. Politicians had two reasons for forming this federation. One was to gain access to the copper mines of Northern Rhodesia and the cheap labor of Nyasaland. The other was to calm the fears of white settlers who were concerned about losing their grip on power over the region.

Although some of its founders hoped the federation would lead to a multiracial society, black leaders opposed this idea from the beginning. In fact, the creation of the federation spurred the growth of black nationalist parties that called for independence. The white governments of the area reacted by trying to crush the black political parties and imprisoning their leaders. However, by 1960 black citizens had won the right to vote, and in time political power was transferred to the black majority. The Central African Federation dissolved after Nyasaland (now MALAWI) and Northern Rhodesia (now ZIMBABWE) became independent in 1963. (*See also* **Colonialism in Africa**.)

Central African Republic

* **savanna** tropical or subtropical grassland with scattered trees and drought-resistant undergrowth

Located in a broad, rolling plateau just north of the equator, the Central African Republic varies from tropical rain forest in the southwest to savanna* woodlands in the northeast. Although most of the country receives abundant rainfall, the extreme—and very dry—northeast receives only about 0.2 inches annually. The Oubangui River, the most important waterway, runs past Bangui, the capital, and along the nation's southern border.

ECONOMY

The Central African Republic contains immense natural resources that could easily make it one of the richest countries in Africa. These resources include fertile land, plentiful wildlife and timber, and exten-

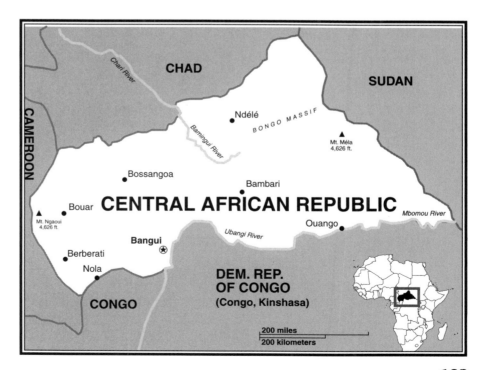

Central African Republic

* **subsistence farming** raising only enough food to live on

* **infrastructure** basic framework of a society and its economy, which includes roads, bridges, port facilities, airports, and other public works

* **indigenous** native to a certain place

* **cash crop** crop grown primarily for sale rather than for local consumption

See map in Archaeology and Prehistory (vol. 1).

* **cede** to yield or surrender

* **coup** sudden, often violent overthrow of a ruler or government

sive mineral deposits. However, partly as a result of poor economic planning, the nation has not fully benefited from its rich resources.

In spite of its fertile land and reliable rainfall, the Central African Republic imports more food than it exports. About 80 percent of the inhabitants work in agriculture—mostly subsistence farming*. The main export crops are cotton, coffee, and tobacco. Central Africans also raise cattle, sheep, goats, and pigs, except in areas where the tsetse fly—an insect that spreads disease—is found.

Mining in the Central African Republic focuses on gold and diamonds, with diamonds producing over half of export revenues. The country also has rich reserves of copper, uranium, iron, and other minerals. The timber industry processes hardwood from the tropical rain forests. Light industries include food processing, breweries, textiles, and footwear. Petroleum and durable goods such as appliances and automobiles are imported. Because the cost of imports exceeds revenues from exports, the country is deeply in debt.

The poor infrastructure* of the Central African Republic limits economic growth. The nation has no railroad and a critical shortage of good roads. Less than 5 percent of the existing roads are paved. In addition, the health care system is poor. Although tropical diseases are widespread and epidemics occur frequently, the country has only one major hospital, in the city of Bangui.

HISTORY

Before the arrival of Europeans in the late 1800s, the region that is now the Central African Republic was frequently invaded by Islamic slave raiders from the north. Weakened by the slave raids, the local population was unable to oppose the European merchants and settlers who followed. In 1894 France established a colony in the region, known as Oubangui-Chari.

The French forced the indigenous* people to work for them, to perform military service, and to pay taxes. Farmers had to grow cash crops* such as cotton instead of the food crops they needed to survive. These policies, as well as cruel treatment of local inhabitants by the French, led to uprisings in 1909 through 1911 and again from 1928 to 1945. In 1960 France granted independence to the colony, which took the name Central African Republic.

David Dacko, the country's first president, introduced a single-party system of government. In 1966 Dacko was overthrown by Captain Jean-Bédel BOKASSA, who committed brutal acts against civilians and squandered much of the nation's wealth. In 1977 Bokassa proclaimed himself emperor of the newly renamed Central African Empire. Two years later, his government—already very unpopular—reached a crisis. Riots broke out in Bangui. French troops took over the airport and the capital, and restored David Dacko to power.

In 1981 Dacko was forced to cede* power to General André Dieudonné Kolingba, who suspended the constitution and assumed absolute authority over the government. After a failed military coup* the following year, Kolingba's rule became even harsher. He introduced

 Central African Republic

POPULATION:
3,512,751 (2000 estimated population)

AREA:
240,324 sq. mi. (622,436 sq. km)

LANGUAGES:
French (official); Sango, Arabic

NATIONAL CURRENCY:
CFA franc

PRINCIPAL RELIGIONS:
Christian 50%, Traditional 24%, Muslim 15%, Other 11%

CITIES:
Bangui (capital), 524,000 (1999 est.); Baoli, Berbérati, Bambari, Bossagoa, Carnot

ANNUAL RAINFALL:
Varies from 75 in. (1900 mm) in the south to 0.2 in. (50 mm) in the extreme northeast

ECONOMY:
GDP per capita: U.S. $1,000

PRINCIPAL PRODUCTS AND EXPORTS:
Agricultural: cotton, coffee, timber, tobacco, cassava, yams, millet, bananas, corn
Manufacturing: diamond cutting, textiles, sawmills, brewing, footwear, bicycle/motorcycle assembly
Mining: diamonds, uranium, gold

GOVERNMENT:
Independence from France, 1960. Multiparty republic; president elected by universal suffrage. Governing bodies: Council of Ministers appointed by president.

HEADS OF STATE SINCE INDEPENDENCE:
1959–1966 President David Dacko
1966–1979 Colonel Jean-Bédel Bokassa; president, 1967–1976; emperor, 1976–1979
1979–1981 President David Dacko
1981–1985 General André Kolingba; president, 1985–1993
1993– President Ange-Félix Patassé

ARMED FORCES:
2,700 (1998 est.)

EDUCATION:
Compulsory for ages 6–14; literacy rate 60%

a new constitution in 1986 and was elected for another six-year term as president.

A poor economy forced Kolingba to cut spending. In addition, the government fell behind in paying civil servants' salaries. These difficulties and Kolingba's harsh policies led to riots and strikes. As the result of elections held in 1993, Ange-Félix Patassé became president. Since that time, violence has broken out over living conditions and a lack of representation for opposition parties.

The Central African president continues to hold considerable power. As head of state and commander of the armed forces, the president appoints the prime minister and the members of the Council of Ministers. There is an elected legislature, but the president has the power to dissolve it and call for new elections.

PEOPLES AND CULTURES

The Central African Republic is home to about 3.5 million people, and more than 40 percent of them are under 15 years of age. Almost half of the inhabitants live in cities and towns such as Bangui.

Of the eight major ethnic groups in the Central African Republic, the largest are the Banda and the Baya (or Gbaya). Other groups include the Mbum, the Zande, and the Aka (or Bibinga), a Pygmy people. Although the role of traditional leaders diminished during the era of French control, ethnic identity is still strong, particularly in the countryside. French is the official language and most of the population speaks Sango, a Bantu language.

Central African Republic

About one-half of Central Africans consider themselves Christians, about 15 percent are Muslim, and 24 percent practice traditional religions. In reality, though, these are little more than labels because most people maintain traditional beliefs and customs. (*See also* **Agriculture, Bantu Peoples, Colonialism in Africa, Forests and Forestry, Health Care, Minerals and Mining, Pygmies, Slave Trade.**)

Cetshwayo

1832–1884
Zulu king

* **annex**   to add a territory to an existing area

Cetshwayo kaMpande was king of Zululand, in southeastern Africa, from 1872 to 1879 and again from 1883 to 1884. Although he fought with great skill and courage to keep his kingdom free and undivided, his efforts were overwhelmed by British colonial forces.

During his early reign, Cetshwayo developed ties with Britain's coastal colony of Natal. He hoped the British would support him in his border dispute with Transvaal, Zululand's inland neighbor. However, in 1877 the British annexed* the Transvaal as part of a plan to establish a confederation in southern Africa. Cetshwayo resisted, and war broke out. Although the Zulu had the upper hand in the early stages of fighting, the British won a decisive victory in the summer of 1879 and sent Cetshwayo into exile.

Three years later Cetshwayo visited Britain and convinced the British government that he was not the warlike tyrant described by British colonial officials. He was restored to his throne in 1883, but local colonial officials supported Cetshwayo's enemies. Civil war followed. Cetshwayo was defeated and died a refugee in a part of Zululand controlled by Natal.

Chad

* **savanna**   tropical or subtropical grassland with scattered trees and drought-resistant undergrowth

* **archaeological**   referring to the study of past human cultures and societies, usually by excavating ruins

Chad is a large, landlocked country that lies south of LIBYA. Its history since independence has been marked by civil war, which has left Chad one of the poorest countries in the world.

The Land and the People.   Chad lies on a vast plain that is divided into two very different regions. The northern part of the country is very dry, and desert dominates the far north. Most of the inhabitants are nomadic Muslim groups such as the FULANI, who raise livestock and camels.

The south consists of relatively well-watered savanna* and contains the country's main rivers, the Shari and Logone. About half of the people of Chad live in the south, which also has most of the country's urban centers. The main livelihood of southerners is agriculture. Many of the people have converted to Christianity, but large numbers still hold on to traditional religious beliefs and practices.

History and Government.   Rock paintings and other archaeological* evidence indicate that northern Chad was settled as early as 5000 to

Republic of Chad

POPULATION:
8,424,504 (2000 estimated population)

AREA:
495,792 sq. mi. (1,284,000 sq. km)

LANGUAGES:
French, Arabic (official); Sara, Sango, others

NATIONAL CURRENCY:
CFA franc

PRINCIPAL RELIGIONS:
Muslim 50%, Traditional 25%, Christian 25%

CITIES:
N'Djamena (capital), 826,000 (1999 est.); Sarh (Fort Archambeault), Moundou, Bongor, Doba, Lai, Abéché, Koumra

ANNUAL RAINFALL:
Variable, from 35–47 in. (900–1200 mm) in subtropical zone to 18–20 in. (200–500 mm) in Saharan zone

ECONOMY:
GDP per capita: U.S. $600

PRINCIPAL PRODUCTS AND EXPORTS:
Agricultural: cotton, cattle, sorghum, millet, peanuts, rice, cassava, sugarcane, livestock, fish
Manufacturing: livestock products and meatpacking, beer brewing, textiles, tobacco processing
Mining: petroleum, uranium, natron, kaolin

GOVERNMENT:
Independence from France, 1960. President elected by universal suffrage. Governing bodies: 57-member Conseil Supérieur de la Transition, elected by a national conference, and Council of State, appointed by president.

HEADS OF STATE SINCE INDEPENDENCE:
1960–1975 President FranÇois-Ngarta Tombalbaye
1975–1979 General Félix Malloum, chairman of Supreme Military Council
1979– President Lol Mahamat Chaoua
1979–1982 President Goukouni Oueddei
1982–1990 President Hisséne Habré
1990– President Lieutenant General Idriss Déby

ARMED FORCES:
25,400 (1998 est.)

EDUCATION:
Compulsory for ages 8–14; literacy rate 48%

2000 B.C. The southern portion of the country was not occupied until about 500 B.C. BERBER peoples moved into northern Chad around the A.D. 700s, pushed southward by the spread of the SAHARA DESERT into borderland regions. A series of kingdoms arose in central Chad between 1000 and 1600. They gained power and wealth by conquering peoples of the region and demanding tribute* and by controlling the southern part of the trade route across the Sahara. Much of their wealth came from capturing people from the south and selling them as slaves to Arab peoples in the north.

The French colonized Chad in 1900, combining the northern and southern sections for the first time. Under the French the south received far more assistance than the north. Some southerners held positions as teachers and businessmen, and some entered government service. After World War II, these groups played a major role in organizing the movement for independence. Chad gained its independence from France in 1960.

The first president of the new country, François-Ngarta TOMBALBAYE, outlawed all political parties except his own and installed an overwhelming number of southerners in the government. This led to protests and uprisings in the central and northern parts of Chad, where rebel groups gained control in the early 1970s. A military coup* in 1975 was followed by a long civil war, and during this time warlords ran much of the country.

The authority of the central government was finally reestablished in 1982, but its harsh rule led to renewed fighting. In 1990 troops under

* **tribute** payment made by a smaller or weaker party to a more powerful one, often under the threat of force

See map in Archaeology and Prehistory (vol. 1).

* **coup** sudden, often violent overthrow of a ruler or government

127

* **guerrilla** type of warfare involving
sudden raids by small groups of warriors

the command of General Idriss Déby defeated President Hissène Habré, and Déby became president. In 1996 the country held the first multiparty presidential elections. Déby won. However, Chad continues to be plagued by political violence and low-level guerrilla* warfare.

Under Chad's constitution the people elect the president, while a national conference chooses the prime minister. The conference also chooses the national assembly, which oversees the government and has the power to dismiss the prime minister.

Economy. Chad has few natural resources, and many of these have been devastated by continual war. Most Chadians are engaged in agriculture, with cotton accounting for about 60 percent of the country's export earnings. However, Chad's agriculture does not always produce enough to feed the people, and the country must import food in years when rainfall is not adequate. Chad has very little industrial development and relies heavily on foreign assistance to meet its budget. The discovery of oil in the late 1990s may help relieve some of the country's economic problems.

Childhood and Adolescence

* **socialization** process by which children acquire the values of the community and learn to live by its rules and customs

See color plate 7, vol. 1.

For most Africans in the past, growing up meant helping the family produce food, learning the community's values, and gradually taking on new tasks, privileges, and responsibilities. After about 1900, however, patterns of childhood education and socialization* began to change. Three major influences for change have been Western-style schooling, religious schooling in the Islamic nations of northern Africa, and the growth of cities. Yet many aspects of childhood and adolescence continue to reflect distinctly African values and cultures.

Children's Lives. African children are considered to be infants while they breast-feed, typically from 12 to 24 months. Infants sleep next to their mothers at night, and during the day they are the main focus of the mothers' parenting activities. Mothers quiet their crying babies quickly, and infants generally do not develop the habit of crying loudly to express emotions. Mothers also use warnings and commands to keep their infants safe and to teach them to respect authority—an important lesson in most rural African communities. On the whole, male and female infants are treated fairly equally.

When mothers work away from the home, infants are usually tended by other women, such as sisters, grandmothers, or other mothers within the extended family. An older sister—perhaps as young as five years old—may become responsible for carrying an infant on her back. In some eastern African cultures, a woman who carries her younger brother on her back has an especially close relationship with him when they are adults.

Once out of infancy, young children are expected to join their brothers and sisters and other related children in the home and eventually the neighborhood. They begin learning about their roles and responsi-

People and Culture

Plate 1: The Herero are Bantu-speaking people of southern Angola, Namibia, and Botswana. Those living in Botswana are descendants of Herero who fled the German colony of Southwest Africa (now Namibia) in 1904. The dress of this Herero woman is said to be based on the style of clothing worn by the wives of German missionaries in the 1800s.

Plate 2: Music and dance play an essential role in many African cultures. Masked figures in ritual dances often represent spiritual beings, and the dancer's identity may be kept secret. This masked dancer performs in Eastern Nigeria.

Plate 3: Following an Islamic tradition, royal courts in western Africa often have musical ensembles that play on ceremonial occasions. The musicians pictured here with side-blown horns and a drum are attached to the court of the Sultan of Cameroon.

Plate 4: Many Africans societies hand down information orally through stories, poems, and songs. Men and women with a knowledge of local culture and history and a gift for storytelling are held in high regard. In Namibia, a Khoisan woman tells a story.

Plate 5: Christianity probably arrived in Ethiopia during the 300s. The Ethiopian Orthodox Church that developed remains an important force in the country. An Orthodox priest in the ancient city of Gondar displays a picture of St. George and the dragon.

Plate 6: The Basotho (or Sotho) live in the small kingdom of Lesotho, a land completely surrounded by South Africa. This Basotho woman is steaming corn bread over a fire.

Plate 7: The colorful *souks*, or markets, of Marrakech, Morocco, sell just about everything, and bargaining is part of the process. This stall is devoted to the sale of wool.

Plate 8: During their first two years, African children are protected, indulged, and taught to respect authority. Older brothers or sisters often care for the infants during the day. Here a toddler in Uganda plays with her doll.

Plate 9: The Asante make up a large and powerful chiefdom within southern Ghana and Ivory Coast. When Osei Tutu II became the sixteenth Asante king in 1999, he took the name of the ruler who founded the Asante kingdom in the late 1600s. The new king also received the traditional symbol of Asante unity—the Golden Stool.

Plate 10: Jomo Kenyatta of Kenya led his country to independence and became its first president in 1964. He is shown in 1977 at one of his last public appearances. He died the following year.

Plate 11: In 1993 F. W. de Klerk, the president of South Africa, and Nelson Mandela, the leader of the African National Congress, received the Nobel Peace Prize for working together to end the system of racial segregation in South Africa. The following year brought free elections in which all races could vote. Mandela became the nation's first black president.

Plate 12: African athletes have excelled in international competitions. Runner Paul Tergat of Kenya is shown arriving first at the finish line of a half-marathon in Mexico.

Plate 13: Rwanda has been torn by conflict between the Hutu and Tutsi people since 1959. During this time, millions of Rwandans have fled to neighboring countries. Here Rwandan refugees cross the Kagera River, seeking safety in Tanzania.

Plate 14: During the holy month of Ramadan, Muslims fast during daylight hours and eat after sundown and just before dawn. In Cairo a man prepares sweets traditionally eaten at the early meal.

Plate 15: The Sakalava, a large ethnic group in Madagascar, live on the western coast of the island. They have a long history as seafarers, trading food, spices, and slaves in the Persian Gulf, Asia, and the Americas. The Sakalava wear distinctive clothing, such as the colorful waist wraps seen here.

African infants are often carried on the back of their mother or another relative, who can tend to the baby's needs while performing other tasks.

bilities. Children as young as two to four years old may help adults with household tasks or with livestock herding. Older children care for younger siblings during the day, supervising their learning and work. During these early years, African children rapidly acquire knowledge about the societies and environments in which they live. They learn the customs that govern speech, behavior, and facial expressions; the relationships among men, women, and children; and the routines of work, play, and ceremonies.

During middle childhood, African children are given increased responsibility. Between the ages of five and seven, many urban children enter school. In rural areas, children of this age may take on new tasks such as carrying pots of water or watching infants. By the age of ten, African children are contributing significantly to their families' eco-

Childhood and Adolescence

Creative Solutions

With few factory-made goods available, children in Africa often invent their own toys. They make dolls, spinning tops, boats, flying objects, and musical instruments. Children create toys from whatever is at hand, including tree branches, leaves, seeds, and scraps of manmade materials.

In the 1990s, the government of Zambia held a children's toy-making contest. Children produced an impressive array of inventions, such as bicycling dolls, cars, trucks, and other vehicles. Most of the toys were made of tin, cloth, and wire. While admiring the children's creativity, some Zambians noticed new holes in their wire fences.

* **exploit**   to take advantage of; to make productive use of

nomic life. They help with farming or herding, or they perform household chores so that the adults can work. Children who are good workers are considered to show maturity and the prized values of respect and obedience.

Between 5 and 12 years of age, some African children are sent by their families to live with relatives who are wealthier or more privileged. In exchange for working for the relatives, the children are expected to receive opportunities not available at home. A rural family, for example, may send a child to live with and work for an uncle in the city, hoping that the uncle will pay for better schooling than the child could receive in the village. Sometimes such arrangements benefit both sides, but in other cases they take advantage of young children. As more Africans move to the cities and divisions between poor and well-off family members grow wider, the temptation to exploit* children's labor increases.

From 12 to 20. Africans experience adolescence differently than teenagers in Western countries. In the West, adolescence leads to sexual and social maturity and to making choices about work—all at about the same time. The teen years are seen as a movement toward eventual individuality and independence. In Africa, however, young people are not automatically considered independent adults when they reach their twenties. Even young people who have arrived at sexual maturity and engaged in courtship may not be considered adults. To Africans, adolescence is not a preparation for independent life but a furthering of the childhood process of fitting into family and community structures.

For African teens, personal choice may be limited. Young men and women are expected to mirror the roles and activities of their fathers and mothers or to accept the choices made for them by their families. A girl's father, for example, may arrange her marriage to a rich man she has never met. In addition, African men and women usually marry at very different ages. It is common in most African cultures for girls to marry in their middle teen years, while men marry later and at a much larger range of ages. That range often spans from age eighteen to age thirty. African adolescents do not expect to live on their own in the near future. Even when they are married and raising their own children, young men and women often belong to the household of the husband's parents or other senior relatives. However, as more and more young Africans live in cities, attend school, and choose their own occupations, their experience of adolescence is coming closer to that of Western teenagers.

Many African adolescents are affected by rituals and customs inherited from the past. In some groups, INITIATION RITES have traditionally marked the passage out of childhood for both boys and girls. Such ceremonies in eastern Africa have involved surgery on the young person's sexual organs. In western Africa, boys and girls have been brought into separate SECRET SOCIETIES, living in the forest apart from their families during their initiations. Although some of these practices are changing in modern Africa, they are still woven into the fabric of community life in many places. (*See also* **Age and Aging, Education, Family, Gender Roles and Sexuality, Kinship, Marriage Systems.**)

Chilembwe, John

**1871–1915
Malawian nationalist**

John Chilembwe was a church leader and opponent of European colonialism in Africa. His activities helped inspire the independence movement in his country of MALAWI and nationalism in Africa.

Schooled at a Scottish Presbyterian mission in Malawi, Chilembwe broke with the Presbyterians in 1892 after meeting Baptist missionary Joseph Booth. Booth took Chilembwe to the United States to attend a black Baptist seminary in Lynchburg, Virginia. Upon his return to Malawi in 1900, Chilembwe established the Providence Industrial Mission. In addition, he criticized local European estate holders for their treatment of African workers.

In 1914, on the eve of World War I, Chilembwe published a letter titled "The Voice of African Natives in the Present War." The letter was an early expression of African nationalism. Chilembwe also secretly organized an uprising against colonial rule. Authorities put the rebellion down quickly, and Chilembwe was killed. His reputation, however, lived on. The memory of Chilembwe played a major role in Malawi's eventual independence and the breakdown of colonial rule in central Africa. (*See also* **Colonialism in Africa**.)

Chinese in Africa

From the late 1700s to the early 1900s, Chinese traders and laborers traveled to southern and eastern Africa to earn a living in the colonies established by Europeans. A large number of Chinese also moved to African islands such as MAURITIUS, RÉUNION, and MADAGASCAR. A second wave of immigrants settled in Africa in the 1920s and 1930s, a time of great unrest in China.

Although many Chinese were recruited as mineworkers in the South African gold mines, others became involved in local business and formed social ties. Traders often lent money to local farmers and bought their crops, which they resold to European firms. Many of these early Chinese settlers produced children with local women. They accepted these children into their own families but sometimes sent them to China for schooling. In recent years the Chinese of SOUTH AFRICA have interacted more with their white neighbors than with black Africans. Many Chinese have left African countries that won their independence during the 1960s and 1970s.

Almost all African Chinese trace their roots to the southern Chinese province of Guandong. They are descended from the original Chinese traders, rather than from Chinese laborers brought to Africa by Europeans at the same time. The current Chinese population in Africa totals about 70,000. Most of these people live in the southeastern part of the continent, where they make a living primarily as grocers and restaurant owners. However, many younger Chinese pursue professional careers. A few have taken high government positions in countries such as ZIMBABWE and Mauritius.

Since the 1950s a commercial community of Hong Kong Chinese has developed in West African nations such as GHANA and NIGERIA. Hundreds of Taiwanese businessmen have also moved to South Africa and the surrounding countries to set up industrial plants. These entrepreneurs, however, have been criticized for taking advantage of local labor in their factories.

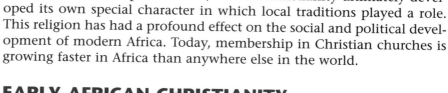

African Christianity goes back to very early times, and the Christianity that developed in Africa influenced the religion's later growth in Europe. However, African Christianity ultimately developed its own special character in which local traditions played a role. This religion has had a profound effect on the social and political development of modern Africa. Today, membership in Christian churches is growing faster in Africa than anywhere else in the world.

EARLY AFRICAN CHRISTIANITY

According to tradition, shortly after the founding of Christianity the apostle Philip baptized a member of the royal court of ETHIOPIA. The early church historian Eusebius wrote that the apostle Matthew also spread the new faith in Ethiopia. In this way, Christianity arrived in Africa before it reached Europe.

Roots of African Christianity. Christianity took root in North Africa at a very early date. Many important figures in the early church came from this region, including the church fathers Clement and Origen of ALEXANDRIA in EGYPT, and St. Augustine of Hippo, a city in present-day ALGERIA. From the A.D. 100s to 400s, Christianity spread throughout much of North Africa. Perhaps the most important force in this development was the monastic* movement, which began in Egypt and only later made its way to Europe.

By the 300s, Christianity had spread to Ethiopia and ERITREA, centered on the city of AKSUM. Most of the region is still Christian today. Beginning in the 500s, Christian kingdoms also flourished on the upper Nile River in NUBIA (in what is now SUDAN). In the 1300s, the Nubians were conquered by Muslims from Egypt.

Spreading Christianity. Despite the early introduction of Christianity in Ethiopia and North Africa, the religion did not penetrate sub-Saharan* Africa for several hundred years. Christianity reached those regions by way of Europe during the great age of exploration. The Portuguese arrived in the kingdom of KONGO in 1483. Eight years later the king of Kongo was baptized under the name of João I, in honor of the Portuguese king João II.

As Europeans established outposts on the coast of Africa in the 1400s and 1500s, they brought along missionaries, who settled among indigenous* populations. At first, the introduction of Christianity was limited to Africans in coastal areas. With a few exceptions, missionaries did not carry Christianity into the interior of the continent until the 1800s.

Europeans considered converting Africans to Christianity to be part of the process of colonization. As a result, their exploitation* of Africa's wealth was accompanied by missionary activity. However, the primary interest of most of the conquerors and traders who journeyed to Africa was to enrich themselves. This goal often involved enslaving and even killing local populations. Although Christian missionaries had come to Africa to save souls, they were often associated with the greed of their fellow Europeans. For this reason, many Africans resisted the missionaries and their message.

See color plate 5, vol. 1.

* **monastic** relating to monasteries, monks, or nuns

* **sub-Saharan** referring to Africa south of the Sahara desert

* **indigenous** native to a certain place

* **exploitation** relationship in which one side benefits at the other's expense

The stone church of St. George in Lalibela, Ethiopia, is more than 700 years old. Designed in the form of a cross, it was cut from the surrounding rock.

After a while, instead of trying to impose Christianity on the Africans, Europeans began to look for ways to use local institutions to gain converts. Missionaries attempted to win over rulers and then use their authority to spread Christianity among the people.

The long-term success of efforts to convert Africans to Christianity often depended on local political developments. The Christian nature of African kingdoms could prove short-lived if the ruling group was overthrown or challenged by a group opposed to Christianity. Attempts to spread the faith by reaching out to ordinary Africans did not occur for many years.

NEW DIRECTIONS IN AFRICAN CHRISTIANITY

For hundreds of years the Roman Catholic Church was the only church active in Africa. The Protestant outcry against the SLAVE TRADE in the late 1700s and early 1800s marked a turning point for African Christianity. Significantly, the first Protestant missionaries to arrive in West Africa were former slaves who had supported the British in the American Revolutionary War. These black preachers and their successors transformed the face of African Christianity.

Christianity in Africa

A variety of Christian denominations are found in Africa. The members of this church belong to the Assemblies of God, a Protestant group.

* **evangelist** person who preaches and spreads the Christian gospel

Black Evangelism. In 1792 more than a thousand former slaves accepted a British offer of free passage to Africa. Most of them were had fought on the British side in the American War of Independence and had later been resettled in Nova Scotia, Canada. There in what is now SIERRA LEONE they founded the city of FREETOWN. Although not formally authorized as Protestant ministers, some of these former slaves became enthusiastic leaders of the effort to convert indigenous Africans to Christianity. In preaching to Africans, they saw much common ground between the lessons found in the Bible and traditional African beliefs and values. This link between the Christian message and African culture was an important factor in the spread of Christianity across the continent in the 1800s and 1900s.

The Protestant evangelists* who founded missionary movements in Africa around 1800 adopted a different course from the Catholics who came before them. They stressed the important contributions that indigenous Africans could make to missionary activity. In 1861 a missionary named Henry Venn took the bold step of transferring nine churches in Sierra Leone to local control. He later named Samuel Ajayi CROWTHER, a former slave who had come to Freetown in 1822, as the first African bishop.

From this point on, black preachers played a leading role in spreading Christianity throughout the continent. They used their familiarity with the people and their culture to relate the Christian message in a uniquely African context, one that combined elements of European Christianity with African traditions.

* **vernacular**   native language or dialect of a region or country

African Scriptures. One of the tasks Crowther set himself as bishop was to translate the Bible into an African language. His first Bible, written in the Yoruba language, was followed by versions in other African languages. These vernacular* Bibles were a major factor in spreading Christianity among indigenous populations.

Few African languages had been written down before. The impact of the grammars, dictionaries, and other works needed for the translation of vernacular Bibles was immense. Reading the scriptures in native languages gave white missionaries and scholars a chance to grasp the African point of view. At the same time, giving Africans access to written forms of their language allowed them to connect with their own history and cultural heritage. The work of Crowther and others like him ensured that Africans, not Europeans, would now lead the missionary efforts in Africa.

White Missionary Activity. Opposition to the slave trade fueled the great missionary efforts of the 1800s and led to the creation of many new orders. Protestant missionaries, such as Scottish explorer David LIVINGSTONE, not only spread Christianity but also played a major role in mapping the land, documenting African social systems, and recording African languages. In addition, they identified the rich natural resources that would be the targets of later colonial exploitation.

Catholic mission activity was re-energized and reorganized at this time as well. The Catholic Church set out to train indigenous clergy to establish an African Catholic Church led by Africans themselves. Until that happened, white missionaries were urged to adopt African dress, language, and customs. The Catholic Church also moved to decentralized control of its missions, giving each one more independence and responsibility for its activities.

Twentieth Century Christianity. The early 1900s produced a number of charismatic African religious leaders, including Yohana Kitigana and William Wadé Harris. A former Buganda chief, Kitigana converted to Christianity, gave up his title, wives, and possessions, and traveled through central Africa preaching. Harris was a Protestant teacher in LIBERIA who abandoned his Western style of life and traveled through western Africa baptizing tens of thousands of people. Both men continued and reinforced a particularly African form of Christianity that blended indigenous and European religious traditions.

Beginning in the early 1900s, education became a major focus of Christian activity in Africa. Schools set up by both Protestants and Catholics during this period educated many of the people who became leaders of postcolonial Africa. Another concern was health. Christian missions established hospitals and clinics, and many religious leaders and independent churches focused even more attention on healing than on education.

In the 1960s the Catholic Church officially adopted the position that local African churches should lead Catholic missionary efforts in Africa. Later, in the 1990s, it stated that African churches would not be forced

Christianity in Africa

to accept pre-existing religious structures and ideas but could develop their own based on local traditions and needs.

The result of Protestant and Catholic activity over the centuries has been the spread of Christianity throughout Africa. Today the continent has more than 300 million Christians. While remaining true to its basic beliefs, Christianity in Africa has become a distinctly Africanized faith with elements of traditional belief and culture. The impressive growth, energy, and vitality of indigenous churches have transformed the continent into a new Christian heartland. (*See also* **Copts; Education; Equiano, Olaudah; Ethiopian Orthodox Church; Islam in Africa; Kingsley, Mary; Missions and Missionaries; Prophetic Movements; Religion and Ritual; Tutu, Desmond Mpilo.**)

Cinema

People in Africa have been watching, acting in, and making movies since the early 1900s. Until the 1950s, films were generally controlled by European colonial powers. The colonial governments oversaw production and decided which movies could be shown to the public. In the years since African nations gained independence, Africans have developed their own cinema with their own directors and actors. Many of their films have gained worldwide attention for their passionate portrayal of social and political issues such as apartheid*.

Cinema During Colonial Times. The early history of African film was dominated by movies made by and for non-Africans. Imported films were shown in West African colonies as early as 1900, and soon afterward colonists in South Africa were making their own movies. One of the first very successful African pictures was *De Voortrekkers (Winning a Continent),* a movie about white South African history made in 1916 by Afrikaner* and British producers.

Many American and British moviemakers came to Africa to film stories of adventure and colonial conquest. These were often enormous productions, with crews and leading actors brought from overseas. The story of H. Rider Haggard's British novel *King Solomon's Mines* was filmed in Africa several times. In the first version in 1918, thousands of ZULU extras acted in a battle scene. For Metro-Goldwyn-Mayer's 1950 version, the film crew traveled for 12,000 miles and five months through four countries. They gathered truckloads of footage of animals and scenery that was used in movies for years afterward. Several foreign actors gained fame for their roles in such films, including African American actors Paul Robeson in the 1930s and 1940s and Sidney Poitier in the 1950s.

Beginning in the 1920s, feature-length documentaries about African people, animals, and geography became popular with foreign audiences. In 1928 Americans Martin and Osa Johnson made *Simba: The King of Beasts,* a film about lions; in 1959 Henri Storck, a Belgian director, filmed *Les seigneurs de la forêt (Masters of the Congo Jungle).* Documentaries about animals were often broadcast on American television.

* **apartheid**   policy of racial segregation in South Africa intended to maintain white control over the country's blacks, Asians, and people of mixed ancestry

* **Afrikaner**   South African of European descent who speaks Afrikaans

More numerous than movies of dramas and documentaries, however, were the many educational and research films produced in Africa during colonial times. Anthropologists* and explorers used film to record their research on African peoples and cultures. Colonial officials and missionaries created educational films to teach black Africans "correct" political and cultural views. The viewpoints expressed in such works are now considered outdated and even racist. However, the films remain valuable historical documents that provide unique images of places and peoples.

Occasionally foreign-made films dealt with issues that troubled the colonial powers in Africa. Such films were usually banned by the colony they criticized. René Vautier of France was jailed for his 1950 movie *Africa 50,* an unflattering look at French rule in Ivory Coast. As late as the 1980s, the white South African government prohibited movies that criticized apartheid.

Many people view Sembène Ousmane as the father of African cinema. His films have dealt with such issues as colonialism, poverty, and the role of women in Africa.

Cinema

The Rise of African Cinema. North Africa's film industry dates from the 1920s. The first Arab film, *Ayn al-ghazal (Gazelle's Eye)* was shot in Tunisia by Tunisian Shemama Chicly. His daughter, Hayde Chicly, wrote the script and starred in the picture. In 1927 the first Arab film company was founded in Cairo. Its *Layla*, made with an Egyptian producer, director, and cast, was the first Egyptian movie. The Egyptian film industry went on to become one of the most productive in Africa, making films shown widely throughout the Arab world.

In addition to creating popular entertainment, such as romance movies, North African filmmakers have also addressed serious subjects. They have documented revolutions and other events that transformed their nations in modern times. For example, Algerian director Mohammed Lakdar Hamina has made several films about the effects of Algeria's revolution and independence from France. One of his best-known works is *Vent de sable (Desert wind),* produced in 1982.

Other Africans have also used movies to explore social themes and present them to wide audiences. Senegalese director Sembène Ousmane is considered by some to be the founder of African filmmaking. He produced African-language films dealing with such topics as colonialism, poverty, corruption, and the role of women. Between 1972 and 1982, Ola Balogun of Nigeria made ten feature films, some of which are based on traditional plays of the YORUBA people.

During the 1970s and 1980s, many African filmmakers explored political subjects. Pictures such as *Sambizanga* (1972) portrayed Angola's revolutionary struggle. Ethiopian Haile Geraima studied film in California before making *Harvest: 3,000 Years* in his country in 1974. He also produced *Sinkofa,* a 1993 movie about slavery in Ghana. One of the most famous African filmmakers is Souley-Mane Cisse of Mali. His 1995 picture *Waati (Time)* is a vision of the African continent as discovered by a young girl. As people throughout the world gain greater appreciation for different cultures, the distinctly African cinema of these artists may reach movie and television audiences everywhere. (*See also* **Popular Culture.**)

Cities and Urbanization

The image of Africa as a continent of traditional villages and small towns has never been correct. Africa has always included both highly urban and rural settlements. However, its cities have grown dramatically in recent years, and some researchers who study population trends have predicted that by the early 2000s about half of all Africans will live in urban areas.

Urbanization—the growth of cities and surrounding areas—has followed different patterns in sub-Saharan* Africa and North Africa. In both areas, however, the recent rapid growth of cities has been fueled by two factors: the high birth rate of city dwellers and the migration of large numbers of people from rural to urban areas.

African cities are a magnet. For those living in agricultural areas devastated by drought or war, moving to the city offers the opportunity for a better life. But many African cities are plagued by problems, including

* **sub-Saharan** referring to Africa south of the Sahara desert

North Africa's Tin Towns

Many urban areas in Tunisia, Algeria, and Morocco are surrounded by unplanned, hastily built shantytowns called bidonvilles. The original bidonvilles sprang up in the late 1800s. Their name comes from bidon, *the French word for kerosene tin. The villagers and countryfolk who migrated to the cities built homes of these tin containers, and in time the bidonvilles became permanent settlements. In response to sometimes violent protests by the residents of the bidonvilles, local governments eventually began to provide water, electricity, and other city services to some of the communities. Still, these settlements remain the drabbest and poorest parts of the North African urban landscape.*

unemployment, lack of housing, crime, and poverty. They also suffer from inadequate public services such as water, electricity, schools, and health care. With urbanization likely to continue, African governments and international aid agencies are under pressure to create plans for managing the growth of Africa's cities.

AFRICA SOUTH OF THE SAHARA

Until about 1980, sub-Saharan Africa was overwhelmingly rural, and experts believed it would remain that way. African governments focused on programs for rural and agricultural development, paying little attention to the rapid growth of their cities. Now urbanization is recognized as a major trend in sub-Saharan Africa. But it has not been accompanied by the modernization and economic growth needed to improve the quality of urban life and support expanding city populations.

Precolonial Cities. In the centuries before European colonization, western Africa was the most urbanized region south of the Sahara. Cities arose there as centers of religion and government in ancient kingdoms, and a web of trade routes linked these centers with Muslim cities in North Africa and the Saharan borderlands.

Jenne-jeno, located in MALI, is thought to be the oldest city in West Africa. Already nearly a thousand years old by A.D. 800, Jenne-jeno consisted of many round brick houses surrounded by a wall. At that time, it was actually two cities: a native town and a nearby settlement of Arab merchants. This mixture of Islamic and African elements was typical of many sub-Saharan cities with links to North Africa. The town of TIMBUKTU in Mali, founded around A.D. 1000, became a major trading hub and a center of Islamic learning in the 1400s and 1500s

Farther south in present-day NIGERIA, the YORUBA established city-states that controlled areas of the surrounding countryside. Ile-Ife, the Yoruba capital, was centered on the king's palace. Radiating out from the palace were 16 residential areas, one for each of 16 major family groups. When the European trade for gold and slaves began along the West African coast in the 1400s, new cities emerged to extend the trade northward into the interior. Despite the presence of European trading posts, the organization and the population of these cities remained African.

Cities existed in other parts of Africa during the precolonial period. In ETHIOPIA, the city of AKSUM was an important economic, political, and religious center. Along the Indian Ocean coast in East Africa, urban centers sprang up at ports that served seafaring traders from the Arabian and Indian peninsulas. Kilwa, with magnificent mosques, palaces, and baths, was the most splendid East African city in the 1400s. However, larger but less splendid cities, such as Mombasa, and in the 1800s ZANZIBAR, came to dominate coastal trade.

Colonial Urban Development. Between the 1500s and mid-1900s, European influence and colonial rule created a number of major urban centers in sub-Saharan Africa. Some of these cities arose from settlements founded by Africans, which the Europeans changed and enlarged. Others were new settlements established to serve as colonial adminis-

139

Cities and Urbanization

Tripoli, Libya, is a modern city with an ancient history. Here, a merchant sells fresh melons in front of a Roman arch.

trative or trading centers. But most cities developed near the sites of natural resources—such as gold, tin, coal, or diamonds—that were being mined by the Europeans.

In the early colonial period, Europeans established small forts and trading posts, often on or near the coasts. These settlements eventually developed into major urban centers, including ACCRA in GHANA, LAGOS in Nigeria, and CAPE TOWN in SOUTH AFRICA. Most of the inland cities, such as JOHANNESBURG and Nairobi, were not founded until the late 1800s and early 1900s. The urban areas became centers of industry. At first, the African populations in urban areas consisted largely of adult men who had come in search of industrial jobs and left their families behind. The high proportion of males continued until the mid-1900s, when more and more families began moving to cities from the countryside.

One of the main features of colonial cities in sub-Saharan Africa was the separation of blacks and whites. Europeans established residential and commercial areas in the more desirable sections of the city, forcing black Africans to establish their neighborhoods elsewhere. Colonial administrators also created parklands or industrial areas to serve as buffer zones between the European and African quarters. While colonial officials made an effort to ensure the comfort and safety of Europeans and to provide them with various services, they generally devoted much less attention to the African quarters.

Cities Since Independence. Sub-Saharan Africa is still the least urbanized region in the world, with less than one third of its population living in cities. However, sub-Saharan Africa is also experiencing the fastest urban growth in the world, and researchers predict that more than half of the region's population will be urban by the year 2025.

Although southern Africa ranks as the most urbanized part of sub-Saharan Africa, the cities in western and eastern Africa are expanding much more rapidly than those in other areas. Lagos, Nigeria, one of the fastest-growing cities, is becoming what experts call a megacity—a very

Tall modern buildings line this busy street in Nairobi, Kenya. Although Nairobi is the financial, commercial, and tourist center of East Africa, unemployment and inadequate housing make life difficult for many of the city's residents.

Cities and Urbanization

* **shantytown** poor, run-down section of a city, often inhabited by immigrants

See color plate 14, vol. 3.

large urban center. If growth rates continue, Africa will contain more megacities than any other continent by the end of this century. Managing the growth of these urban centers and solving their problems are among the most serious challenges now facing African governments.

One of the most common features of modern African cities is the growing number of people who live in shantytowns*. Usually overcrowded and filled with inadequate housing, these communities have little or no sanitation or other public services. People in shantytowns build shelters with whatever materials they can find—boards, tin sheets, or even cardboard and plastic—generally on land they do not own. Since African governments cannot afford to replace inadequate housing or provide basic services, many shantytowns have been accepted as unavoidable.

Another problem facing African cities is a shortage of jobs. The economies of most African nations are just not able to create enough jobs for their growing populations. Unemployment and the high cost of living in cities combine to create a serious problem of poverty. Linked with poverty and unemployment are various other problems, such as crime, illiteracy, and disease. Because these conditions can lead to social and political unrest, they threaten not only the stability of cities but of African nations as well.

Some experts believe that one way to improve prospects for Africa's urban future is to encourage the growth of small and midsize cities, reducing the burden on large urban centers. These smaller cities could also serve as a link between megacities and the agricultural countryside. However, such plans require reliable transportation systems, and in much of Africa highway and rail connections between cities and rural areas are inadequate.

Another way of dealing with the future is the development of national urban plans. Such plans would look beyond the immediate needs of cities and focus instead on long-range efforts to provide housing and services and to create jobs and build economic connections between urban centers and the rest of the country. African leaders realize that continued urban growth is unavoidable, and that city life will be in the future of more and more Africans.

NORTH AFRICA

North Africa, home of the ancient Egyptian civilization and site of ancient Phoenician, Greek, and Roman colonies, has a long history of urban life. Today, it is the most urbanized part of Africa. In Morocco, Tunisia, Algeria, and Libya, more than half the total population lives in cities or towns.

Large cities have existed in North Africa for thousands of years, and some present-day towns stand on the sites where they were founded. The Egyptian culture that built the pyramids and other monuments also established cities that show evidence of careful urban planning. Alexandria, a major port on the Mediterranean coast, dates back more than 2,000 years.

The Arabs who conquered North Africa during the Middle Ages

founded many of the region's major cities, including Marrakech and Fez in Morocco, Tripoli in Libya, and Tunis in Tunisia. At the heart of each Arab city was the Casbah, a fort that served as the center of government, and a mosque* with an accompanying tower called a minaret. Around the city was a wall pierced by several gates.

After European powers took control of North Africa in the 1800s, urban areas expanded rapidly. Colonial trade, in particular, contributed to the growth of port cities, such as Casablanca, in Morocco, ALGIERS, and Tunis. As Europeans settled in large North African urban centers, they became dual, or twin, cities. One half of the dual city was the medina, the old walled Arab city with narrow, twisting streets. The other half was a new European-style city with wide, straight, tree-lined streets and houses built on large lots.

The rapid growth of cities that began in the colonial period continued after North African nations gained their independence in the mid-1900s. Governments of North Africa have faced two challenges in regard to their cities. The first has been to unify the native and European areas of the cities and modernize them. This has proved very difficult, and in many cases the divisions remain. The second challenge has been to provide housing, employment, and services for the people who flock to cities in ever-increasing numbers. (*See also* **Architecture; Colonialism in Africa; Development, Economic and Social; European Communities; Houses and Housing; North Africa: Geography and Population; Population.**)

* **mosque** Muslim place of worship

Class Structure and Caste

* **precolonial** referring to the time before European powers colonized Africa

African societies, like those in nearly all areas of the world, are divided into various groups or classes. Each class has its own distinct characteristics, roles, privileges and limitations, and relations with other groups. Only a few societies based on hunting and gathering have no formal division into classes.

The class structure of African societies today is a patchwork. Some of the traditions that shape it have been carried over from precolonial* times. Other elements can be traced to Western influence. The result is a complex structure that is still developing as new forces of change reach African societies.

TRADITIONAL CLASS SYSTEMS

* **hierarchy** organization of a group into higher and lower levels

Traditional African societies are stratified—organized into levels like the layers of a cake. Three basic principles define the hierarchy* within African class systems. The first of these is elderhood, the quality of being older than someone else. The second is servitude, the condition of controlling or being controlled by others. And the third is rank, or a person's level in society relative to the ruler.

Elderhood. Peasant society, made up of fairly simple agricultural communities, is widespread in Africa. In such societies, everyone lives in much the same way. Differences in wealth and occupation have little or

Class Structure and Caste

* **exploitation**   relationship in which one side benefits at the other's expense

* **artisan**   skilled crafts worker

* **patron**   special guardian, protector, or supporter

* **caste**   division of people into classes based on birth

no importance. Instead, hierarchy is based on the concept of precedence, that is, who came first. Status—respected position—and power belong to old and established groups rather than to the new.

Respect for elderhood is the key to the social organization of these societies. For example, a group that has cleared an unoccupied piece of land gains precedence, or the right to be honored, as the first settlers on that land. To maintain peaceful relations, newcomers who want to live nearby must acknowledge the precedence of those who were there first. The first settled family usually heads local councils. Other families assume duties according to their abilities, and some may gain influence because of their wisdom, strength, courage, or fertility.

Within most communities and families, status is linked to age. Each person has less status and authority than older individuals but more than those who are younger. Final authority rests with the eldest person in the community. But even that person must respect the authority of the dead elders—the ancestors. In some societies, the entire community is organized into age sets—groups of people at the same stages of life. As the members of an age set become older, they gain greater power and status in the community.

Servitude. In other traditional African societies, class structure has been based on levels of control or servitude. After about A.D. 500, several centrally organized, warring states appeared in parts of Africa. In these states, violence and exploitation* led to societies ruled by classes of military aristocrats or nobles.

Slaves and servants were at the bottom of the social structure. Slaves were people who had been captured or defeated in war. Servants were the descendants of slaves and other servants, born into bondage on their masters' estates. Just above slaves on the social ladder were commoners, including peasants and merchants. They could not be enslaved, but they could own slaves. With more rights and authority than commoners, aristocrats were still higher in society. Only people from this class could rise to the highest level of all—rulership.

Many African societies share a similar three-part class structure. Among the TUAREG of northwestern Africa, for example, kings or leaders come from the *imajeghen,* a class of nobles who make up less than one percent of all Tuaregs. Below this class is the *imghad,* the common people. The third and lowest class, the *iklan,* consists of farmers, herders, laborers, and artisans* whose ancestors were black Africans enslaved by the Tuareg.

A form of hierarchy called patronage or clientage has also shaped African societies. It is a relationship between people of unequal status, wealth, or power. The higher-status patron* provides protection or security to the lower-status client, who in turn is expected to give loyalty and obedience to the patron. A patron may have many clients, and clients may have clients of their own. Complex webs of patronage are part of the structure of social and political life in both traditional and modern communities.

In some aristocratic societies, patronage grew into a system called caste*. Patrons protected and took care of members of certain castes—such as blacksmiths, leather workers, or musicians—who produced

In many African societies people gain respect and significance with age. Senior members of a group, such as these community elders from Swaziland, often hold positions of leadership.

things that the patrons wanted. Although caste members were considered free, they were under the authority of kings and nobles and could not marry outside their own groups. Castes tended to become closed, hereditary groups within the larger societies.

Rank. As aristocrats competed for power and status, systems of rank emerged, creating hierarchies within the courts of kings and emperors. Some of these hierarchies included many subdivisions. Ranking gave rise to elaborate systems of etiquette by which individuals acknowledged each other's rank.

Class Structure and Caste

* **clan** group of people descended from a common ancestor

Heirs to a throne and aristocrats were not the only individuals who could reach high rank. Because rival heirs and ambitious aristocratic clans* could threaten a king's power, rulers often appointed trusted slaves to high-ranking positions as advisers or military officers. Sometimes, as in the kingdom of TOGO, court slaves eventually took over the throne.

Islamic societies in northern Africa adopted an Arab-influenced system of rank in which warrior clans held power. Elsewhere, even small communities of Muslim merchants created Islamic-style local governments. Judges and holy men had high rank because they administered the laws and advice needed to conduct business, manage slavery, and settle disputes.

MODERN SYSTEMS

Although many Africans remain deeply loyal to traditional social systems, Western institutions and policies dominate modern Africa. Social class affects everyone's daily behavior, yet the class structure is too complex and varied to be easily summarized. Indeed, the class structure of African society is still taking shape.

Class. In urban settings and societies undergoing modernization, the elite class—people with power and influence—is expanding. In the 1960s, the African elite consisted of small groups of men and women, generally from the same schools and universities. Today the elite class has become both larger and more diverse. Its members serve as links between African societies and a global elite—the owners and executives of international corporations and agencies such as the United Nations. Although the African elite are at the top level of their own local or national status system, they form the lower level of the international superclass.

Members of the global elite also form a permanent social class in African society. Non-African officials of international companies and agencies are not citizens of any African nations where they live and work. They do not vote. They have no local ancestors and usually no descendants who will remain in Africa. However, their Western lifestyles and behavior have a far-reaching effect on African society.

In contrast to the elite is a mass of peasants, workers, migrants, shopkeepers, small businesspeople, clerks, schoolteachers, soldiers, police, and minor officeholders. These people cannot rightly be called a class because they have little in common to unite them. However, they generally share resentment over the widening gap between them and the elite.

Ethnicity. African peoples are divided into thousands of ethnic groups. Ethnic ties and loyalties connect people across the lines of class. Workers belonging to one ethnic group are likely to feel closer to elite members of the same group than to workers from another group. In Africa, where nations often contains many different ethnic groups, ethnic ties can hinder the growth of national identity. Individuals may regard themselves as Ganda or YORUBA, for example, rather than

Ugandan or Nigerian. Ethnic ties may also affect class divisions. Heads of state sometimes favor members of their own ethnic group with positions of power and profit. Such favoritism has led to civil war among competing groups in many African nations.

SOUTH AFRICA was formerly the continent's prime example of a social structure based on ethnic and racial identity. Under the system called APARTHEID, social groups were legally organized into a hierarchy, with whites at the top, followed by Indians, "Coloureds" (people of mixed race), and Africans at the bottom of the social ladder. Although apartheid has ended, its social and economic inequalities linger, and South Africa's class structure still has strong ethnic and racial elements.

Rank. In modern Africa, rank has little influence on social organization. Rank has lost most of its importance because it has no place in the foreign economic and political systems that now dominate much of Africa. Only in a few cases, including SWAZILAND, LESOTHO, and BOTSWANA, have systems of hereditary rank been preserved. The ethnic kings of these nations are heads of state. Elsewhere, ethnic rulers—such as the Buganda king in UGANDA and the Muslim emirs of northern NIGERIA—have become regional leaders with limited power.

In a few situations in which rank remains important, it may have religious as well as political meaning. Following Islamic tradition, some groups of BERBERS in North Africa give the highest place in their social order to people who claim to be descended from Muhammad, the prophet of Islam. Catholic churches in Africa also maintain a rigid, elaborate, and formal hierarchy of ranks. (*See also* **Age and Aging, Ethnic Groups and Identity, Gender Roles and Sexuality, Islam in Africa, Kings and Kingship, Kinship, Slavery, Women in Africa.**)

Cleopatra

69–30 B.C.
Egyptian queen

Cleopatra, one of the most famous figures of ancient history, was the last ruler of EGYPT in the tradition of the pharaohs who had governed the land for several thousand years. She came to the throne in 51 B.C. as the wife of her brother, Ptolemy XIII.

For several hundred years before that time, Rome had been increasing its control over Egypt. The young Cleopatra needed an ally in a struggle with enemies in Egypt. According to legend, she had herself rolled in a carpet and delivered as a gift to the powerful Roman general Julius Caesar. With Roman support, Cleopatra defeated Ptolemy and ruled as pharaoh. She also began a love affair with Caesar. Caesar built a palace in Rome for Cleopatra and their son, Caesarion.

After Caesar was assassinated in 44 B.C., Cleopatra allied herself with Mark Antony, another leading Roman. Antony hoped that the riches of Egypt would help him become ruler of Rome. Cleopatra bore Antony three children. She hoped that he would make her children his heirs and Rome's future rulers. In 32 B.C. Octavian, Antony's great rival in the Roman government, declared war against Antony and Cleopatra. The two lovers lost their navy in a battle near Greece and retreated to

Cleopatra

ALEXANDRIA, where both committed suicide. Although she lost her life and her kingdom, Cleopatra is remembered in history as an intelligent, ambitious, and passionate ruler.

Climate

The diverse climates of Africa range from scorching deserts to icy glaciers, from steamy rainforests to grassy plains. Climate is a long-term weather pattern, the sum of features such as temperature, rainfall, and wind. The amount of heat from the sun plays a major role in determining climate. The equator receives more solar heat than any other part of the earth, and the zones on either side of the equator are called the tropics.

Africa, with the equator cutting across its center, is the world's most tropical continent. Only its northern edge and southern tip are outside the tropics. Half of Africa lies north of the equator and half to the south. This symmetry, or balance, produces matching belts of climate at approximately equal distances north and south of the equator.

The center of the continent has a wet tropical climate, with extremely heavy rainfall. To the north and south are belts of tropical climate with a dry season. Beyond lie belts of tropical climate with longer dry periods and occasional droughts, such as those that have caused famines in the SAHEL. North of the Sahel lies the almost rainless SAHARA DESERT, but in the narrow southern part of Africa cool, moist air masses moving inland from the oceans bring some summer rainfall to the KALAHARI DESERT. Finally, north and south of the desert regions are belts of Mediterranean climate, with hot dry summers and mild moist winters.

Climate Shapers. Other environmental factors, such as winds, ocean currents, and the surface features of the land, create variations within these climate belts, giving different regions of Africa their particular local climates. One of the chief climate shapers in sub-Saharan* Africa is the Intertropical Convergence Zone, or ITCZ, which is the point where warm, moist tropical air masses meet. The regular cycle of movements of the ITCZ carry it north of the equator between March and June and south of the equator between September and December. These movements determine the number and timing of rainy seasons throughout Africa. Areas within the path of the ITCZ have two rainy seasons; those at the northern and southern reaches of the ITCZ's path have only one rainy season. The Sahara in the north and the Namib-Kalahari desert region in the south lie outside the influence of the ITCZ and receive little precipitation.

Mountains and ocean currents influence climate as well. Mountains force the air masses of the ITCZ to rise, grow cooler, and shed their moisture in the form of rain or even snow, giving mountainous areas greater annual precipitation. The cold Benguela Current in the Atlantic Ocean cools the surrounding air and keeps the ITCZ away from southwestern Africa. As a result, that region generally receives little rain. It does, however, get some moisture from fog that forms along the coast.

* **sub-Saharan** referring to Africa south of the Sahara desert

Maritime Madagascar

The large island nation of Madagascar, located off Africa's southeastern coast, has a maritime climate, which means that it is influenced mainly by the ocean. Strong regular winds called trade winds blow from the southeast, bringing moisture from the Indian Ocean to eastern Madagascar, which gets up to 137 inches of rain a year. More than any other part of Africa, eastern Madagascar is affected by cyclones, large tropical storms with high winds that sweep over the island from the Indian Ocean between November and April.

Africa's tropical rainforests receive heavy rainfall year round, which supports lush vegetation and a canopy of tall trees.

Seasonal movements of the atmosphere over the North Atlantic Ocean affect the climate of North Africa. In the summer, an area of high atmospheric pressure known as the Azores High blocks moist Atlantic air from reaching the region's Mediterranean coast. For this reason, summers in North Africa are hot and dry, influenced by winds blowing north from the Sahara. In winter, however, the Azores High moves southward, allowing cool, damp air from the Atlantic to reach the coast, bringing milder and wetter weather.

Regional Climates. Each climate region has its local variations. The Mediterranean climate of North Africa brings its coast at least 16 inches of rainfall a year, with some mountainous areas getting several times more. However, the region's southern interior has a desert climate with fewer than 4 inches of precipitation. Between these two areas is a region of dry, flat plains, called steppes, where annual rainfall ranges from 4 to 16 inches and summer droughts last five months or longer. Rainfall in the steppes can cause devastating flash floods.

Equatorial Africa includes the southern coast of West Africa and the rainforests of Central Africa. This region receives heavy rain throughout the year, although there are two periods with even more rainfall. These rainier seasons generally last from September to November and from February to June, although they are longer near the coast.

Climate

The interior of West Africa, the Sahel, Sudan, and the Ethiopian highlands form another, drier climate region. The northern parts of this area receive less precipitation than the southern parts and have a single rainy season from October through June. In addition, rainfall in the region generally decreases from west to east. Parts of eastern Ethiopia and Somalia near the Indian Ocean have a desert climate.

East Africa, consisting of Uganda, Kenya, and Tanzania, straddles the equator. It has a hot, humid climate along the coast and around Lake Victoria, but cooler climates in the highlands and mountains. The rainiest areas are the Lake Victoria basin, the mountains, and the coastal islands, which receive more than 59 inches of rain annually. Other parts of the region average 30 inches of annual rainfall. April and May form one rainy season, October and November the other.

Southern Africa has a climate somewhat similar to that of West Africa and southern Sudan. The rainy season is longest in the northern part of the region, where it lasts from November to March. Precipitation decreases from north to south and increases from west to east—the reverse of precipitation patterns north of the equator. The dry season in southern Africa can bring drought. The tip of southern Africa, along the coast, has a Mediterranean climate, with rainfall from April to September and a dry season during the rest of the year. (*See also* **Deserts and Drought, Ecosystems.**)

Coetzee, J. M.

1940–
South African novelist

* **apartheid** policy of racial segregation in South Africa intended to maintain white control over the country's blacks, Asians, and people of mixed ancestry

The South African writer and literary critic John Michael Coetzee is known for novels that explore the effects of apartheid in his homeland. Coetzee studied at the University of Cape Town and at the University of Texas, where he received a Ph.D. in literature. He then returned to SOUTH AFRICA despite his opposition to the government's racial policies.

Among his best-known works is the *Life and Times of Michael K*, which won Britain's prestigious Booker Prize in 1983. The book tells the story of an uneducated man struggling to understand and deal with the civil war in his country. His 1986 novel *Foe*, a retelling of Daniel Defoe's classic *Robinson Crusoe*, examines how people can be enslaved by language. In 1999 Coetzee won a second Booker Award for *Disgrace*, a novel that looks at the problems of South Africa after apartheid.* In addition to writing and literary criticism, Coetzee teaches English at the University of Cape Town and translates works from Afrikaans (a language based on Dutch) into English. (*See also* **Literature.**)

COINS

See *Money and Banking.*

Colenso, John William

**1814–1883
British missionary**

*John Colenso was an outspoken critic of conventional missionary work who condemned the way colonial authorities treated Africans. Born in England, Colenso became the first bishop of the Diocese of NATAL in 1853 and established a mission station in the town of Bishopstowe. He was well-read in both Christian teaching and modern scientific thinking and discoveries. He was also familiar with the way Africans understood Christian teaching and supported many of their views about religious belief and experience.

This knowledge and his early experiences in Africa led Colenso to write a book called *The Pentateuch and the Book of Joshua Critically Examined* (1870). In it he argued that the Bible was not the literal word of God. The book greatly upset religious authorities, and Colenso was excommunicated, or expelled, from the church.

In the early 1870s, Colenso exposed Britain's unjust treatment of the Hlubi people of Natal and their chief, Langalibalele. Later when the British invaded the ZULU kingdom and deposed its ruler, CETSHWAYO kaMpande, he championed the cause of the Zulu people. Unfortunately, Colenso did not succeed during his lifetime in his efforts to reform religious thought and colonial political activity. His protests, however, highlighted the violence and injustice that were basic elements of European imperialism* in Africa. Colenso had three daughters who carried on the struggle for African rights in SOUTH AFRICA after his death. (*See also* **Christianity in Africa, Missions and Missionaries**.)

* **imperialism** domination of the political, economic, and cultural life of one country or region by another country

Colonialism in Africa

Colonialism, which refers to the establishment of political and economic control by one state over another, had an enormous impact on Africa. The colonial experience began in the late 1400s, when Europeans arrived and set up trading posts in Africa. It reached a peak in the late 1800s and early 1900s, when European powers dominated many parts of the continent. Colonialism in Africa created nations and shaped their political, economic, and cultural development. The legacy continues to influence the history of the continent.

OVERVIEW OF COLONIALISM

Between the 1400s and 1800s, Europeans began to take an interest in Africa, mainly the coastal regions. Sailing along the shores of the continent, they established trading posts and engaged in commerce with local peoples. They made little attempt to explore the interior. During this period, Europeans had very little influence in Africa.

From the mid-1700s to 1880s, Europeans became more involved in the continent. One reason for this increased involvement was growing opposition to the SLAVE TRADE. In 1787 the British founded a colony for freed slaves in SIERRA LEONE. About 30 years later, a group of Americans established LIBERIA for freed slaves and their descendants. Along with efforts to end slavery, Europeans also tried to bring Christianity to Africa. Their missionaries traveled throughout the continent, seeking to convert Africans and spread Western culture.

Colonialism in Africa

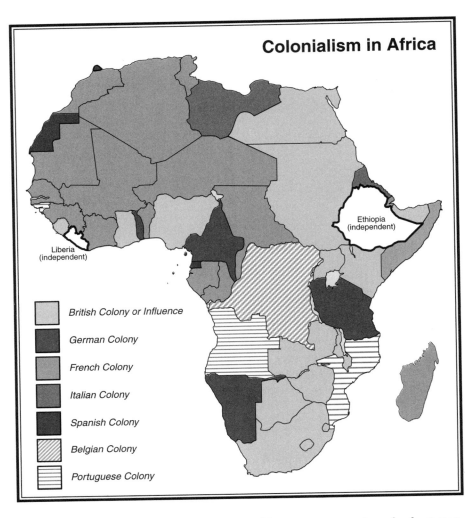

Colonialism in Africa

Ethiopia (independent)

Liberia (independent)

- British Colony or Influence
- German Colony
- French Colony
- Italian Colony
- Spanish Colony
- Belgian Colony
- Portuguese Colony

By the late 1800s many Africans had begun to accept and adapt various elements of European civilization. At the same time, the nature of European interest in Africa changed dramatically. Impressed by the continent's abundant supply of natural resources, Europeans sought to exploit* the potential wealth. To achieve this goal, they attempted to overpower African peoples and force them to accept foreign rule. In the 1870s rival European nations raced to colonize as much African territory as possible. By the late 1880s, they had divided up most of the continent among themselves, without permission from the African peoples.

Patterns of European Expansion. The first European settlements in Africa were established by traders. Although merchants generally operated independently, from time to time they called on their home governments for help in dealing with hostile Africans. Eventually, European nations negotiated alliances and trading treaties with the coastal peoples. They also appointed officials to protect commercial interests at strategic points along the coasts.

Christian missionaries were the first Europeans to establish outposts in the interior of Africa. The missionaries acted as intermediaries* between Africans and Europeans and often helped settle disputes

* **exploit**   to take advantage of; to make productive use of

* **intermediary**   go-between

152

The "Scramble" for Africa

The competition for territory in Africa was truly a "scramble," as explorers, traders, and adventurers of all kinds fanned out across the continent signing treaties with local rulers.

Many people feared that this haphazard approach would create overlapping claims. In November 1884, German chancellor Otto von Bismarck called a meeting in Berlin to discuss colonization in Africa. Representatives from 14 countries, including the United States, the Ottoman Empire, and most European nations, attended. They agreed to guarantee free trade and the neutrality of the Congo Free State. Moreover, the guidelines they established influenced the way in which European nations carved up Africa.

* **indigenous** native to a certain place

* **entrepreneur** person who organizes, manages, and takes risks of a business venture

* **cede** to yield or surrender

* **annex** to add a territory to an existing area

* **imperialism** domination of the political, economic, and cultural life of one country or region by another country

between indigenous* communities. However, Christian missionaries also became a disruptive force in African society. After converting to Christianity, many Africans would no longer recognize the authority of their local chiefs. In addition, some missionaries provided essential information to European armies and supported military expeditions against African groups that refused to accept Christianity.

African rulers did not develop a common policy toward the Europeans. Some tried to regulate or prohibit contact with Europeans. Many coastal states, however, had already become too dependent on overseas trade to cut their ties with Europe. Meanwhile, Europeans took advantage of rivalries between African peoples and forged alliances with some groups against others.

By the late 1870s, Africa had begun to attract other kinds of Europeans: adventurers and entrepreneurs*. Many of these individuals were interested only in obtaining riches or in recreating European culture in Africa. They urged their governments to establish colonies that would serve as sources of raw materials and as markets for European goods.

The drive to establish colonies and obtain raw materials led to the so-called "scramble" for Africa. At first four nations—Belgium, France, Great Britain, and Portugal—struggled to claim territory and establish colonial outposts. Various individuals tried to get African rulers to sign treaties that would cede* control of land.

Between 1884 and 1885, representatives from several European nations met in Berlin, Germany, to discuss ways to avoid conflict over the competition for African colonies. The European powers agreed on a set of rules for annexing* territory. In the years that followed, they signed various treaties that resulted in the partitioning, or division, of Africa into colonies with clearly defined borders.

As the pace of European imperialism* increased, many African peoples became very concerned. Fears that Europeans would seize all the land led to a number of armed conflicts. Some of these developed into full-scale wars as well-equipped armies from Europe invaded Africa to secure territorial claims. By 1914 Europeans had taken over the entire continent except for ETHIOPIA and Liberia. European imperialism now moved into a new phase—establishing colonial administrations that would maintain order and provide economic benefits for the governing nations.

The Colonial Order. European policy in Africa had two parts: the colonial government and the colonial economy. The colonial government was concerned with the affairs of a colony at the central and local levels. European officials directed the central government, which made and carried out laws and oversaw the judicial system. The local governments were supposedly run by traditional African leaders. In most instances, however, local chiefs and kings were allowed little real authority.

European officials dominated almost all colonial governments until after World War II, when some countries permitted Africans to play a greater role. Although colonialism brought stability to some regions, it

Colonialism in Africa

did little to promote the development of African political institutions or to provide administrative training for local people.

The colonial economy was perhaps the most important aspect of European policy in Africa. Before the 1800s Africa had developed a system of local and foreign trading networks, and Africans and Europeans were fairly equal trading partners. This situation changed, however, as Europeans took steps to control trade and natural resources in Africa.

The colonial powers flooded Africa with European-made goods, causing many African industries to fail because they could not compete. Europeans also encouraged the growth of cash crops* in Africa, with each colony specializing in a different crop. The emphasis on cash crops destroyed many traditional forms of agriculture. In some colonies white farmers received special treatment. They claimed the best land, forcing Africans to work less desirable plots. Some colonial governments imposed taxes on Africans. To pay them, many Africans had to abandon their land and work for wages on white-owned farms and in mines.

* **cash crop** crop grown primarily for sale rather than for local consumption

Impact of Colonialism on African Societies. Colonial governments brought roads, railroads, ports, new technology, and other benefits to Africa. However, their policies also damaged traditional economies and dramatically changed patterns of land ownership and labor. Although the colonial system provided opportunities—such as

Opened in 1869, the Suez Canal created a passageway for trade between the Mediterranean and Red Seas. By gaining control of the canal in 1876, Britain was able to invade Egypt and conquer it.

King Leopold's Colony

Crowned king of Belgium in 1865 at the age of 30, Leopold II soon became fascinated by the vast unexplored regions of Africa. With the help of explorer Henry Morton Stanley, he laid claim to a region of the Congo river basin about 80 times the size of Belgium. Although Leopold's main interest in the colony was the personal power and prestige it brought him, he also sought to profit from its abundant supply of natural rubber. This led to his downfall. When word spread about the mistreatment of rubber workers in the Congo under Leopold, Belgium stepped in to take over the colony.

education, jobs, and new markets for goods—for some Africans, it left many people poor and landless. In addition, the emphasis on cash crops raised for export made African societies dependent on foreign nations. Little was done to develop trade between colonies. As a result, many African nations still trade more with overseas countries than with neighboring states.

Colonial rule disrupted the traditional political and social institutions that had developed in Africa over centuries. As Europeans carved out empires, they destroyed existing kingdoms and split up or combined many ethnic groups. In time, the colonies they created became African nations consisting of diverse groups with little in common with their fellow citizens. Furthermore, European powers destroyed much of the political and social control of traditional African chiefs and rulers. They failed, however, to establish lasting replacements for these authorities. Finally, European colonialism introduced Africans to various aspects of Western culture. African schools and universities are based on European systems of education and religion. But other parts of Western culture have not taken root as firmly.

The impact of colonialism varied somewhat with each European power. Moreover, some governments used various approaches from one colony to the next. The handful of European nations that dominated Africa—Belgium, Great Britain, France, Germany, Italy, Portugal, and Spain—developed different sets of policies for their colonial possessions.

BELGIUM

In some ways, Belgium became a colonial power by accident. Unlike Britain, France, and Spain, it had no history of conquest and colonization in the Americas or in Asia. The nation's involvement in Africa came about because of the actions of one individual—King Leopold II of Belgium.

The Congo Free State. In the late 1870s King Leopold hired British adventurer Henry Morton STANLEY to obtain territory for him in Africa. Experienced in exploring central Africa, Stanley traveled to the Congo region and made treaties on Leopold's behalf with a number of local chiefs.

When European powers agreed on plans for colonizing Africa at the Berlin Conference, Leopold received control of an area around the Congo River basin. The colony became known as the Congo Free State and was owned by the king and not by Belgium. Leopold ruled it with an iron hand, directing all his economic and political policies toward increasing profits. He introduced harsh measures, such as forced labor, and allowed the brutal treatment of workers.

By 1904 other nations began to put pressure on Leopold to end the cruel conditions in the Congo Free State. After investigating the situation there, the Belgian government decided to annex the region in 1908, making it a Belgian colony rather than a personal possession of the king.

The Belgian Congo. Under Belgian rule, the Congo Free State became known as the Belgian Congo. Belgian authorities ended forced

Colonialism in Africa

* **League of Nations** organization formed to promote international peace and security; it functioned from 1920 to 1946

* **diplomacy** practice of managing relations between nations without warfare

labor and gave greater recognition to traditional chiefs. Furthermore, they made no attempt to impose European culture on the African peoples. At the same time, the Belgian authorities allowed other groups—including missionaries and private companies—a great deal of freedom to pursue their own interests in the region.

Belgian colonial authorities, the Catholic Church, and big business generally worked together, although they sometimes found themselves at odds. The Catholic Church, for example, objected to government attempts to support the authority of traditional African chiefs, which might weaken the influence of missionaries. Both the church and the government criticized Belgian companies for their methods of recruiting workers, which often disrupted rural communities.

In the mid-1950s some Belgians and Africans began calling for decolonization—a gradual ending of colonial rule. By this time Belgian authorities had granted Africans certain limited rights, but no voting privileges. After rioting broke out in 1959, the Belgian government announced that it would grant independence to the Congo in June 1960. This abrupt change from colony to independent state left Africans in the Congo unprepared to govern or manage the economy. As a result, the new nation—later known as Zaire and then as Democratic Republic of Congo or CONGO (KINSHASA)—remained dependent on Europeans for guidance and assistance.

Ruanda-Urundi. For a time, Belgium also held the territory to the east of the Congo known as Ruanda-Urundi. Ruled by Germany from 1899 to 1917, the region was transferred to Belgium by the League of Nations* after World War I. Belgium administered the colony until 1962, when it split into the independent nations of RWANDA and BURUNDI.

GREAT BRITAIN

Great Britain acquired a huge colonial empire in Africa during the late 1800s through a combination of diplomacy* and military force. In ruling this vast territory, Britain's policies varied according to local conditions and the nature of British settlement. In some areas, colonial authorities favored a form of "indirect rule," in which local African rulers had some degree of power. In others, British officials took a more direct approach to governing, controlling all aspects of society. Although a few well-educated Africans—mostly lawyers—held high government posts in the late 1800s, they were replaced by British officials after 1900.

West Africa. The British colonies in West Africa were NIGERIA, the Gold Coast (present-day GHANA), Sierra Leone, the GAMBIA, and—after World War I—CAMEROON. Throughout West Africa, Britain tended to exert its power indirectly, often cooperating with African kings. In areas without established rulers, the British generally chose Africans to serve as chiefs.

The British established a system of law and order in these colonies. They also built a network of roads, railways, and ports for the movement of cash crops and other goods. They imposed taxes on Africans, which had to be paid in cash, to increase the labor force. The only ways Africans could make these tax payments were to sell products or work for wages. Colonial authorities sometimes allowed forced labor as well.

The British provided few benefits for Africans. Although the colonial governments established some schools, most educational institutions were run by missionaries. Services such as medical facilities and electricity were concentrated in major cities and, as a result, reached only a small number of Africans.

In the early 1940s, British authorities began to offer more services and to involve Africans in economic planning and government. Ultimately, however, such policies were not enough to satisfy the desire of Africans for self-government. By the mid-1960s Britain had granted independence to all its colonies in West Africa.

East Africa. Britain's colonies in East Africa were UGANDA, KENYA, ZANZIBAR, British Somaliland, and Tanganyika, a former German colony known as German East Africa. The British also governed the islands of MAURITIUS and the SEYCHELLES in the Indian Ocean. They began to take control of East Africa in the late 1800s and eventually set up quite different administrations in each colony.

In Uganda the British adopted a policy of indirect rule, giving considerable autonomy* to local leaders. They encouraged Africans to produce cash crops, which made Uganda one of the richest colonies in Africa.

The British authorities in Uganda gave their political support to the Ganda, one of the country's many ethnic groups. However, the Ganda became too powerful and other African groups came to resent them. The Ganda tried to prevent the British from interfering in Uganda's affairs and providing social services, education, and agricultural improvements to the people. During the 1940s, other Ugandan groups organized protests against the Ganda. Eventually opposition to European and Asian control of the cotton industry united the people of Uganda, and Britain granted the country independence in 1962.

In contrast to Uganda, the colonial government of Kenya was dominated by European settlers. The fertile highlands of Kenya attracted many European farmers who established huge plantations, taking the best land and forcing Africans to resettle elsewhere.

For many years, British policies in Kenya benefited the white settlers. As the population grew, Africans began to press for the right to expand onto white-owned lands. This expansion was strongly resisted by the settlers. In the early 1950s, a group known as the MAU MAU, made up of members of the GIKUYU people, began a violent uprising against the settlers. After attempting to put down the rebellion, colonial authorities realized that they would have to agree to some of the Mau Mau's demands. The government allowed Africans to farm in the highland regions, making some white settlers give up their land. In addition, the British began discussions with Kenyans about independence, which was granted in 1963.

Located south of Kenya, Tanganyika was a German colony until World War I, when Britain took it over. Initially, the colony attracted few

* **autonomy** independent, self-government

157

Colonialism in Africa

British settlers and little investment. In the 1950s, however, Britain became more involved in Tanganyika, encouraging settlement and introducing various political and economic measures. Although the Africans resisted some of the British policies, the move toward independence—granted in 1961—was relatively peaceful.

Zanzibar had been a colony of the Arab state of Oman since the mid-1800s, used mainly as a source of slaves. It had been ruled for years by an Arab upper class. When the British took Zanzibar over, they continued the tradition, appointing Arabs to most government posts. Rivalries between the Arabs and the indigenous population led to conflicts that Britain was unable to resolve. The colony was granted independence in 1963. The following year, Zanzibar and Tanganyika united to become the nation of TANZANIA.

British Somaliland was located in the northern portion of present-day SOMALIA, near DJIBOUTI. Britain established a protectorate* there in the 1880s. In 1960, the region joined with Italian Somaliland, farther south, to form the independent Republic of Somalia.

* **protectorate**   control of a weak state by a stronger one

Britain captured the island of Mauritius in 1810 and then formally received control of it under the Treaty of Paris (1814), signed by several European nations at the end of the Napoleonic Wars. The same treaty gave Britain the islands of the Seychelles. Mauritius gained its independence in 1968, followed eight years later by the Seychelles.

Central and Southern Africa.   Britain's colonial possessions in central and southern Africa included Southern Rhodesia (present-day ZIMBABWE), Northern Rhodesia (ZAMBIA), Nyasaland (MALAWI), Bechuanaland (BOTSWANA), Basutoland (LESOTHO), and SWAZILAND. Before 1910, when SOUTH AFRICA became independent, Britain also had two colonies in that region—the Cape Colony and Natal.

Involvement in South Africa dated from the early 1800s, when Britain acquired the Cape Colony from the Dutch. British immigrants flooded into southern Africa in the late 1800s. They never gained more than partial control there, however, because of the presence of large numbers of Dutch settlers, known as Afrikaners, or Boers. As British settlement increased, many Afrikaners tried to move north into Bechuanaland. The African rulers of Bechuanaland, fearing an invasion of the Dutch settlers, asked Britain for help in 1885. Britain agreed and Bechuanaland became a British protectorate. Britain maintained a system of indirect rule there until Bechuanaland gained independence in 1966.

A similar situation occurred in Basutoland, a mountainous land that the Afrikaners had originally considered unsuitable for settlement. In the 1850s, however, the Afrikaners began to expand into Basutoland. In response to an appeal from the local people for help, Britain established a protectorate in Basutoland. Originally governed as part of the Cape Colony, Basutoland came directly under British rule in 1884. However, most of the administration of the area was left in the hands of indigenous authorities.

Swaziland also became a British protectorate. In this case, the British stepped in to end warfare between two African peoples, the Swazi and

Zulu. Once again, Britain established a system of indirect rule. It granted Swaziland self-government in 1967 and full independence in 1968.

In 1889 Britain gave the British South Africa Company, headed by Cecil RHODES, rights to the area that became known as Southern Rhodesia. Attracted by the offer of large tracts of land, white settlers flooded the region. Attempts by Africans to rebel against the settlers were brutally crushed, and Southern Rhodesia became a highly segregated society, dominated by whites. Forced to live on poor farmland in special areas known as reserves, many Africans had to work for the settlers to earn a living.

The British South Africa Company also gained the rights to Northern Rhodesia. At first, the British administered the region mostly through local African authorities, and there was little opposition to colonial rule. As in Southern Rhodesia, however, the settlers took over the best land and gained political and economic control of the colony and its rich copper mines.

The area to the east of Northern Rhodesia became known as Nyasaland. Ruled after 1904 by British colonial officials, it never attracted as many white settlers as the Rhodesias. Nevertheless, the spread of European-owned plantations in the region eventually aroused opposition among Africans, which led to armed rebellion in 1915. For many years, Nyasaland served as a source of labor for other colonies. Whites in Northern and Southern Rhodesia relied on Africans from Nyasaland to work on farms and in mines.

In 1953, in an effort to promote the economic and political development of the region, the two Rhodesias and Nyasaland joined together as the Central African Federation. Meanwhile, African protests against colonial policies grew stronger. By the early 1960s, the colonial administrations of Nyasaland and Northern Rhodesia began allowing Africans greater participation in government. Both regions won independence in 1964; Nyasaland took the name Malawi and Northern Rhodesia became Zambia.

In Southern Rhodesia, settlers fiercely resisted any attempts to increase African power. In 1965 the white-dominated government declared independence for the colony. African opposition to the government erupted in guerrilla* warfare, and in the 1970s the administration's power began to crumble. By 1980 a majority black African government ruled the nation, which was renamed Zimbabwe.

* **guerrilla** type of warfare involving sudden raids by small groups of warriors

North Africa. Britain was involved in governing two large territories in North Africa—EGYPT and the SUDAN. Egypt had been conquered in 1517 by the Ottoman Empire, based in Turkey. Ottoman influence spread to northern Sudan and other parts of North Africa. In the 1800s Britain gained control of Egypt as a result of dealings over the newly built SUEZ CANAL, which provided a shipping route between the Mediterranean and Red seas. Facing a financial crisis in 1876, the Egyptian ruler sold all of Egypt's shares in the canal to Britain. The sale made Britain the majority shareholder. As Egypt's finances continued to worsen, British power in the region increased. In 1882 Britain responded to an Egyptian revolt by invading and occupying the country.

Colonialism in Africa

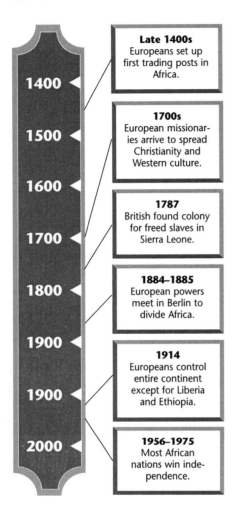

Timeline	Event
1400	**Late 1400s** Europeans set up first trading posts in Africa.
1500	**1700s** European missionaries arrive to spread Christianity and Western culture.
1600	
1700	**1787** British found colony for freed slaves in Sierra Leone.
1800	**1884–1885** European powers meet in Berlin to divide Africa.
1900	
1900	**1914** Europeans control entire continent except for Liberia and Ethiopia.
2000	**1956–1975** Most African nations win independence.

* **bureaucracy** large departmental organization within a government

At the start of World War I, Britain made Egypt a protectorate. After the war, local opposition arose to the British, who introduced harsh policies to keep the peace. Tensions continued to grow and Britain granted Egypt limited autonomy in 1922. Britain continued to maintain some control until the mid-1930s.

South of Egypt along the Nile River, the Sudan was conquered by British and Egyptian forces in 1898. Britain set up a joint administration with Egypt to govern the region. As in Egypt, the British had to use brutal measures to maintain control in the Sudan during World War I. British and Egyptian rule continued until 1956, when the Sudan gained independence. The new nation faced bitter regional differences between the Muslim-controlled north and the Christians of the south.

FRANCE

The French colonization of Africa took a number of years, beginning in the 1830s in North Africa and extending into Central Africa in the early 1900s. A number of territories began as "military colonies," conquered and then governed by the French armed forces. Over time, however, civilian administrations replaced military rule.

In principle, France maintained a policy of direct rule in Africa. French officials had full authority for governing and directing the affairs of the colonies. In practice, however, Africans often played important roles in the colonial bureaucracy*. The French relied on local rulers to support their administration. Unlike the British, who left local matters pretty much in the hands of African authorities, the French intervened constantly in the affairs of their African subjects.

An important feature of French colonial administration was the distinction between "citizens" and "subjects." Only citizens had the same rights as French colonists, and very few Africans became citizens. All other inhabitants of the colonies were subjects. Subjects had no political rights, but they had various obligations, such as serving in French armies. France recognized African laws and allowed the people to be judged by them. At the same time, the authorities tried to get Africans to adopt certain aspects of French culture, such as the French language.

As with other European powers in Africa, an important aim of French colonization was economic development. However, France had a difficult time stimulating its colonial economies. Many of its colonies were thinly populated and could not supply many workers. Moreover, for many years private businesses and trading companies controlled the economies of a number of colonies. France exercised little influence over these companies.

North Africa. France's North African colonies consisted of ALGERIA, TUNISIA, and MOROCCO. French forces invaded Algeria in 1830 in an effort to stop pirates based there from attacking ships in the Mediterranean. After placing a number of coastal towns under military rule, the French eventually gained control of the rest of the country. In the 1860s and 1870s, French settlers began colonizing many areas of Algeria.

Habib Bourguiba of Tunisia helped to negotiate independence from France and became his country's first president.

* **vulnerable**   open to harm or attack

* **nationalism**   devotion to the interests and culture of one's country

In Tunisia, France competed with Britain and Italy for economic control. When violence broke out in Tunisia in 1881, a French naval force invaded and established a protectorate. Morocco escaped European domination for many years. In 1880, however, the European powers forced the Moroccans to sign a treaty guaranteeing the rights of foreigners in the country. In the 1890s political disorder in Morocco left the country vulnerable*. France and Spain took control in 1906, governing jointly for three years until Spain withdrew its claim to the country.

French control of Algeria, Tunisia, and Morocco was never secure. Throughout the colonial period, the inhabitants of the region were in an almost constant state of rebellion. In some of the more remote areas, the people never came to accept French rule. As early as the 1930s, popular resistance began to fuel movements for independence.

When France was occupied by Germany in World War II, its Vichy government maintained loose control over the North African colonies. American and British forces invaded and took over the region in 1942, but returned it to France when the war ended. In the following years, Algeria, Tunisia, and Morocco all experienced a surge of nationalism*, and local opposition to French rule grew dramatically. Faced with spreading violence, terrorism, and rioting, the French granted the countries independence—Morocco and Tunisia in 1956, and Algeria in 1962.

Colonialism in Africa

See
color plate 7,
vol. 2.

West and Central Africa. French colonies in West and Central Africa included Senegal, Guinea, Ivory Coast, Togo, Dahomey (present-day Bénin), Cameroon, Central African Republic, Gabon, and French Congo, (now Congo, Brazzaville). Before the mid-1800s, France had little interest in these areas except to establish trading posts and missionary stations along the coasts. During the "scramble" for Africa, however, the nation set its sights on a number of areas in each region, hoping to get territories with valuable resources.

France used military force to take over most of its colonies in West Africa. In some areas—such as Guinea, Ivory Coast, and Dahomey—the French met fierce resistance from the Africans. After establishing control of the coasts, it sometimes took a number of years to move inland and gain possession of the interiors. In 1904 France's colonies in West Africa, including some in the southern Sahara, were formally organized into a large administrative unit known as French West Africa. Eventually, French West Africa included Senegal, French Sudan (present-day Mali), Guinea, Ivory Coast, Dahomey, Upper Volta (present-day Burkina Faso), Niger, and Mauritania. Some of the people of Senegal were granted French citizenship and a few became members of the French legislature in Paris. After World War I, the former German colony of Togo was divided between France and Britain.

France acquired Cameroon in Central Africa as a result of World War II. Formerly the German colony of Kamerun, it was divided into East Cameroon (or Cameroun, controlled by France) and West Cameroon (or Cameroons, controlled by Britain). France gained Congo, Gabon, and the Central African Republic as the result of treaties with local rulers and military force. In 1910 Gabon, Congo, Central African Republic, and Chad were combined in an administrative unit known as French Equatorial Africa.

Serious challenges to French colonial rule began after World War II, when Africans began agitating for greater autonomy. Drained financially by the war and by problems with its territories in Southeast Asia, France was unable to put up much resistance to African demands. The Overseas Reform Act in 1956 gave the African colonies autonomy in their internal affairs, while France remained responsible for defense and foreign policy. By 1960 all the French colonies of West and Central Africa had gained full independence.

The Southern Sahara. The French colonies in the southern Sahara, which included the area known as the Sahel, were Mauritania, Mali, Upper Volta, Niger, and Chad. France colonized this arid region primarily to link its other territories and to prevent other Europeans from claiming it.

Although France gained control of most of the southern Sahara in the 1890s, the nomadic peoples of the area continued to resist foreign rule for many years. The French governed the vast and thinly populated region through local rulers, who had a great deal of autonomy. Most of the colonies were administered as part of French West Africa, with Chad included in French Equatorial Africa.

There were no strong independence movements in the southern Sahara after World War II. In 1958 France created the French

Community, an organization that gave internal autonomy to its African colonies. Although created mainly to satisfy independence movements in other parts of Africa, the French Community also benefited the colonies of the southern Sahara. When France granted independence to its West and Central African colonies in 1960, it did the same with its southern Sahara colonies.

East Africa. France's colonies in East Africa included MADAGASCAR, RÉUNION, the COMORO ISLANDS, and French Somaliland (present-day Djibouti). During the late 1700s and early 1800s, France competed with Britain for control of the island of Madagascar. For a number of years, France dominated the coastline of Madagascar while Britain held the interior. At the Berlin Conference of 1884–1885, Britain agreed to let France establish a protectorate over the island. Resistance to French rule led to a bloody but unsuccessful rebellion in 1916. When Germany occupied France in World War II, the British took charge of Madagascar because of its strategic location along shipping routes between Asia and Europe. After the war France regained control but faced a growing movement for independence, which it granted in 1960.

The island of Réunion came under French control in the early 1700s. An important sugar-growing area, it was dominated by white plantation owners who used slaves to tend the sugar crop. By 1848 the French government had abolished slavery. In 1946 the island became an overseas department of France. The French established a protectorate for the four Comoro Islands in 1885, then made them into a colony in 1912. The islands declared their independence in 1975, but France still claims one of them—Mayotte—as a territory.

France obtained the tiny colony of French Somaliland as a result of treaties signed with local African rulers in 1862. Located at the southern end of the Red Sea, the colony allowed France to guard the shipping lanes leading to the Suez Canal and the railway to Ethiopia. France granted the colony independence in 1977.

GERMANY

See color plate 11, vol. 3.

German colonialism in Africa lasted only from 1884 to 1914. Germany's defeat in World War I resulted in the loss of all its colonies. The nation gained little economic benefit from its African possessions, and opposition to colonial policies led to a number of bloody rebellions.

German colonies in Africa included Togo and Kamerun (Cameroon) in West Africa, South-West Africa (present-day NAMIBIA), and German East Africa (present-day Tanzania, Rwanda, and Burundi). Germany's policies in these areas differed somewhat, reflecting the history of its involvement in the region.

Germany began establishing commercial and missionary activities in Togo and Kamerun in the mid-1840s. During the "scramble" for Africa in the 1880s, the nation acquired both areas as colonies. Two distinct colonial systems developed under German rule. In Togo, traders and missionary societies worked together to influence colonial policies that would favor their interests in the colony. In Kamerun, plantation owners exerted a great deal of power in the colonial administration. In both

Colonialism in Africa

colonies, Germany's primary aim was to exploit the natural resources. The colonial administration's policies were often brutal and harsh.

German missionaries entered South-West Africa in the 1840s. Settlers soon followed and established farms and towns, and the area became a German colony in 1885. Following the discovery of mineral resources in the late 1800s, a mining industry developed. Resistance from Africans to colonial policies led to a bloody revolt from 1904 to 1908. Germany responded by sending troops into the colony, and afterward the military dominated the colonial administration. South-West Africa became one of the most brutal colonial societies on the continent, and many Africans (mainly members of the Herero people) were killed as part of a strategy of genocide*.

German exploration of East Africa began in the 1860s, and Germany's claim to the region was established at the Berlin Conference. At first, the colony was ruled by a trading company, the German East Africa Company. However, after violent uprisings by Arabs in the coastal regions, the German government took control. As in other German colonies, colonial rule in East Africa tended to be ruthless.

After Germany's defeat in World War I, Britain and France acquired Togo and Kamerun and divided the territories between themselves. The League of Nations authorized South Africa to administer South-West Africa, and it gave control of most of German East Africa to Britain. The rest of German East Africa, known as Ruanda-Urundi (present-day Rwanda and Burundi), went to Belgium.

* **genocide** deliberate and systematic killing of a particular ethnic, religious, or national group

ITALY

Like Germany, Italy's rule in Africa was relatively short-lived. Also like Germany, Italy lost its colonies in Africa as a result of war—in this case, its defeat in World War II.

Italy had no history of conquest and colonization in other parts of the world. As a result, it had few officials experienced in colonial matters. Moreover, the Italian government and people had little interest in colonization. Consequently, Italian colonial polices were rather haphazard and disorganized, and colonial rule depended largely on local decisions and situations. Because of their inexperience, Italian authorities often had to rely on the military to help administer and control the colonies.

Italy's first colonies were in the "horn" of Africa, a region wedged between the Red Sea and Indian Ocean. In 1885 Italy signed various treaties with Muslim rulers in that region, obtaining rights to ERITREA and Italian Somaliland (present-day Somalia). Both colonies were hot, dry regions that other European powers had considered worthless. However, because Italy was a weak nation at the time, it could not compete with other countries for more valuable territories.

In 1936 Italian forces based in Eritrea invaded and took control of ETHIOPIA, an ancient African kingdom that had remained independent during the "scramble" for Africa. Italy combined the conquered territory with Eritrea and Somaliland to form the colony of Italian East Africa. In 1937 an assassination attempt on the Italian governor of Ethiopia led to a reign of terror, in which many Ethiopians were arrested and exe-

Portugal, the first European power to explore Africa, established settlements on the continent's west and east coasts. This Portuguese fort in Mombasa, Kenya, was built in 1593.

cuted. Unrest in the country continued to grow, and by 1940 Ethiopian resistance groups had gained some power. During World War II, British forces invaded Ethiopia, restored the monarchy, and ended Italian rule.

Italy's other colony was LIBYA, on the coast of North Africa. For many years, Italians had crossed the Mediterranean Sea to settle in Libya. However, Italy made no attempt to colonize the area until the early 1900s. In 1911 Italian forces invaded Libya and tried to take control from the Ottoman Turks, the Muslim rulers of the country. After occupying a number of coastal areas, the Italians claimed the region as a protectorate. Muslim resistance to Italian rule led to an organized revolt that continued in some places until about 1931. During World War II, Britain, France, and their allies launched extensive campaigns against the Italians in Libya. After the war, the colony was split between the British and the French, but a united Libya gained its independence in 1951.

PORTUGAL

The Portuguese were the earliest explorers of sub-Saharan Africa, first sailing along its coasts in the 1400s. Their first colony there, the CAPE VERDE islands off the north coast of Africa, was established in the 1440s. Cape Verde settlers pioneered new systems of tropical agriculture and developed a distinctive culture that blended African and Portuguese elements.

165

Portugal went on to carve out four more colonies in Africa: Portuguese Guinea (present-day GUINEA-BISSAU), SÃO TOMÉ AND PRÍNCIPE, ANGOLA, and MOZAMBIQUE. Guinea-Bissau, a small administrative post in Portuguese Guinea, became the capital of the Portuguese colonies of West Africa in the 1900s. An international trading zone since the 1400s, Guinea-Bissau over the centuries supplied ivory and gold to Europe and slaves to the Americas.

In the 1600s and 1700s, Angola was also a source for slaves. Portugal established its claim to Angola through treaties with other European powers in the late 1800s and early 1900s. In 1914 Portugal gave Angola a degree of autonomy, although white Portuguese still ruled the colony. The African population staged periodic uprisings until Angola gained its independence in 1975.

The tiny island colonies of São Tomé and Príncipe also gained their independence in 1975. Primarily agricultural, these islands had been controlled by Portugal since the 1400s. For many years they served mainly as way stations on the Portuguese slave route from Africa to the Americas.

The Portuguese presence in Mozambique dated from the late 1400s, when explorers established a number of trading posts along the coast. Portuguese claims to the colony were recognized during the European negotiations over Africa in the late 1800s. At that time, a commercial firm, the Mozambique Company, was put in charge of administering the colony. Mozambique gained independence in 1975.

Portuguese colonial rule in Africa focused on trade and economic development. Some Africans in Portugal's colonies acquired commercial skills, while others received enough education to become clerks and administrators. In general, however, little attempt was made to involve Africans in colonial government. Moreover, colonial economic policies often supported forced labor and other harsh measures.

By the early 1900s, significant numbers of Portuguese began migrating to the African colonies in search of opportunity. This migration increased in the 1930s. The presence of the immigrants, who took jobs and land away from Africans, heightened racial tensions and led to political and social unrest. In some colonies, particularly Angola and Mozambique, this unrest played a major role in the drive toward independence.

SPAIN

From the late 1400s to early 1800s, Spain maintained a large colonial empire in the Americas. However, by the time European nations divided Africa into colonies in the late 1800s, the Spanish had little power. As a result, Spain acquired only a few colonies in Africa: Spanish Sahara (present-day WESTERN SAHARA), Spanish Guinea (EQUATORIAL GUINEA), and a group of tiny territories on the north coast of Morocco.

Spain's claim to Spanish Sahara—a barren, desert area—dates from 1884, but only in 1934 did Spain gain control of the interior. By the early 1960s, Morocco and Mauritania had begun to claim parts of the region, and this fueled an independence movement in Spanish Sahara. Finding the colony increasingly difficult to govern, Spain withdrew in 1976.

> **Remember:** Words in small capital letters have separate entries, and the index at the end of this volume will guide you to more information on many topics.

Spain gained control of the small colony known as Spanish Guinea on the west coast of Africa at the Berlin Conference of 1884–1885. In 1902 Spain formed a special council to administer the colony and oversee its development. Two years later it established basic rules of land ownership, including protection of the landholdings of some of the indigenous peoples. The Spanish left local affairs largely in the hands of traditional African rulers and groups. In the 1950s Spain's sub-Saharan territories became "overseas provinces," which made them integral parts of Spain. Africans in Spanish Guinea were granted Spanish citizenship in 1959, and the region gained autonomy in 1963 and independence in 1968.

Spain's tiny territories of Ifni, Ceuta, and Melilla along the coast of Morocco were remnants of a time when both Spain and Morocco were controlled by the Moors*. During the colonial period, Spain and France jointly ruled Morocco, although France actually governed the colony. When France granted Morocco independence in 1956, Spain gave up all claims to the region except for Ifni, Ceuta, and Melilla. It returned Ifni to Morocco in 1968, but Ceuta and Melilla still remain Spanish territories. (*See also* **Afrikaner Republics; Arabs in Africa; Christianity in Africa; Development, Economic and Social; Economic History; History of Africa; Independence Movements; Missions and Missionaries; Nationalism; Neocolonialism; Plantation Systems; Southern Africa, History; West African Trading Settlements; World Wars I and II.**)

* **Moors** North African Muslims who conquered Spain in the A.D. 700s

COMMERCE

See *Markets; Trade.*

Comoro Islands

The Comoros are a group of four islands lying in the Indian Ocean between MOZAMBIQUE and MADAGASCAR. Mayotte, the easternmost island, is an administrative territory of France. The other three—Grande Comore (Ngazidja), Anjouan (Nzwani), and Mohéli (Mwali)—make up the Federal Islamic Republic of the Comoro Islands.

All the islands are volcanic in origin. Mayotte, the oldest, is fairly flat; the other islands are mountainous. Rising to 7,790 feet, Mount Karthala is the highest peak on the islands and an active volcano. The Comoros enjoy a tropical climate, featuring a wet season from October to April and a dry season from May to September. The temperature averages around 66°F during the dry season and between 75°F and 79°F in the rainy season.

The islands' fertile volcanic soil and mild climate provide favorable conditions for agriculture. Most of the inhabitants depend on local farming, raising livestock, and fishing for a living. However, the population has increased so much over the last 50 years that there is some question about the continuing ability of the Comorians to feed themselves. In addition, crops grown for export are producing less income because of reduced demand for the islands' main agricultural products—vanilla, cloves, and perfume oils.

Comoro Islands

Federal Islamic Republic of the Comoros

POPULATION:
578,400 (2000 estimated population)

AREA:
838 sq. mi. (2,170 sq. km)

LANGUAGES:
French, Arabic (official); Comoran (a Swahili dialect)

NATIONAL CURRENCY:
Comorian franc

PRINCIPAL RELIGIONS:
Sunni Muslim 86%, Roman Catholic 14%

ISLANDS:
Grand Comore (Ngazidja), Anjouan (Nzwani), Mohéli (Mwali), Mayotte (Maore); Capital: Moroni, 30,000 (1999 est.)

ANNUAL RAINFALL:
Varies from 43–114 in. (1,100–2,900 mm)

ECONOMY:
GNP per capita: U.S. $685

PRINCIPAL PRODUCTS AND EXPORTS:
Agricultural: vanilla, cloves, perfume oils, copra, coconuts, cinnamon
Manufacturing: perfume distillation, textiles, jewelry, construction materials
Tourism is also an important industry.

GOVERNMENT:
Independence from France, 1975. President elected by universal suffrage. Governing bodies: Assemblée Fédérale elected by universal suffrage.

HEADS OF STATE SINCE 1990:
1990–1995 President Said Mohamed Djohar
1996–1998 President Mohamed Taki Abdulkarim
1998 President Tadjiddne Ben Said Massounde (interim)
1999– Colonel Azali Assoumani

ARMED FORCES:
520 (1996 est.), serving under approximately 20 French officers.

EDUCATION:
Compulsory for ages 7–15; literacy rate 57%

* **coup** sudden, often violent overthrow of a ruler or government

* **mercenary** hired soldier

* **secede** to withdraw formally from an organization or country

In recent years, the islands have made a major effort to build up the tourist industry. With their beautiful beaches, coral reefs, and warm climate, the Comoros have long attracted visitors. Tourism provides an opportunity for economic growth in the near future.

The Comoros have been inhabited for over a thousand years, but during most of that time each island was separate, ruled by its own sultan or sultans. As a result, the islands developed independent traditions and dialects of the language known as Swahili. Even today inhabitants of the various islands have difficulty understanding one another.

For hundreds of years the Comoros prospered as Indian Ocean winds brought sailing ships engaged in trade between Asia and Africa to the islands. This trading activity resulted in a very diverse population made up of Africans, Arabs, Indians, Europeans, and Malagasy (peoples from Madagascar). The invention of the steamship put an end to this era, and the islands eventually became dependent upon the French.

France gained control of the Comoros in the late-1800s and in 1912 placed them under the authority of its colony of Madagascar. The islands continued to be attached to French Madagascar until the end of World War II. Three of them gained independence in 1975, but the inhabitants of Mayotte chose to remain under French control.

Since independence, the government has been toppled several times by coups* backed by foreign mercenaries*. Twice the French have stepped in. The country became the Federal Islamic Republic of the Comoro Islands (FIRCI) in 1978 with Ahmed Abdallah as president. An attempt by the island of Anjouan to secede* from the republic led to another coup in 1999 and to military rule under Colonel Azali Assoumani. The island of Mayotte is still claimed by FIRCI, but it remains a territory of France. (*See also* **Colonialism in Africa, Government and Political Systems, Islam in Africa.**)

Conakry

Conakry, capital of GUINEA, lies at the tip of the Kaloum Peninsula on the western coast of Africa. The surrounding land is swampy, and its climate is tropical. During the rainy season, about 144 inches of rain fall in five months. About 1 million people live in the city.

In the 1200s and 1300s, Conakry was part of the Mali Empire, and descendants of Mali nobility, the Malinke, still live in Conakry. From the 1880s to the 1950s, the city—and the rest of Guinea—was ruled by French colonists. After Guinea won independence in 1958, residents of Conakry and the rest of the nation suffered under the radically anti-French leadership of President Sékou TOURÉ. The city grew extremely poor.

Since Touré's death in 1984, Conakry has experienced new life. Streets in the city's center are now paved and shaded with mango trees. Modern shops, nightclubs, and restaurants have appeared, and utilities such as electricity have become more reliable. Conakry's deep-water port services a lively export trade in bauxite, bananas, iron ore, and other products. The city is also home to Guinea's only international airport. Roads connect Conakry with IVORY COAST, MALI, and SENEGAL, and railways connect it to other Guinean cities, including Kankan, Fria, Boké, and Kamsar.

Congo (Brazzaville)

Congo, Republic of

* **exploitation** relationship in which one side benefits at the other's expense

The Republic of Congo lies along the equator and stretches northeast from the Atlantic coast into the heart of the African continent. Its dominant feature is the CONGO RIVER, one of Africa's most important waterways and the main highway for trade in the area. Many different ethnic groups live together in Congo's cities, often contributing to political and social unrest.

HISTORY, GOVERNMENT, AND ECONOMY

Two kingdoms and several smaller chiefdoms once occupied what is now the Republic of Congo. France took control of the region in the 1800s and claimed it as a colony for more than 150 years. Since gaining independence, Congo has struggled to achieve a stable government and economy. But internal conflict and continued exploitation* by European powers have made this task especially difficult.

History and Government. The most important of the precolonial kingdoms were the Kingdom of Kongo and the Kingdom of Téké. The Kingdom of Kongo occupied the southwestern Congo region, with its capital in what is now northwestern ANGOLA. The Kingdom of Téké was located along the center of the Congo River, where it controlled the flow of goods between the region's interior and the coast.

The Portuguese were the first Europeans in the Congo area. Arriving in the 1480s, they maintained a strong presence there for more than 200 years. However, French traders and missionaries gradually pushed out the Portuguese, and by the late 1700s France had become the major

169

Congo (Brazzaville)

Before signing the treaties that established the French Congo, Pierre de Brazza (1852-1905) explored much of western and central Africa for France. Brazzaville, Congo's capital, was named for him.

European power in the Congo. Between 1875 and 1885, a representative of the French government, Pierre Savorgnan de Brazza, signed a treaty with the Téké king and established military posts in the region. Brazza—after whom Congo's capital city BRAZZAVILLE is named—later became the first commissioner of French Congo. However, he was replaced when he refused to open the country to exploitation by French companies. Under colonial rule, the local population was forced to work under brutal conditions to extract the region's natural resources and to build roads and the railroad to the Atlantic coast.

After World War II, France granted the Congo a degree of self-rule and allowed limited political and social reforms. Congo won its independence in 1960, and Fulbert Youlou became its first president. In 1963 Youlou declared Congo a single-party state with himself at its head. Three days of rioting followed the announcement, and Youlou was overthrown. His successor, Alphonse Massemba-Débat, ruled for four years

Republic of Congo

POPULATION:
2,830,961 (2000 estimated population)

AREA:
132,000 sq. mi. (342,000 sq. km)

LANGUAGES:
French (official); Kongo, Lingala, Teke, Monkutuba, other Bantu dialects

NATIONAL CURRENCY:
CFA franc

PRINCIPAL RELIGIONS:
Christian (mostly Roman Catholic) 50%, Traditional 48%, Muslim 2%

CITIES:
Brazzaville (capital), 1,004,000 (1999 estimated population); Pointe-Noire, Kayes, Loubomo, Ouesso, Impfondo, Fort Rousset, Djambala

ANNUAL RAINFALL:
Varies by region, averaging about 60 in. (1,520 mm) per year

ECONOMY:
GDP per capita: U.S. $1,500

PRINCIPAL PRODUCTS AND EXPORTS:
Agricultural: cassava, sugarcane, rice, corn, peanuts, vegetables, coffee, cocoa, timber
Manufacturing: lumber and plywood, petroleum refining, cement, textiles, food processing
Mining: potash, petroleum, lead, zinc, copper, uranium, phosphates, natural gas

GOVERNMENT:
Independence from France, 1960. Military dictatorship, officially declared multiparty in 1991. President elected by universal suffrage. Governing bodies: Assemblée Nationale and Sénat (elected legislatures), Council of Ministers (appointed by president)

HEADS OF STATE SINCE 1979:
1979–1992 President Colonel Denis Sassou-Nguesso
1992–1997 President Pascal Lissouba
1998– President Denis Sassou-Nguesso

ARMED FORCES:
10,000 (1998 est.)

EDUCATION:
Compulsory for ages 6–16; literacy rate 75%

---

* **coup** sudden, often violent overthrow of a ruler or government

* **infrastructure** basic framework of a society and its economy, which includes roads, bridges, port facilities, airports, and other public works

before being replaced in a military coup* led by Captain Marien Ngouabi. Like his predecessors, Ngouabi tried to gain complete control over the government. In 1977 he was assassinated and replaced by General Joachim Yhombi-Opango.

Two years later another coup brought Colonel Denis Sassou-Nguesso to power. Sassou was more successful than previous Congolese leaders in securing control over the nation. He eliminated political rivals and placed his supporters in government posts. But Sassou heeded calls for greater democracy in 1991, when he allowed the formation of a national convention that stripped him of his powers. The following year Pascal Lissouba was elected president. Sassou and others organized resistance to Lissouba's rule, and by 1997 the nation was engaged in a violent civil war. Lissouba was forced to flee the country, and Sassou again assumed the presidency. Outbreaks of fighting and civil war continued in the following years.

Economy. Congo is rich in natural resources including timber, diamonds, gold, and many different minerals. However, political unrest and a lack of infrastructure* have slowed the nation's economic development. Although many Congolese people are engaged in farming, agriculture accounts for only a small percentage of national wealth. As a result, Congo imports much of its food. Oil was discovered offshore in the early 1970s and quickly became the chief source of the nation's income. However, a large portion of this revenue goes to the European firms that have helped Congo develop its petroleum resources. Other

171

Congo (Brazzaville)

industries—including food processing and textile production—are located in the three main cities of Brazzaville, Pointe-Noire, and Nkayi.

LAND AND PEOPLE

Congo consists of four main regions: the coastal plain, the Nyari Valley, the Téké Plateau, and the Congo Basin. All the regions experience two dry and two rainy seasons per year. The coastal plain has a cooler and drier climate than the rest of the country. The Nyari Valley, just northeast of the coastal plain, features fertile soil that produces many of the nation's crops such as coffee, cocoa, and sugar. The Téké Plateau, lying north of the capital, is a region of low hills and rolling, sandy plains. The Congo Basin in the northeast consists of tropical rain forest and flat, swampy valleys. Because of its rugged terrain, the northern part of the country is much less developed than the south.

The population of Congo is highly concentrated in the south, with almost two thirds of the people living in or around the cities of Brazzaville and Pointe-Noire, which are the two end points for the Congo-Océan railroad. In addition, many people live in the small towns that sprung up along the rail line, towns that were created mainly to serve as railway stations. Nearly one-third of the country's entire population lives in Brazzaville alone. Although most of the people share an urban lifestyle, the Congolese are extremely diverse and can be divided into about 75 distinct groups. About half of Congo's population belong to the Kongo ethnic group, who live between Brazzaville and the coast. The other major ethnic groups are the Téké of south central Congo and the Mbochi of the north. These different groups have maintained strong traditions and rivalries, and most Congolese still identify with their own ethnic group rather than with the nation as a whole. This has made unifying the country under shared political leadership a particularly difficult task. (*See also* **Colonialism in Africa, Ethnic Groups and Identity, French Equatorial Africa.**)

Congo (Kinshasa)

Congo, Democratic Republic of

* **sub-Saharan** referring to Africa south of the Sahara desert

The Democratic Republic of Congo—formerly known as Zaire—is the second-largest country in Africa. Located in the center of the sub-Saharan* region, the Congo is huge and diverse and blessed with abundant natural resources. But the nation's history is troubled. Since gaining independence in 1960, it has been plagued by violence, dictatorial rule, economic mismanagement, and political corruption. Once a land of promise, the Congo has become the prime example of the problems facing modern Africa.

GEOGRAPHY

The Democratic Republic of Congo is about the size of the United States east of the Mississippi River. Except for a very small section of coastline along the Atlantic Ocean, the country is landlocked.

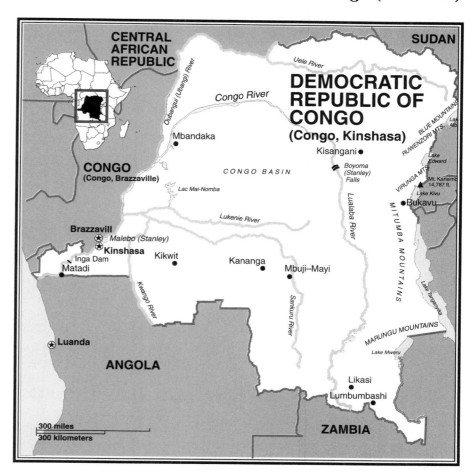

The Congo is dominated by the CONGO RIVER, one of the largest rivers in the world. The river divides the country into four distinct geographic regions. In the center of the country is the immense Congo Basin, or Central Basin, an area of roughly 300,000 square miles covered by dense tropical rain forest. This hot, humid region contains a number of large plantations that produce coffee, cocoa, palm oil, and rubber. It is the most thinly populated area of the country.

North and south of the rain forest are woodlands. These areas, which enjoy abundant rainfall, a fairly temperate climate, and two growing seasons per year, produce most of the country's food. The majority of the nation's inhabitants live in the woodland areas.

The easternmost part of the Congo features high mountains rising to nearly 17,000 feet. With rich volcanic soils, this fertile region produces a variety of food crops as well as coffee and tea. The southernmost part of the Congo consists of forested savanna* and has a much drier climate and relatively few inhabitants.

HISTORY AND GOVERNMENT

The history of the Democratic Republic of Congo has been marked by violence and exploitation* of the people by their leaders. This pattern,

* **savanna** tropical or subtropical grassland with scattered trees and drought-resistant undergrowth

* **exploitation** relationship in which one side benefits at the other's expense

Congo (Kinshasa)

See map in Archaeology and Prehistory (vol. 1).

* **indigenous** native to a certain place

* **Soviet Union** nation that existed from 1922 to 1991, made up of Russia and 14 other republics

established under Belgian colonial rule from 1885 to 1960, continued after independence under MOBUTU SESE SEKO.

Precolonial and Colonial History. The first large state to emerge in the region was the kingdom of Kongo, which by 1500 covered an area of about 30,000 square miles. Kongo dominated the region until 1665, when civil war broke out after the death of the king. The Portuguese, who had been active in the area since the late 1400s, tried to take advantage of the confused situation by invading Kongo. Kongolese forces defeated the Portuguese, but the continuing war and internal rivalries greatly damaged the kingdom. It never regained its former power.

In the late 1800s, the Belgian king Leopold II sent American adventurer Henry Morton STANLEY to explore the Congo River basin. Although Stanley had already traveled parts of the region, he had never journeyed so far inland. On his mission for Leopold, Stanley signed several treaties with local chiefs. Leopold then used the treaties to lay personal claim to the area. In 1885 an international agreement in Europe gave the king ownership of the region, then known as the Congo Free State. Leopold leased parts of his territory to private companies that wanted to profit from the region's riches. The companies used brutal tactics to force the local population to work for them on rubber plantations, in the mines, as porters, and to serve in the colonial army. Some scholars estimate that violence, overwork, and starvation killed perhaps as many as 10 million Congolese people in 20 years.

Leopold ran the Congo Free State as his own private kingdom until 1908, when in disgust at his greed, the Belgian government declared it a colony of Belgium. Many of Leopold's practices continued under Belgian rule, although treatment of the indigenous* population was slightly less brutal. Virtually all state resources and services were controlled by colonial authorities and foreign companies, and the local people had little or no say in economic or political matters.

Independence and the Congo Crisis. By the 1950s the independence movements sweeping through Africa spread to the Belgian Congo. In response to Congolese demands for greater rights, the Belgian government proposed a 30-year timetable for independence. Most Congolese found this unacceptable, and mounting political and economic unrest in the late 1950s forced the Belgians to grant the Congo independence in 1960.

The first president of the new nation was Joseph Kasavubu; Patrice LUMUMBA, a political rival, served as prime minister. Within weeks of independence, the Congolese army mutinied and civil unrest spread throughout the country. Hundreds of Europeans were massacred and thousands fled the country and returned to Europe.

As the revolt continued, Prime Minister Lumumba asked the UNITED NATIONS (UN) to send troops to restore order. Lumumba also sought assistance from the Soviet Union*, and soon the United States became involved in the conflict as well, raising the prospect of a major war. During this time, the important copper mining region of Shaba in the southeast declared its independence from the new nation.

Congo (Kinshasa)

Heart of Darkness

"An empty stream, a great silence, an impenetrable forest... At night sometimes the roll of drums behind the curtain of trees would run up the river and remain... as if hovering in the air high over our heads." These images of Congo's remote interior are found in Joseph Conrad's short story "Heart of Darkness"—one of the most famous works of English literature. The tale was inspired by Conrad's own experiences as a young steamboat captain journeying through the unexplored Congo in the late 1800s. It explores not only the darkness of the African jungle, but also the darkness—greed and corruption—Conrad felt existed in the heart of man.

* **communism** system in which land, goods, and the means of production are owned by the state or community rather than by individuals

Cold War period of tense relations between the United States and the Soviet Union following World War II

The Congolese military soon stepped in to help Kasavubu, aided by the U.S. Central Intelligence Agency. The military arrested Lumumba and turned him over to the leader of the Shaba rebels, Moise TSHOMBE, who had Lumumba killed. Meanwhile, civil war continued to rage between Shaba and the Congo. In 1962 the UN proposed a peace plan, but Tshombe resisted it, believing he could conquer the entire country. But the forces against him were too powerful, and he surrendered to Kasavubu the following year. In 1965 Kasavubu was himself overthrown by Colonel Joseph Désiré Mobutu, who would rule for more than 30 years with the help of U.S. financial support.

The Mobutu Years. Mobutu immediately moved to consolidate power in his own hands by eliminating political opponents and stirring up rivalries between competing ethnic groups. He also dissolved the parliament and created a single party to control political life.

In 1971 Mobutu changed the country's name from Congo to Zaire, which he claimed was an African word for "big river" (it was actually a Portuguese mispronunciation of the word for river.) He also took the name Mobutu Sese Seko ("the all-powerful") and declared European names illegal. He even went so far as to outlaw neckties because they were part of Western clothing.

Instead of building up the country, Mobutu and his allies robbed it. Mobutu took possession of foreign-owned businesses and gave them to his friends and supporters, who proceeded to destroy much of the nation's economy. In addition, political corruption became widespread because poorly paid public officials had to accept bribes to make a living. In the mid-1970s Mobutu issued some reforms in an attempt to ease some of the economic conditions his policies had created. The reforms had little effect.

Mobutu's dictatorship allowed no opposition, and many of his policies were very harsh. Yet Mobutu received support in the 1970s and 1980s from the United States and other Western countries because of his opposition to communism*. During this period, Zaire's southern neighbor ANGOLA was in the midst of its own civil war, and Western nations saw Mobutu as a stronghold against the Communist forces battling in Angola.

By the 1980s Mobutu faced increasing criticism at home and abroad. Zaire's economy was in a disastrous state, public servants were unpaid and restless, and public order was disintegrating. When the Cold War* ended in the early 1990s, Mobutu's Western allies no longer needed him as a stronghold against communism.

As Mobutu saw his control of events slipping away, he made a desperate bid to stay in power by approving multiparty elections in 1990. However, he kept postponing them for various reasons. The next year the economy almost totally collapsed, and riots and violence swept through Zaire, killing hundreds of people and destroying much of the nation's infrastructure.

In 1996 rebel forces in eastern Zaire, led by Laurent Kabila, began marching west toward the capital of KINSHASA. Zaire's armed forces were so disorganized and demoralized that they offered almost no resistance. In less than a year, the rebels gained control of the entire country and forced Mobutu from power.

175

Congo (Kinshasa)

Democratic Republic of the Congo

POPULATION:
51,964,999 (2000 estimated population)

AREA:
905,560 sq. mi. (2,345,410 sq. km.)

LANGUAGES:
French (official); Kongo, Lingala, Swahili, Tshiluba, Ngwana

NATIONAL CURRENCY:
Congolese franc

PRINCIPAL RELIGIONS:
Christian 80% (Roman Catholic 50%, Protestant 20%, Kimbanguist 10%), Muslim 10%, Traditional 10%

CITIES:
Kinshasa (capital), 5,064,000 (2000 est.); Kisangani, Lumbumbashi, Kanaga, Likasi, Mbandaka, Mbuji-Mayi, Bukavu

ANNUAL RAINFALL:
Varies from 30–60 in. (800–1500 mm) in south to 80–118 in. (2,000–3,000 mm) in central basin rainforest

ECONOMY:
GDP per capita: U.S. $110

PRINCIPAL PRODUCTS AND EXPORTS:
Agricultural: coffee, sugar, palm oil, rubber, tea, cassava, bananas, corn, fruits
Manufacturing: mineral processing, cement, textiles, leather goods, cigarettes, processed food and beverages
Mining: diamonds, cobalt, copper, cadmium, gold, silver, zinc, iron ore, coal

GOVERNMENT:
Independence from Belgium, 1960. Dictatorship.

HEADS OF STATE SINCE INDEPENDENCE:
1960 Prime Minister Patrice Lumumba
1960–1965 President Joseph Kasavubu
1965–1997 President Mobutu Sese Seko
1997–2001 Laurent Désiré Kabila
2001– Joseph Kabila

ARMED FORCES:
50,000 (2000 est.)

EDUCATION:
Compulsory for ages 6–12; literacy rate 77%

The Congo Today. When Kabila took over as president in 1997, he changed the country's name to The Democratic Republic of Congo and promised that elections would be held after a two-year period of reorganization. However, Kabila made little progress in introducing democracy, and his government proved to be almost as corrupt and brutal as the one it replaced.

By mid-1998 Kabila himself faced a rebellion after ousting the military advisers who had helped him to power. These advisers led a rebel force that nearly captured Kinshasa before Kabila called for support from neighboring Angola and ZIMBABWE. Within months the conflict expanded to include CHAD, ANGOLA, LIBYA, RWANDA, UGANDA, and even Zimbabwe.

By the year 2000, rebel forces controlled the eastern third of the Congo, while Kabila ruled the rest of the country with the military support of his foreign allies. Like Mobutu before him, Kabila ruled by force and by decree, but his hold over the country was largely dependent on the continued presence of foreign forces. In January 2001, Kabila was assassinated and his son, Joseph, was sworn in as president.

ECONOMY

About 75 percent of the people of the Democratic Republic of Congo are engaged in agriculture. Most farms are small, lack modern equipment, and use little in the way of improved seeds or fertilizer. Although some plantations employ more modern, large-scale farming methods, this type of agricultural production has decreased over the past 30 years.

Mining has been an important part of the nation's economy since the colonial era. Copper was the main export until the early 1990s, when it

See map in Minerals and Mining (vol. 3).

was replaced by diamonds. Manufacturing is concentrated in the capital city, Kinshasa, and in a few other urban centers. However, manufacturing represents only a small percentage of the nation's economic activity.

In the early 1970s, high copper prices and political stability led to several years of growth in the country's economy. Then in 1973, the nation's president, Mobutu Sese Seko, seized all foreign-owned businesses and gave them to Zairians who supported his regime*—a policy known as Zairianization. Most of these new owners had little business experience and no particular interest in making their companies profitable. Instead, they enriched themselves on whatever profits they could make.

* **regime**   current political system or rule

Zairianization had a disastrous effect on the nation's economy. Many businesses went bankrupt because of poor management and corruption, and the economy began a long-term decline. Industrial production and mining decreased dramatically. High rates of inflation* made the nation's currency virtually worthless. With no money to spend on maintaining roads and other transportation services, the country saw its infrastructure* deteriorate. As a result, the cost of moving food from the countryside to the cities rose sharply and food prices skyrocketed.

* **inflation**   increase in prices

* **infrastructure**   basic framework of a society and its economy, which includes roads, bridges, port facilities, airports, and other public works

In the 1990s, the economic problems led to rioting, looting, and general civil disorder. Civil war erupted in the mid-1990s. Today, the nation's economy remains in desperate shape and shows little sign of improving in the near future, despite the nation's natural riches and potential.

PEOPLES AND CULTURES

The population of the Congo is unevenly distributed. Most of the people are concentrated in a few areas, more than half of them in cities. About 70 percent are Christian, including many members of the Kimbanguist Church—a Baptist-style church founded in Congo by Simon KIMBANGU. Between 20 and 25 percent practice traditional African religions. The remaining 5 to 10 percent of the Congolese people are Muslim. Many of the Christians include elements of traditional religions in their rituals* and beliefs.

* **ritual**   religious ceremony that follows a set pattern

The Congo is home to about 300 different ethnic groups of varying sizes. The most important factor in determining a person's ethnic identity is LANGUAGE. The country has more than 200 languages, but four BANTU languages stand out above the others. Used for instruction in most schools, these four languages—Lingala, SWAHILI, Tshiluba, and Kongo—also dominate radio and television broadcasting.

Shared histories and participation in the economy and government play a role in ethnic identity in the Congo today. In practice, ethnicity is very flexible, and people often identify themselves with more than one group. A single national culture does not yet exist, although a common national identity is only now beginning to take shape in the nation's cities, especially Kinshasa. (*See also* **Colonialism in Africa, Global Politics and Africa.**)

Congo River

Congo River

For centuries the Congo River has played a key role in trade, travel, and exploration in equatorial* Africa. The Congo and its many tributaries form the largest system of navigable* waterways in Africa. For local peoples, the river is a vital highway of commerce and communication.

The Congo flows for 2,900 miles in a great curve through the center of Africa. It is the world's second most powerful river (after the Amazon in South America), emptying 10 million gallons of water each second into the Atlantic Ocean. Together with its many tributaries, it drains a vast area that covers most of the nations of Democratic Republic of Congo, Republic of Congo, and the CENTRAL AFRICAN REPUBLIC. It also drains parts of ZAMBIA, ANGOLA, and TANZANIA. Much of the river lies within the *cuvette centrale,* a vast, basinlike depression in the plateau of equatorial Africa. The Congo's main tributaries include the Aruwimi, Ubangi, Lulonga, Tshuapa, Sangha, and Kasai Rivers.

The Congo is called the Lualaba at its source in the savannas* near the southeastern corner of the Democratic Republic of Congo. It flows north over many falls and rapids to Wagenia Falls, not far from the city of Kisangani in the heart of the rain forest. Below Wagenia Falls the river's name changes to Congo. Dotted with countless islands, it follows a lazy curve west and then south through the rain forest. In some places the river is more than 9 miles wide, and during periods of high water it spills over its low banks onto wide floodplains on either side. Below the city of Liranga, the river forms the border between the two Congo nations.

At Tchumbiri, the river leaves the swampy flatlands of the *cuvette centrale* and begins carving a path to the ocean through the Téké Plateau and the Crystal Mountains. It narrows and flows rapidly between steep banks, then widens again to form Malebo Pool, also called Stanley Pool. On either side of the pool stand the two capital cities, KINSHASA (The Democratic Republic of Congo) and BRAZZAVILLE (the Republic of Congo). Between Kinshasa and Matadi, the Congo drops steeply, passing over 32 waterfalls. This section of the river could be the largest source of hydroelectric* power in the world, although little has yet been done to harness that power. For its final 150 miles, from Matadi to the Atlantic coast, the river is navigable by oceangoing ships.

The Congo's waterfalls and rapids kept Europeans out of the central basin during the years of the SLAVE TRADE. So little was known of the river that as late as the 1800s Europeans thought that its mouth might be the mouth of the Niger River, far to the north. The upper Congo was familiar, however, to African fishers and traders, who traveled the river in very long dugout canoes with as many as 60 or 70 paddlers.

France and Belgium sought control of the Congo River while they were establishing their colonies in equatorial Africa. The European scramble to colonize the area was started by Henry Morton STANLEY, the first white explorer to travel most of the river's length. Early colonists transported steamboats piece by piece from the river's estuary* to Stanley Pool. Once assembled, the boats were used to control commerce and impose colonial rule on the central stretch of the Congo. Later, railroads carried people and goods from the coast to the steamboat networks.

After the nations of equatorial Africa achieved independence in the mid-1900s, Africans reclaimed control of the Congo waterway network. At first, African fishermen began to gain power by working on the steamships that traveled the river or by carrying on trade from their own dugout canoes. Those early African traders often had to travel at night to avoid colonial river patrols. Since then, riverboats and the barges they pull have become floating marketplaces, sometimes even described as floating cities. For a large part of equatorial Africa, the Congo River remains the principal route of trade and travel. Local people often call it simply *Ebale* (the river). (*See also* **Congo (Kinshasa)**, **Congo (Brazzaville)**.)

Copts

* **sect** religious group

T he Copts, a Christian sect* in EGYPT, trace their history back almost 2,000 years. They follow customs and beliefs that they adopted long before Islam, the dominant religion in Egypt today, arrived in the region.

According to tradition, Christianity was introduced to Egypt in the A.D. 40s. The city of ALEXANDRIA became a center of Christian scholarship, and the religion spread down the Nile river basin to NUBIA and southeast into ETHIOPIA. In the 200s Saint Antony, an Egyptian Copt, founded a movement to establish monastic communities—religious colonies where Christians could seek spiritual growth. Many Christians from Greece, Rome, Syria, Nubia, and Ethiopia spent time in Coptic monasteries.

Over time, a conflict arose between the church in Rome and the Egyptian church. The church in Rome held that Jesus Christ had two separate natures—divine and human. The Egyptian church—along with certain other eastern churches—claimed instead that Christ had a single, divine nature. This eastern belief came to be known as Monophysite Christianity, from the Greek words for "single nature." In 451 a church council held at Chalcedon (near present-day Istanbul) condemned the monophysite view. As a result, the Egyptian Christians and the other eastern churches split with Rome.

In the 640s the ARABS conquered Egypt and introduced Islam to the region. They began to refer to the Egyptian Christians as "Copts." Under Arab rule, the Copts slowly abandoned the use of their own language (a version of ancient Egyptian) and began to speak Arabic. Many Copts worked in the civil service or ran businesses.

* **discrimination** unfair treatment of a group

* **ritual** religious ceremony that follows a set pattern

Today between 6 and 9 million Copts live in Egypt. Some are farmers and others work in various trades in the cities. Although the Copts' right to practice their religion is guaranteed by Egyptian law, they often face discrimination* from Muslims. The Coptic Church (also known as the Coptic Orthodox Church) runs its own schools as well as a college connected to the Institute of Coptic Studies in CAIRO. Its rituals* are similar in many ways to those of the ETHIOPIAN ORTHODOX CHURCH, which is also sometimes called Coptic. (*See also* **Christianity in Africa, Religion and Ritual.**)

Correia, Mãe Aurélia

Correia, Mãe Aurélia

**Early 1800s
Trader in Guinea-Bissau**

* **artisan** skilled crafts worker

* **commodity** article of trade

Mãe Aurélia Correia was a wealthy and powerful trader in the GUINEA-BISSAU region from the 1820s to the 1840s. Among the many women traders of African or mixed ancestry at the time, Mãe Aurélia was the most successful.

Little information exists about Mãe Aurélia's birth and family because the Portuguese colonial authorities in Guinea-Bissau kept poor records. Her sister (or aunt), Mãe Julia da Silva Cardoso, worked closely with her. They operated trading vessels and maintained many slaves, including sailors and skilled artisans*. As the business grew, the two women accumulated large quantities of gold and silver jewelry and expensive garments, and they lived in European-style houses.

Around 1825 Mãe Aurélia married Caetano José Nozolini, an army officer from CAPE VERDE. It is certain that Nozolini must have had excellent leadership skills and other positive attributes, for Mãe Aurélia would have been very careful to choose a husband that could be of the most help to her in building her business ventures. Together, the couple continued to gather great wealth, dominating the war-torn and untamed Guinea-Bissau region. No other leader in the region could mobilize as many people as Mãe Aurélia could to defend her family's interests. Nozolini's leadership abilities, combined with Mãe Aurélia's shrewd business skill, enabled the couple to dominate trade in slaves and other commodities* along the Geba and Grande rivers and on various nearby islands.

Portuguese colonial officials lacked soldiers and supplies, and they depended on Mãe Aurélia, Nozolini, and other traders to help maintain order in the region. In 1826 Mãe Aurélia and her husband played an important role in putting down a mutiny at the Portuguese fort in Bissau. In 1842 the Portuguese asked for Mãe Aurélia's assistance when the inhabitants of Bissau laid siege to the fort.

When British authorities took notice of the slave trading activities of Mãe Aurélia and Nozolini, the couple claimed the slaves they were shipping to Cape Verde were members of their extended family. During the 1830s, Mãe Aurélia and her husband used slaves to develop peanut plantations on the easily accessible island of Bolama along the coast. The island's location gave the British an opportunity to strike at the two slave traders. In a series of raids on the island, British naval squadrons took hundreds of slaves to freedom in SIERRA LEONE.

A son and three daughters of Mãe Aurélia and Nozolini survived infancy. The son, who was educated in France, took over the family business; two of the daughters married doctors involved in commerce; and the third daughter married a wealthy trader. Through their own ventures, the children maintained the family's prominence in Guinea-Bissau. (*See also* **Slave Trade, Trade.**)

CÔTE D'IVOIRE   See *Ivory Coast.*

Crafts

See
color plate 7,
vol. 3.

* **wattle-and-daub** method of construction that consists of mud or clay laid on a framework of poles

See color
plate 12,
vol. 3.

For centuries Africans have produced handmade items such as cloth, baskets, and pottery to meet the practical needs of everyday life. Such handicrafts are also expressions of their makers' skills and of personal, regional, and cultural styles. Many are produced specifically for sale or for export to markets in other countries.

Basketry. Both men and women make many kinds of baskets and mats out of plant materials such as wood, palm leaves, reeds, grasses, and roots. They decorate their handiwork with patterns of differently colored and textured materials or with leather stitched onto the basketwork. There are two basic basket-making techniques. In plaited basketry, strands of plant fiber are soaked and then twined, woven, or twisted together. In sewn basketry, a thin strip of continuous material—usually grass—is stitched onto itself in a coil. Some baskets made this way are so tightly sewn that they hold liquid.

Baskets serve a wide range of practical purposes. Most are used as containers for serving food, storing items, or carrying goods. Some baskets function as tools, such as traps for fish and animals and strainers for flour or homemade beer. Basketry techniques are applied to other tasks, including fashioning the framework for thatched roofs and wattle-and-daub* walls.

African baskets have decorative and social purposes as well. Hats are often made of basketwork adorned with fiber tufts, feathers, fur, and leather. The traditional beaded crowns of the YORUBA people of Nigeria, for example, have basketry foundations. Groups such as the Chokwe of Angola and Zambia create dance masks of basketry or bark cloth on a wicker frame. Over much of eastern Africa, baskets ornamented with shells, beads, dyed leather, and metal dangles are presented as special gifts. They may also be included among a bride's wedding decorations.

Flat mats, another form of basketry, often serve as ground covering on which to sit or sleep. The nomadic Somali people use mats to roof their temporary shelters. In the Congo region, traditional houses are often walled with rigid mats, patterned in black on a background of natural yellow.

Beads and Jewelry. Africans use beads to adorn their bodies, their furnishings, and their burials. Nigerians had developed a glass bead industry by 1000 B.C., and ancient trade routes circulated beads of bone, stone, ivory, seed, ostrich eggshell, metal, and shell. Cowrie shells from the Indian Ocean were highly valued. Once used as money, they still serve as symbols of wealth in many places.

Western and central Africans traditionally used beads to cover furniture, sculpture, and clothing. Groups in Nigeria and Cameroon fashioned complicated pictures out of tiny colored beads. For many nomadic peoples, beadwork, which could be carried with them, was the main form of visual art. In eastern Africa, beadwork ornaments displayed the wearer's social position through a complex system of color and design. In many regions children wore beads to bring good health and luck.

Crafts

Foreign contact and modern materials have changed the types of beads used in Africa. Glass beads from India were imported into sub-Saharan* Africa more than 1,000 years ago. By the late 1800s, colored glass beads manufactured in Europe were being shipped by the ton to Africa, where they served as trade goods. Despite the widespread use of these imported beads, native African bead-making techniques survived. However, craftspeople began using new materials in their work. For example, MAASAI groups have recently incorporated blue plastic pen caps into their beadwork in place of traditional feather quill pens. Today, people produce beads and other kinds of jewelry from coins, buttons, wire, and discarded aluminum and plastic, working these materials into their traditional styles.

African artists and craftspeople also make metal ornaments and jewelry. Many parts of western Africa have a long history of producing fine gold jewelry. The country that is now Ghana was formally named the Gold Coast. The name came from the fact that the local ASANTE kings wore so many gold necklaces, bracelets, crowns, rings, and anklets. In Ancient Egypt, craftspeople used gold to create spectacular jewelry, burial items, vessels, and furniture for their kings, the PHARAOHS. The TUAREG people of northeastern Africa specialize in making silver jewelry. Today many Africans produce jewelry and beadwork to sell to tourists.

Pottery. Pottery is among Africa's oldest crafts. Archaeologists have discovered evidence that people in the Sahara desert were making pottery more than 10,000 years ago. Deposits of clay are found throughout the continent. This versatile material is used to make containers for cooking, storing, and measuring foodstuffs, as well as for jewelry, furniture, coffins, toys, beehives, musical instruments, household utensils, and tiles. Even broken pottery has value in Africa—as game pieces, floor tiles, and raw material for making new pottery.

Traditionally, each piece of African pottery was made by hand. Potters, some of whom were traveling craftspeople, developed a variety of techniques that could produce sturdy pottery quickly and inexpensively. They baked it over open bonfires, in fire pits, or in simple furnaces called kilns. Although these methods remain in use, some African manufacturers now make pottery by pressing or pouring clay into molds for mass production.

Africans often decorate their pottery with texture. They carve or raise patterns and designs on the surface of the clay. Craftspeople in Islamic cultures, especially in North Africa, paint clay tiles with elaborate geometric patterns and designs inspired by Arabic script. These are generally used to decorate mosques* and Muslim religious schools.

Africans tend to draw a line between clay sculpture and functional pottery vessels. Traditionally, in much of the continent, sculpture is produced by men and the pottery by women. This division of labor came in part from a belief that making clay images of people or animals was considered similar to a woman's ability to have children. However, in many cultures, powerful women and women beyond childbearing age may create figurines.

African pottery vessels sometimes carry meanings beyond their everyday functions. The style of a pot may reflect a person's position in soci-

See color plate 8, vol. 4.

People in various parts of Africa create jewelry and other ornaments from colorful beads. This Zulu woman of South Africa is stringing glass beads on cotton thread.

See color plate 9, vol. 3.

See color plate 8, vol. 3.

Raffia Artists

Textiles in the Congo region and other parts of central Africa were traditionally made of raffia. Today the finest raffia weavers come from the former central African kingdom of Kuba. Men weave the raffia cloth in small rectangles. Women decorate these pieces with embroidery or by cutting patterns into the fabric surface. One garment of the region is the ntshak, a long skirt made of many rectangles sewn together. The ntshak is decorated by a group of relatives, either men or women, depending on whether it is to be worn by a man or a woman. The resulting garment belongs to the 6 or 12 people who helped create it.

* **raffia** type of palm used for weaving and basketry

ety. A widow, a married man, and a child might each be expected to use a pitcher of a different shape. A flour jar marking a tomb may indicate that a fertile mother is buried within. Pottery vessels may also act as containers of spiritual forces. A dead woman's spirit could be thought to inhabit the pot that she used for years to haul water.

Textiles. Textiles are cloths woven of threads. In Africa, they have great cultural as well as practical significance. People offer textiles as gifts on important social occasions and often bury them with the dead. Textiles may indicate the wearer's importance in the community. Their patterns or color combinations sometimes carry symbolic messages. In some parts of Africa, cloth was once used as money. Textiles remain an important item in the economy, especially in West Africa, where more workers are engaged in the production and trade of cloth than in any other craft profession.

Barkcloth, traditionally used throughout much of central and eastern Africa, is not a true textile. It is pounded from the bark of the *ficu* tree. However, Africans have long used barkcloth in the same way they use textiles. Textile weaving and the production of barkcloth rarely occur in the same area.

African textile makers have traditionally used at least five types of hand-operated looms to weave their cloth. Some types are worked on only by men, others by women. All of these looms produce long, narrow strips of material, ranging from less than an inch to about 10 inches in width. When sewn together, the strips make rectangular cloths. Today African textiles are often manufactured on automatic looms in factories.

Africans produce many distinctive cloths woven from cotton, wool, wild silk, and raffia* fibers. Egyptian weavers have been making fine linen for over 1,600 years. The FULANI people of Mali are known for their *kaasa* covers, a tightly woven wool fabric that offers protection against cold and insects. The weavers of southern Ghana and Togo are famous for their *kente* cloth, large, richly colored textiles worn by men at important ceremonies. The most valuable of these are made of silk. BERBER women produce colorful wool rugs woven in unique geometric designs. Manufactured fibers such as rayon play an important part in the modern textile trade of Africa.

Carving. African carvers—usually men—produce sculpture and other art works, such as masks. They also create a wide range of everyday items, including stools, axe handles, dugout boats, headrests, containers for food and liquid, and spoons. Such items are generally made of wood. Artworks and high-quality handicrafts may be adorned with carved patterns and figures of people or animals. Some carvers decorate their woodwork with a technique called *pyrogravure,* which involves blackening the wood with a hot iron blade.

The carving of very simple items, such as an axe handle, may require no special ability. Often the local blacksmith combines the skills of ironworking and woodworking and will fit a handle to the metal tool he has made. On a higher level, there may be one man in an area who is widely known for his craftsmanship. He might spend most of his time carv-

Crafts

Many African artisans specialize in creating useful items. The Sudanese women shown here are weaving baskets from natural materials.

ing. In some North African societies, noblemen paid skilled carvers to create highly decorated wooden objects, from delicate spoons to carved camel saddles.

Not all carving is done in wood. African artists have a long tradition of working with ivory (from hippopotamus and elephant tusks), bone, and horn. In Cameroon and the Congo region, carvers craft buffalo horn into ceremonial drinking vessels. Some groups have carved figures and pipes from soapstone, and in Egypt, great temples still display detailed images and hieroglyphics* cut into the stone by ancient craftspeople. (*See also* **Art, Body Adornment and Clothing**.)

* **hieroglyphics** ancient system of writing based on pictorial characters

Creoles

In Africa, the term *Creole* refers to any people with some mix of African and non-African racial or cultural heritage. Creole populations can be found on most African islands and along many of the continent's coasts, areas where Africans first mingled with Europeans and Arabs. From these contacts, six major Creole types emerged: Portuguese, black American, French, Dutch, British, and Arab.

Portuguese, Black American, British, and French Creoles. Portuguese Creoles were the first of the European Creoles. They emerged during the late 1400s when the Portuguese traded and settled along the west and east coasts of Africa. Creoles living in the islands of CAPE VERDE are offspring of Europeans and enslaved Africans from the mainland. They speak either Portuguese or a Creole language based on Portuguese. Creoles who live near the coast of ANGOLA trace their origin to mestizo*, Brazilian, and African ancestors. They have considerable influence on the country's affairs. Creoles in the area of MOZAMBIQUE disappeared during a series of wars between 1830 and 1911.

Black American Creoles are found in SIERRA LEONE, LIBERIA, and in scattered communities along the coast of GHANA. They are descendants of liberated slaves and, in Liberia, of free black Americans from the southern United States. The Creoles of Sierra Leone are descended from freed Africans who lived in Britain, Jamaica, and Nova Scotia.

The islands of MAURITIUS and SEYCHELLES as well as the French territory of RÉUNION are home to most of Africa's French Creoles. They are the descendants of French settlers and slaves brought from east Africa and MADAGASCAR in the 1700s. They speak a French-based Creole language.

Dutch and British Creoles. More than 3 million Dutch Creoles, known as Coloureds or CAPE COLOURED PEOPLE, live in SOUTH AFRICA. There are also small populations in NAMIBIA and other southern African countries. They emerged during the 1600s and 1700s through a mixture of individuals of European and KHOISAN origin with Asians from Malaysia, Sri Lanka, and India, and enslaved Africans from Madagascar and southern Africa. Most are Christian, although there is a small Muslim minority known as Cape Malays. The vast majority of those living in South Africa speak Afrikaans, a Dutch-based language.

A few thousand British Creoles, known as Fernandinos, live in the island of Bioko in EQUATORIAL GUINEA. They are descendants of liberated slaves from Sierra Leone and Cuba who intermarried with settlers from CAMEROON, Ghana, Sierra Leone, and NIGERIA during British colonial rule. Their Creole offspring became cocoa planters.

Common Features of Creole Culture. Creole groups today have more in common with one another than they have with any African ethnic groups. On African islands, Creole languages predominate; on the mainland, Creole languages are national languages in Guinea-Bissau, Sierra Leone, Liberia, and South Africa. In island societies, Creoles occupy a wide range of positions, from plantation workers to members of the wealthy and powerful upper class. On the coast of mainland Africa, Creoles were often given economic and political opportuni-

* **mestizo** person of mixed European and Native American ancestry

185

ties by foreign rulers. They developed a strong sense of identity and formed their own political parties. When African nations were struggling for independence in the mid-1900s, many Creoles supported colonial rule. Some Creoles fought for independence and afterward held positions of power. However, in most countries, Creoles gradually lost their political power to inland ethnic groups that were considered more African.

The Creole community of Africa has grown in several ways. On the islands, elements of Creole culture, including language and music, came to dominate popular culture. In Creole cities on the mainland, some non-Creoles tried to become part of Creole society, which often enjoyed special status. Most people seeking to join the Creole community converted to Christianity, the religion shared by nearly all Creoles except for Comoran Creoles and Cape Malays. (*See also* **Ethnic Groups**.)

CRIME

See *Laws and Legal Systems.*

Crowther, Samuel Ajayi

ca. 1806–1891
Anglican bishop

* **Anglican** Church of England

Samuel Ajayi Crowther was an educated traveler, translator, and missionary who was named the first African bishop in the Anglican* Church. Born in what is now Nigeria, Crowther was captured and sold into slavery at the age of 12. A British antislavery ship rescued him at sea, however, and took him to Freetown, Sierra Leone. There he was baptized and educated by the Christian Missionary Society (CMS). Crowther soon began to study and to preach in the Yoruba language, and in 1843 he became a minister in the Anglican Church. He served as a pioneering member of CMS Yoruba missions and helped translate the Bible into Yoruba. In 1857 Crowther became leader of the Niger Mission and opened five new mission stations, including one for the Niger Delta.

In 1864 the Anglican Church named Crowther Bishop of Western Equatorial Africa with responsibility for missions in Liberia, Rio Pongas, and other places. In 1890, however, European missionaries critical of Crowther's administration of the Niger Mission forced him to resign. Before his death a year later, Crowther helped plan the reorganization of the Niger Delta Mission, and his son later became its pastor.

DA GAMA, VASCO

See *Gama, Vasco da.*

DAHOMEY

See *Bénin.*

Dakar

* **cash crop** crop grown primarily for sale rather than for local consumption

Dakar, the capital and largest city in SENEGAL, is one of the most important ports of West Africa. The Portuguese landed near the site of modern Dakar in 1444, and several European powers fought over the region until the French gained control in the mid-1600s. The area was originally valued as a source for slaves. After the banning of SLAVERY in 1815, however, the French forced the local population to grow peanuts as a cash crop*.

For many years Dakar served as the capital of the colony of FRENCH WEST AFRICA. In 1887 some of the city's inhabitants were granted French citizenship, including the right to vote and to participate in local government as well as representation in the parliament in Paris.

During World War II Dakar was first occupied by the pro-German Vichy French government, but American forces captured the city in 1942. Dakar remained the political center of Senegal after the country gained its independence in 1960. Today this city of about 1.7 million people is home to the University of Dakar, an art museum, and a center for nutritional research. It boasts a thriving port, manufacturing industry, and Senegal's only international airport. Dakar is also a popular tourist spot. Even so economic growth has stalled and the city is heavily dependent on foreign aid.

Dance

* **hierarchical** referring to a society or institution divided into groups with higher and lower levels

Through dance, African people celebrate, worship, educate, and express social organization. Styles vary greatly from culture to culture, but most African dance shares some common features. In particular, it emphasizes rhythm. Elements of traditional dance and music often blend with contemporary or foreign styles to create new kinds of African dance.

Purposes of Dancing. In all African cultures, dance is an expression of social structure. People of the same status, age, or occupation usually perform together. In their dances, these groups demonstrate behavior that is considered appropriate to their place in the community and to the occasion. Dance unites them and reinforces their identities. For example, among the TUAREG of northeastern Africa, each social class has its own style of dance and music and even its own musical instruments.

In traditional societies with hierarchical* organizations, dance can be an expression of leadership. A ruler is expected to proclaim his authority in formal dances. If he fails to meet the required standard of performance, his subjects may lose some respect for him. A ruler's wives and lesser chiefs also have their own specific forms of dance to show their position in society. Followers may pledge loyalty and honor their leaders through still other dances. One example of a royal dance is that

187

Dance

* **deity**   god or goddess

* **rite**   ceremony or formal procedure

* **ritual**   religious ceremony that follows a set pattern

* **sub-Saharan**   referring to Africa south of the Sahara desert

of the ASANTE kings of Ghana, who wave ceremonial swords while dancing. Pointing the swords toward the sky symbolizes the kings' dependence on the gods and the ancestors. Pointing the swords toward the earth represents the king's ownership of the land.

For many traditional African religious leaders, dance is a vital part of their role. Priests and priestesses use movement to describe the gods they serve. In Nigeria, YORUBA priests who serve the thunder god Shango show his wrathful nature with fast arm motions that represent lightning. They roll their shoulders and stamp their feet to indicate thunder. The leaders of many women's religious societies in western Africa use dance as therapy. They employ songs and dances to cure women of various disorders.

Masquerade dancers, who represent spiritual beings, play a central role in many religious societies. Often the masquerade dancer's personal identity is a closely guarded secret. The dancer performs completely covered by cloth and wearing a metal or wooden mask that symbolizes a particular deity* or spirit. Before performing special rites*, dancers may train for many years beginning at an early age.

In societies that are organized into sets, or groups, by age, individuals pass through many age-grades in their lifetime. The dances of each age-grade promote qualities that the society admires in people of that age. The dances of elders are usually sedate and dignified, while those of younger men and women may show off such characteristics as strength, endurance, and beauty.

Dance is an important form of education in traditional African societies. The repeated patterns of dances teach young children physical coordination and control. Dance can also introduce children to the community's social customs and standards of behavior. Children may form their own dance and masquerade groups or join adults at the end of a dance line.

Features of African Dance.   In North Africa, some dance forms have sprung from the region's Arab and Islamic heritage. One example is the whirling dance of the Sufi Muslims known as dervishes. In their rituals*, the dervishes enter a religious trance and dance wildly, spinning and twirling around. Other traditional North African dances share the emphasis on rhythm that is found throughout sub-Saharan* Africa. The BERBERS of Morocco dance to the beat of drummers who assemble around a bonfire. The dancers form two lines. Individuals in one line call out a phrase or line, and someone in the opposite line responds. As the calling continues, the dancers move as one—shuffling, bending back and forth at the waist, and raising and lowering their arms. In some Berber groups, men and women mix; in others, the women form their own line.

Rhythm is the central element in sub-Saharan dance. Music and dance are usually inseparable. Normally musicians lead the dancers, using drums, rattles, and other percussion instruments to sound a beat for the dancers to follow. But in some cultures the dancer may take over, challenging the musicians to follow his or her rhythm. Sometimes dancers wear leg or ankle rattles that emphasize the rhythm of their movements. In Western cultures, people focus on the shapes created by

Funerals in Africa often include ceremonial music and dances. Here, a group of Mossi people participate in a funeral dance in Ivory Coast.

See color plate 2, vol. 1.

a dancer's body. African audiences also judge a dancer's skill by his or her ability to follow rhythms.

Styles of African dance range from the simple to the acrobatic. The Kambari people of Nigeria move in a circle around their drummers, sliding one foot forward while the other stamps a repetitive beat. The Ndau of southern Africa perform a more energetic war dance on the theme of "stamping the feet in pain." The style of the dance changes rapidly as accelerating drumbeats encourage the powerful dancers to explode into vigorous new forms of expression.

Dance is a group activity. In addition to age-sets and occupational groups, such as hunters, that perform together, dance groups or clubs are common in Africa. These allow both sexes and various ages to dance together to perfect their skill. Once a dance club has acquired a reputation for excellence, it is invited to perform at major social events, such as marriages or funerals, or to entertain chiefs and important visitors. In some dance groups, the members follow a leader and perform rehearsed movements together, with little or no opportunity for individual expression. Other groups allow each dancer to develop a personal style or to step forward from the group for a solo performance.

Although it is a collective effort, African dancing can be highly competitive, even aggressive. Many traditional dance forms encourage individual dancers or groups to try to outdo each other. In the early 1900s, some wealthy urban Africans learned the formal steps of Western-style

Dance

dances and competed in ballroom dancing championships modeled on those of the United States and other Western countries. With much emphasis on fine clothes, these competitions showed the enduring power of dance to establish a person's position in society.

Dance and Society. Dance reflects the social order, and as African society changes, so does its dance. The Dogon of Mali, for example, have long performed dances in honor of their ancestors in which they carry and manipulate carved wooden masks. In the 1930s foreign promoters discovered their outstanding dancing and took Dogon dance groups to Paris and the United States. The Dogon dancers learned elements of modern choreography*. They also modified their costumes and modernized their masks for foreign audiences. After returning to Mali, they continued to perform traditional ritual dances in their home territories, but their choreographed shows gained popularity with both local and foreign audiences.

* **choreography** designing or arranging a dance

Dance is not always reserved for important social functions. It is also the most popular form of recreation in sub-Saharan Africa. Even on informal occasions, however, Africans usually do not dance simply for individual expression. They often perform for the admiration and attention of others.

Informal African social dance is continually developing into new styles either invented by talented individuals or drawn from foreign influences. In the 1960s a recreational dance called highlife became popular in West African cities. It originated in Ghana, where musicians were playing Western instruments such as saxophones and guitars in open-air cafes. Nigerian musicians began following the same lively style, using local instruments, and dancers adapted their movements to the new sound. Various styles emerged. In some African countries, music and dance took on the flavor of Latin rhythms such as the cha-cha. The people of the Congo excelled at jazz, which in turn gave rise to its own dance forms. Such examples show that although African dance draws on deep and honored traditions, it is an ever-changing expression of life as it is lived today. (*See also* **Masks and Masquerades, Music and Song, Musical Instruments, Religion and Ritual.**)

Dar es Salaam

Dar es Salaam (which means "haven of peace" in Arabic) is the capital and largest city in TANZANIA. In the late 1990s, its population was about 1.5 million. Arabs from Southern Arabia first established fishing villages in the area during the A.D. 1600s, but the city did not really grow until Sultan Sayyid Majid of ZANZIBAR built a palace there in the 1860s.

In the 1890s Dar es Salaam became the capital of the newly established colony of German East Africa. The Germans constructed new buildings and a rail line heading northwest, then they lost the region to Britain during World War I. Renamed Tanganyika, the colony achieved independence in 1961. Three years later it joined with Zanzibar to form the United Republic of Tanzania. In the 1970s the city of Dodoma was proposed as a new capital, but the cost of relocation was too great and the government remained in Dar es Salaam.

Located in a protected harbor along Tanzania's coast, Dar es Salaam has the national university, many foreign embassies, and a lively night life. In the city center is the main market, Kariakoo, built on the site of a former British military camp. On the outskirts, industrial areas have grown up along the rail lines and near the harbor. (*See also* **Colonialism in Africa.**)

Death, Mourning, and Ancestors

* **ritual** ceremony that follows a set pattern

* **funerary** relating to death, burial, or funerals

* **sub-Saharan** referring to Africa south of the Sahara desert

"People who die are not buried in a field, they are buried in the heart," goes a saying of the central African nation of RWANDA. Death of course is more than the physical fact of a life's end. It also brings emotional and social change to families and communities. Africans mark those changes with rituals* that draw on traditional beliefs and customs, as well as on Muslim and Christian practices. These funerary* customs provide ways for people to dispose of their dead, express their grief, and honor the memory of those who have died.

For Muslims in North Africa and other regions in Africa, Islamic writings and beliefs govern burial customs and ideas about the afterlife. In sub-Saharan* Africa, traditions about death and mourning vary a great deal. Across much of that region, death is seen as the act of becoming an ancestor, and funerary practices are related to the important role ancestors play in the lives of those they left behind.

DEATH AND BURIAL

In all cultures, burial customs are a way of separating the dead person from the living. They may also fulfill religious requirements or expectations. In addition, funerals and obituaries generally serve social functions, giving families and communities a public opportunity to display their social position and relationships.

Funerary Practices in Sub-Saharan Africa. Burial customs in sub-Saharan Africa reflect differences in the cultures and histories of various communities. Both European colonial influence and modernization have played a role in shaping these practices.

The Lugbara people of northwestern UGANDA live in densely populated settlements, where death occurs daily and is witnessed—or at least known of—by many. Although death is familiar, the Lugbara give it great importance. Their funeral rituals are longer and more elaborate than ceremonies for birth, coming of age, or marriage. Large numbers of people attend funerals, not just the relatives of the deceased.

In contrast, the Mbeere people of KENYA have traditionally lived in small, roving, widely separated groups. They left their dead in the wild with little ceremony. In the 1930s the British, who controlled Kenya, required burial of the dead, and 30 years later they introduced individual land ownership. Responding to these changes, the Mbeere developed elaborate funeral ceremonies that became indications of property

191

Death, Mourning, and Ancestors

* **deity**   god or goddess

* **clergy**   ministers, priests, or other religious officials

ownership as well as tributes to Mbeere leaders and to the strength of their followers.

Deaths and funerals often involve issues of identity in Africa, where many people follow more than one religious tradition and have ties to more than one ethnic group. In one such case, the death of a wealthy man in GHANA sparked a rivalry between two towns to which the deceased belonged by kinship, marriage, and political and economic ties. The rivalry was complicated by the dead man's links with both the Presbyterian church and the non-Christian deity* of his father. When the Presbyterians buried him and claimed him as one of their own, the question of the dead man's hometown and primary kin was decided in favor of the town with the Presbyterian connection. Yet funeral arrangements can also serve to acknowledge more than one identity. Some Africans favor funeral services led by several clergy* together.

The dead in sub-Saharan Africa are usually buried, typically after being washed and sometimes shaved. Those able to preserve the body of the deceased may do so for several days to allow people to gather for the funeral. The form of the funeral may depend on the dead person's age, gender, ethnic group, class, or religion. Status within the community and type of death also affect the funeral. Sudden and untimely deaths are considered "bad," and someone whose life ends in such fashion may receive no funeral at all. Long life, community service, and wealth, however, are celebrated with large and elaborate funerals. In all cases, death is associated with pollution, and at the end of the funeral guests are expected to cleanse themselves. Young children and pregnant women, thought to be especially likely to be tainted by death, are often forbidden to attend funerals.

In NIGERIA, Ghana, BÉNIN, BOTSWANA, and elsewhere, details about the deceased and funerals usually appear in obituaries. Wealthy people place these death notices in newspapers and on radio and television to draw attention to the coming funerals. Poor folk—and Muslims, who must bury their dead quickly—rely mainly on radio announcements. Obituaries, as well as memorial notices that relatives place in the media months or years after a death, give survivors a chance to celebrate their position in society by dwelling on the career and achievements of the deceased. Some groups create other kinds of memorials to the dead, such as the carved wooden posts made by the Mahafaly of MADAGASCAR and the Giryama of Kenya.

Some traditional African ideas about the soul's life after death focus on journeys or judgments. The Dogon of MALI and the YORUBA of Nigeria, among others, believe that the dead must undertake a long and difficult trip to distant spirit lands. Sometimes the highest deity makes a final judgment about the character of the deceased. While the spirit lands and afterlife are hidden from the living, the dead, in their role as ancestors, remain very much a part of living communities.

Islamic Traditions. Muslims never cremate, or burn, their dead. They bury them. Tradition calls for the burial to take place very soon after death. Whenever possible, someone who dies during the day is buried before sunset; a person who dies at night is buried in the morn-

The Mahafaly of Madagascar bury their dead in remote locations in the countryside. Their box-like tombs are often decorated with geometric forms and carved wooden sculptures.

ing. After being washed, the body is wrapped in a white cloth and buried with its face turned toward Mecca, the Islamic holy city in Saudi Arabia.

Muslim funeral and mourning customs vary. Among the Berbers of Morocco, only men attend funerals, and local schoolmasters or prayer leaders read from the Qur'an, the Islamic holy book. In many Berber groups, relatives of the deceased hold a feast for those who attended the funeral some days or weeks later.

Islamic beliefs about the fate of the soul after death are based on the Qur'an and the Kitab al-run (Book of the Soul). According to these texts, the Angel of Death sits at the head of a dying person and directs the soul toward either the anger or the mercy of God, depending on whether the person has lived a wicked or a good life. Two other angels record the deeds of the deceased. Souls judged to be good, as well as the souls of all Muslims who die in a jihad, or holy war, go to a garden paradise. Wicked souls go to a hell of eternal punishment.

THE ROLE OF THE ANCESTORS

Explorers and scholars of the 1800s described African beliefs and customs about the dead as ancestor worship. More recent study has shown that the relationship between the living and their ancestors varies

Death, Mourning, and Ancestors

among African peoples but is always complex. Some scholars describe such relationships as respect rather than worship. This view is rooted in the idea that families and communities are shaped by those who have gone before. The dead continue to have meaning and authority, as long as the living remember and honor them. In turn, the living are judged by how well and faithfully they perform their duties to their ancestors.

Ancestors in Everyday Life. The Lugbara of central Africa believe that their elaborate and very public funerals are an essential part of a transformation that begins with death: the transformation of the deceased into a spirit whose name will be remembered by descendants. Rituals for the dead may extend over a period of years. The Lugbara plant fig trees at the graves of important elders and may put small stone slabs together to form "houses" honoring the dead. The trees and stones are shrines where people may consult their ancestors. In time, the most senior ancestors lose their ties to a specific location and are considered part of the creator deity.

Shrines, family stories, and genealogies* make ancestors a familiar presence in everyday life throughout much of sub-Saharan Africa. The living interact with the dead in various places and ways. Inherited property, called "the tears of the dead" in ZIMBABWE, represents a link with ancestors. The Nzima people of Ghana regard long-term projects such as orchards and plantations as the work of the dead continuing across generations. Children are named for ancestors, and sometimes the spirits of ancestors are thought to be reborn in the young.

African Muslims honor their ancestors with rituals. Some people perform a ceremony each year that is believed to open the passage between the living and the dead. In exchange for the prayers of the living, the dead return blessings.

Not every dead person is honored as an ancestor—someone whose identity contributes to the social position of descendants. There is ranking among the dead just as among the living. Unmarried or childless individuals, the very poor, orphans, former slaves, criminals, those who commit suicide, and people who died "bad" deaths or from certain "bad" diseases such as leprosy are unlikely to be remembered as ancestors. Someone who has not buried a parent "well" will be regarded as foolish or useless and will probably be forgotten also.

Ancestors and beliefs about them appear in many expressions of African cultures. Some West African stories, for example, feature a type of wayward or unruly spirit who keeps appearing as a newborn child only to die back again into the spirit world. Such beliefs are not limited to literature. Nigerian author Chinua ACHEBE began writing about this spirit after hearing a 16-year-old girl speak of her experiences. He described the pain and bewilderment she felt at being treated as a living person who could disappear into the spirit world at any moment.

Ancestors and Politics. At various times and places in African history, death and ancestry have become political tools. One of the most powerful ways to take away a group's place in society—short of enslavement—is to limit the ability of its members to carry out funeral and

* **genealogy** family history; record of ancestry

See color plate 4, vol. 3.

194

mourning rituals. African governments and societies have done this by enforcing different codes of burial for different classes of people.

In some societies, "proper" burials may be priced so high that poor people cannot afford them. Stripped of these important ties to the rest of the community and to other generations, the poor are seen as having neither past nor future. Africans have responded to this situation by forming burial societies, which date from the time when they began moving into cities in the early 1900s. Members of these societies pool their resources and contributions to provide each other with "proper" burials that meet the standards of their cultures.

Some African political movements in the 1800s and 1900s called upon ancestral figures. They were said to have inspired many prophets or leaders of uprisings or crusades against colonial rule. In the 1850s, for example, a young XHOSA woman named NONGQAWUSE caused some commotion in SOUTH AFRICA. Claiming to speak for the ancestors of her people, she ordered the Xhosa to sacrifice all their cattle as a way to end their quarrels and become strong again. They followed her advice and became very poor.

Burial has also become a political issue in struggles over the corpses of well-known people. One such struggle took place in Uganda in the 1970s. Seeking to win the favor of the country's Ganda people, General Idi AMIN DADA brought the corpse of their former ruler back from Great Britain, where he had died. Amin then staged a public viewing of the body and a large state funeral. However, when the ruler's heir tried to strengthen his own claim to office by burying the body in the royal tomb of the Ganda, Amin Dada dismissed the action as a meaningless ritual. Of course, the action was not meaningless. It was an illustration of the significance that death, mourning, and ancestry hold for many Africans. (*See also* **Ethnic Groups and Identity, Islam in Africa, Kinship, Religion and Ritual, Spirit Possession.**)

De Klerk, Frederik Willem

1936–
South African political leader

Frederik Willem De Klerk served as president of SOUTH AFRICA from 1989 to 1994. He was the driving force behind government efforts to end the country's official system of race discrimination known as APARTHEID. De Klerk was raised in a political environment. His father was a cabinet minister who served as president of South Africa's senate. After graduating from university, De Klerk became an attorney and was active in the National Party. In the early 1970s he was elected to Parliament twice, and later he held several cabinet posts in the national government.

Early in his political career De Klerk supported traditional policies that limited the rights and freedoms of blacks in South Africa. However, he gradually changed his political views, and as president he introduced a new approach to dealing with the country's racial conflicts. Instead of consulting the military on political matters as previous leaders had done, he sought advice from civilians. He also allowed peaceful demonstrations by opponents of apartheid.

See color
plate 11,
vol. 1.

Soon after his election as president, De Klerk released eight members of the outlawed African National Congress (ANC) from prison. Over the next few months he began talks with the ANC, the South African Communist Party, and other political groups about the future of South Africa. One of his most important moves was to release Nelson MANDELA, who had spent more than 20 years in prison for opposing the apartheid regime. In the early 1990s, De Klerk represented the existing government at the Convention for a Democratic South Africa, a meeting that laid the groundwork for a postapartheid state. After stepping down as president in 1994, he took a position in the government of national unity that oversaw the country's transition to full democracy.

De Klerk boldly pushed through reforms leading to a new political order in South Africa in which the opportunities available to citizens would no longer be determined by their race. He did so even though he knew that he and his party would lose their immense political power as a result of his efforts. For his work in helping to end apartheid and grant full civil rights to South Africa's black majority, De Klerk shared the 1993 Nobel Peace Prize with Nelson Mandela.

Deserts and Drought

* **sub-Saharan** referring to Africa south of the Sahara desert

See color
plate 15,
vol. 2.

Africa contains two desert regions, the SAHARA DESERT in the north and the Namib-Kalahari region in the southwest. Traditionally, very few people have lived in Africa's deserts. However, some groups inhabit the semiarid lands bordering deserts—areas that are somewhat wetter than the desert. The well-being of these people depends on rainfall, which varies greatly from year to year.

With an area of about 3.3 million square miles, the Sahara is the world's largest desert. Its extreme dryness (less than about 5 inches of rainfall per year) has long made it a barrier between the Mediterranean world and sub-Saharan* Africa. Nevertheless, through the ages nomads and traders have crossed this formidable desert. Most of the Sahara consists of rock or gravel plains, with several large mountain masses. About 20 percent of the desert is covered by seas of loose sand, called ergs, that form "living" dunes. Moved and shaped by wind, these dunes reach heights of more than 500 feet.

The SAHEL, a semiarid region along the southern border of the Sahara, contains large areas of ancient ergs with "dead" dunes that are held firmly in place by vegetation. The Sahel generally receives from 4 to 8 inches of rainfall annually.

The Namib is Africa's only true desert south of the equator. It stretches along the Atlantic coast for 1,240 miles in a long narrow band. The driest part of the desert, by the coast, receives less than half an inch of rain per year, though moisture from fog and humidity supports some plant and animal life. To the east lies the KALAHARI DESERT, a vast and featureless red sand plain that is really a semiarid region rather than a desert.

Before Europeans took over the continent, Africans had learned to cope with the climate of deserts and semiarid regions. Small, nomadic populations inhabited many dry areas. European colonial rule brought

Low vegetation and rocky soil cover this desert region in Niger.

fixed national borders, which made it difficult for nomads to travel freely.

Since the mid-1900s, as African populations have grown, many people have moved to crowded urban centers. With the best agricultural land already occupied, others have migrated to drier and less fertile areas, such as the Sahel. This population movement has caused more Africans to face the hardships of drought and desertification—the spread or creation of a desertlike landscape.

Drought is a prolonged period of reduced rainfall or of altered rainfall patterns, as when the rain falls at the wrong time of year for local crops. In modern times the western Sahel has seen three major drought periods: 1910–1914, 1941–1943, and 1968–1985. Devastating droughts have also occurred in southern, eastern, and northeastern Africa. Some of these have led to severe food shortages and famines, effects that worsen as Africa's population continues to increase.

Drought also contributes to the problem of desertification. Sometimes climate changes cause an existing desert to expand. Other times, land takes on the properties of a desert when the soil becomes less fertile or begins to erode rapidly. Human activities, such as cutting trees or plowing up natural vegetation that holds soil in place, can also lead to desertification. The process has been most noticeable in the West African Sahel, especially in the years following the drought that began in 1968. (*See also* **Climate, Ecosystems.**)

Development, Economic and Social

In general, development refers to a process by which countries use their natural and human resources to improve the economy and the lives of their people. Many experts also study development in terms of its outcome—the results that are achieved through economic, political, and social programs. A complex concept, development includes economic measures such as income and economic production, political measures such as civil rights and freedoms, and social measures such as literacy and public health. In terms of development, Africa lags dramatically behind most of the world.

THE CHALLENGE OF DEVELOPMENT

Development is not simply a matter of building factories, improving farmland, or investing in new technology. It also involves providing opportunities for all citizens to participate in economic and political activities and to benefit from them. This aspect of development has presented particular challenges to many African nations over the past 40 years.

Trends in African Development. During the colonial period, European powers carried out various improvement projects in their African territories. They built roads, railroads, and airports, expanded cities and ports, and founded schools. In the years immediately following independence, most African nations modeled themselves after their former colonial masters. Economically, this meant building an industrial society that could produce the kind of material wealth enjoyed by Europe and the United States. Government was seen as the institution best able to carry out these tasks, and development activities were centralized within African national governments.

Most African nations at this time began large-scale projects designed to stimulate certain sectors* of the economy, such as mining or manufacturing. Government experts decided what needed to be done and how to do it. The general population had little involvement with the planning or execution of development projects. By the mid-1960s, however, it had become clear that this approach to development was not working. Wealthy and educated people tended to benefit from development projects, while the majority of the population did not.

* **sector**   part; subdivision of society

The Misery Index

Every year the United Nations prepares a report that measures growth in every nation by examining a wide range of social and economic factors. Based on this report, the United Nations then publishes a "misery index," listing the world's poorest and most disadvantaged nations. For the year 2000, 30 of the 35 nations at the bottom of the index were in sub-Saharan Africa. The 10 worst-off countries were all in Africa, led by Sierra Leone, which has suffered from ongoing civil war. Stressing that political freedom is critical for achieving economic progress, the UN report notes that a number of nations at the bottom of the list—including Burundi, Chad, and Niger—are military dictatorships.

* **nationalize** to bring land, industries, or public works under state control or ownership

* **infrastructure** basic framework of a society and its economy, which includes roads, bridges, port facilities, airports, and other public works

In the next phase of development, African nations began to emphasize the redistribution of resources. The aim was to make vital resources, such as land and access to technology, more widely available. Lower-level officials were given greater freedom to make decisions and carry out policies. Projects designed and supervised by central government planners gave way to programs adapted to local needs and priorities.

During the 1970s, Western economists identified government as the main obstacle to effective development. They said governments were trying to do too much, growing too large, and creating too many regulations. Many nations introduced reforms that reduced the size of their governments, cut social services, sold off nationalized* industries, and eliminated policies that protected local businesses against foreign competition. Such actions helped stabilize currencies and increase market efficiency, but they also led to cuts in social services and funds invested in the country's infrastructure*. In many African nations, the level of development actually decreased during this time.

Since the 1980s, economists have placed greater emphasis on the role of the individual in development. Local programs created and run by individuals, families, and community groups are now seen as powerful sources of change. In addition, international agencies and nations that have lent money to African states for development have placed increasing pressure on African governments to change the way they operate. One thing they demanded was the establishment of more democratic forms of government. In recent years, more open government has been seen as the key to development in Africa.

Models of Development. African nations have several models of development that they can follow. Some favor a system of Western capitalism—with the marketplace determining what goods and services are needed and private businesses providing those goods and services. Other nations have adopted a system of socialism—with the government setting priorities and creating state-run institutions to achieve its goals.

So far no single model of development has proved best for all countries at all times. Because many African nations are heavily in debt to other countries and to international lending institutions, those lenders have a good deal of influence on which models the borrower nations adopt.

An important issue facing African nations is whether to try to be self-sufficient and produce all needed goods locally or to rely on the international marketplace for certain goods. Some countries have looked beyond national borders and joined with neighboring states to draw up regional development plans.

DEVELOPMENT AND REFORMS

In the early years of independence, many African nations took steps to control their economies and provide employment for their people. They created state-run industries and passed laws protecting these industries from foreign competitors. They also greatly expanded the government's role in developing the infrastructure and social services. Many govern-

Development, Economic and Social

Workers install a water pipeline in Ethiopia. Access to water supplies can improve public health and increase agricultural productivity.

* **recession**   economic slowdown

* **inflation**   increase in prices

ments borrowed heavily to finance these development plans, but much of that money was lost due to mismanagement and corruption.

In the 1980s worldwide economic developments—a major recession* and very high interest rates—made matters worse for hard-pressed African nations. As their debts mounted, African leaders turned to institutions such as the World Bank and the International Monetary Fund to refinance their loans. To qualify for debt relief, borrowers were required to undergo "structural adjustment." This meant adopting reforms aimed at reducing government spending and control over the economy, promoting the growth of private enterprise, and relaxing trade restrictions to allow foreign businesses to compete with local businesses. It was hoped that these policies would reduce inflation*, make markets more efficient, and stimulate long-term economic growth. This, in turn, was expected to improve social and economic conditions.

The success of structural adjustment programs has been mixed. Many experts agree that they helped stabilize local African markets and

economies, but they did not promote long-term growth. Some experts argue that structural adjustment actually held development back by cutting government funding for improvements in infrastructure and education that are necessary for continued long-term growth. In addition, advances expected in agriculture and industry did not take place. Again, critics charge that development in these sectors of the economy has been hurt by poor transportation and roads, lack of access to credit, and poor education—all areas where funding was cut under structural adjustment programs.

EFFECTS OF ECONOMIC AID

* **capital**   money invested to start a business or industry

According to early theories of development, the best way to promote growth was to increase the amount of capital* in a country and to plan carefully how to invest it. The thinking was that outside financial aid would allow people in developing countries to purchase goods and services while still saving money. This aid would also provide revenue for the nation until its economy was strong enough to generate money from foreign trade.

* **Cold War**   period of tense relations between the United States and the Soviet Union following World War II

Unfortunately, this theory did not work out as hoped in Africa. Its failure can be explained, in part, by the fact that during the Cold War* financial aid was often given for political rather than economic reasons. In many cases, aid went to nations considered strategically important, not necessarily to those that needed help the most.

By the early 1990s, various financial institutions had begun to stress programs run at the local level rather than ones coordinated by the central government. However, for such programs to work, local people had to learn the skills needed to run programs themselves. Unfortunately, at the same time technical assistance decreased, aid for long-term projects was increasingly replaced by short-term aid. This made it more difficult for local people to gain the ability to operate on their own.

International lenders also emphasized that to receive aid in the future African nations would have to develop more democratic and efficient forms of government and to change their economic policies. However, laying off government employees or ending protection for local businesses can lead to political unrest. So African governments often resist such changes and lose their eligibility for international aid. These new lending policies have contributed to a decline in the amount of aid flowing to Africa.

COMMUNITY DEVELOPMENT AND LOCAL GOVERNMENT

Community development is a different approach to development. It combines funding and services from the central government with the participation of local citizens. The goals of community development are modest compared to those of large aid programs. They include digging new wells, improving local sanitation, increasing literacy, and other small-scale works.

Community development programs achieved some successes in Africa, but they also ran into problems. Perhaps the most serious was

Development, Economic and Social

that the government programs and their directors often came into conflict with local officials, who saw the programs as challenges to their authority and considered the directors to be political rivals. Because the programs did not produce large-scale progress, international aid agencies and central governments in many nations lost enthusiasm for community development. In a number of cases, community development programs were taken over by the central government.

The success of community development programs depends largely on a close working relationship between central and local governments. The local governments must have a great deal of independence to set priorities and decide how to achieve goals. They also need to control their own budgets and resources to pursue their goals. Some African countries have relatively independent local governments. In many others, however, local governments are merely an extension of the central government, and they lack the power to set goals and must depend on the central government for money and resources.

Many African countries lost faith in the idea of building up local governments and sharing power with the central government. Some substituted a system in which the central government appointed local officials and controlled their policies and budgets. As Africa's economies went into decline this system was abandoned, and some countries returned to more independent local governments.

Recently, many local African communities have begun to take development into their own hands, often with little or no government help. A new model is emerging in which communities plan their own programs and provide the people to run them, while local government provides financial assistance. This approach cannot provide large-scale development—such as maintaining roads, building, or utilities—but it is changing accepted ways of thinking about the people's and the government's role in development.

Diagne, Blaise

1872–1934
Senegalese politician

The Senegalese politician Blaise Diagne was the first African elected as a deputy to the French National Assembly in Paris. Like all Africans born in SENEGAL during the colonial period, Diagne was an *originaire*—a French citizen with certain limited rights. Educated in France and at the University of Saint-Louis in Senegal, he worked in Africa for the French customs service.

In 1914 Diagne was elected to represent Senegal in the National Assembly. He vowed to work against taxes and laws that treated the Senegalese harshly and to clarify the rights of *originaires*. Soon after Diagne took his seat in the National Assembly, World War I broke out and the French needed soldiers. Diagne offered to help enlist *originaires* in the armed forces if they received full rights as French citizens. The government agreed to his demands. By 1918 Diagne had recruited 60,000 *originaires*. In return the French built veterans' hospitals, agricultural schools, and a medical school in Senegal.

Diagne was reelected overwhelmingly in 1919. Disturbed by Diagne's growing power, the French authorities began to work against him and

he lost the election of 1923. Nevertheless, Diagne stayed in politics, serving as Under-Secretary of State for the French Colonies in the 1930s. In Senegal, some saw Diagne as a hero, while others thought the lives lost in the war and his compromises with the French were not worth the benefits he gained for the colony. (*See also* **Colonialism in Africa, Government and Political Systems, World Wars I and II.**)

DIAMONDS

See *Minerals and Mining.*

Diaspora, African

See map in Slave Trade (vol. 4).

Today, Africans and their descendants are found on every inhabited continent. African traditions have influenced religion and art, and popular music the world over owes much to African rhythms and musical styles. This global presence is due largely to the African diaspora—a movement of people of African descent to areas outside their homeland.

The story of the African diaspora has three parts: dispersion, settlement abroad, and return to Africa. In the dispersion, or spreading out, people left Africa for other parts of the world. Some departed voluntarily, but many did not. The dispersion was driven by a SLAVE TRADE conducted by Arabs, Europeans, and Americans, who forced enslaved Africans to leave their homes and move to other areas. The second part of the diaspora, settlement abroad, concerns the lives of Africans and their descendants in their new countries—including their relationships with people of other races and their legal, social, and economic position in society.

Some dispersed Africans—and people of African descent—actually returned to Africa. Many of them played leading roles in the continent's social and political development. Others never set foot in Africa, but they drew upon the idea of their ancestral homeland for personal identity or for cultural or political purposes.

Africans in Africa and those who are a product of the diaspora share the legacy of the slave trade and of domination by other peoples who saw themselves as superior. Both in Africa and worldwide, Africans have reacted to this history of slavery and racial subjugation and persecution by striving to maintain their own identities and to claim freedom, independence, and equality.

AFRICANS IN ASIA AND EUROPE

For centuries Africans have settled in various parts of Asia and Europe in a dispersion that has included both voluntary migrations and forced movement as a result of enslavement.

Asia. In ancient times Africans traveled across the Red Sea, the Mediterranean Sea, and the Indian Ocean as merchants, sailors, soldiers, adventurers, and slaves. Ethiopian traders settled on the Arabian penin-

Diaspora, African

sula and in the Persian Gulf region long before those areas became part of the Roman Empire. Africans were taken as slaves to Arabia and Persia. In the A.D. 500s, the Ethiopian king Ella-Asbaha occupied parts of Yemen on the Arabian peninsula and left some people behind.

People of African slave descent living in Arabia, the Persian Gulf region, and India became known as Siddis and Habshis. Some modern historians have found evidence that the Arabs and Persians of those regions had strong feelings of contempt for Africans and treated them as inferiors. Several men of African origin became poets known as the Crows of the Arabs. One of them, an African slave named Abu Dulama whose poetry was well known throughout the Arab world in the 700s, described Arabic society's view of his fellow blacks: "We are alike in color; our faces are black and ugly, our names are shameful."

Africans sometimes rebelled against their lowly status. In the part of the Arab world that is now Iraq, enslaved Africans led freedom movements in 694 and again in 868. The second revolt led to the founding of an independent state called Dawlat al-Zanj that survived for 15 years.

Over time, communities of free and enslaved Africans emerged in many Arabian and Indian towns and cities. Africans worked as merchants, dock workers, clerks, and agricultural laborers. Enslaved Africans also appeared in China, taken there by Arab traders in the 650s. The largest number of enslaved Africans in Asia, however, were resettled in India, where they worked as guards, soldiers, and sailors. A few rose to high positions in the armies or governments of various Indian states.

The life stories of some Africans in Asia are known. One of them, Malik Ambar, was captured in Ethiopia by Muslim Arab slave traders and sold in Baghdad, Iraq. There he learned Arabic and became a clerk. Later he was sold to Indians who took him to central India. He became a soldier, organized a revolt, and seized control of the Indian state of Ahmadnagar. He ruled from 1601 to 1626, employing Africans, Arabs, Persians, and Indians at his court. During his reign Ambar founded towns, built canals and roads, and encouraged trade, scholarship, and the arts. He also joined forces with other Siddis against Indian and European foes.

By the 1500s Europeans were competing with Arabs to trade both goods and slaves in Asia. Arab vessels carried Africans to the farthest reaches of Asia, including Indonesia, China, and Japan. The Europeans began abolishing the slave trade in the 1800s, but Arab traders continued to carry slaves from ports such as ZANZIBAR in East Africa to Arabian and Asian markets. By 1830 the city of Karachi in present-day Pakistan was importing about 1,500 African slaves each year.

Some of these Africans gained fame. Zahur Shah Hashmi and Murad Sahir became noted poets, and Mohamed Siddiq Mussafar wrote a compelling eyewitness account of the slave trade and the lives of enslaved Africans in Pakistan. Mussafar praised the achievements and hopes of African Americans such as Frederick Douglass and Booker T. Washington, who fought for black freedom and dignity. His poem "Africa's Gift" recognized the global presence of people of African descent and their contributions to other societies.

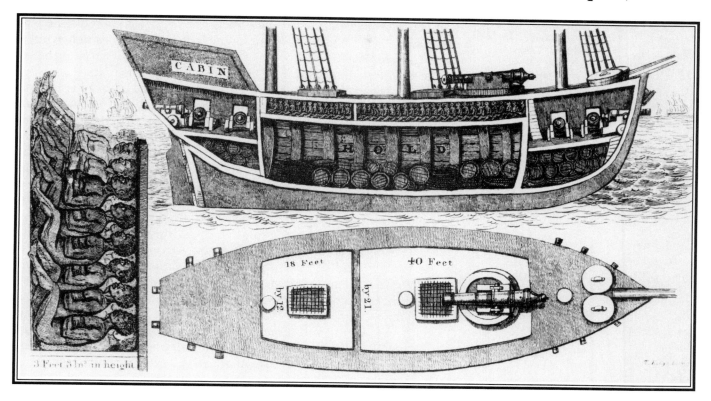

For hundreds of years slave traders captured large numbers of Africans and transported them overseas in ships like the one shown here.

During the early 1800s, free Africans continued to settle in Asia. Some were merchants. Others accompanied Asians for whom they had worked in East Africa. Like earlier African migrants, they adopted various aspects of Asian culture while maintaining some of their own as well. In parts of Pakistan, Habshis still celebrate the Waghu Mela, or Crocodile Festival, which has African roots. In scattered areas of India, people speak SWAHILI, the trade language of East Africa.

Europe. In ancient times trade relations between Europeans and Africans developed around North African cities, attracting merchants from the SUDAN, the Sahara region, and the Nile River valley. These early commercial contacts led to the migration of Europeans to Africa and of Africans to Europe. Enslavement also played a role in the movement of Africans to the Mediterranean region. The ancient Greeks and Romans, like the Egyptians, held Africans in bondage.

The African presence in Europe increased after the A.D. 700s, when Muslim Arabs from North Africa invaded and occupied Spain. The Muslims dominated the Mediterranean Sea until the 1400s. Throughout this time, Arabs and Europeans traded in African slaves. During the medieval* period, a number of Africans were settled along stretches of the northern Mediterranean coast and on Mediterranean islands such as Sicily.

Free and enslaved Ethiopians also visited and lived in medieval Europe. ETHIOPIA, a Christian state since the A.D. 400s, was reaching out for connections with European Christians, and Europeans sought an alliance with Ethiopia against the Muslims. During the Middle Ages, a

* **medieval** referring to the Middle Ages in western Europe, generally considered to be from the A.D. 500s to the 1500s

Diaspora, African

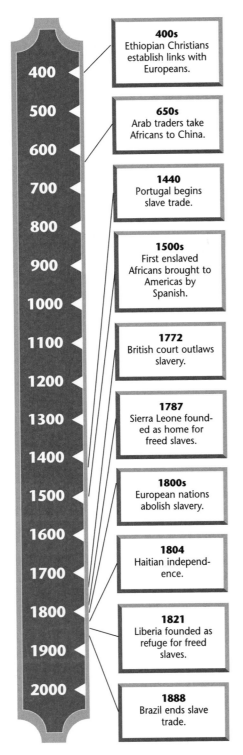

400s
Ethiopian Christians establish links with Europeans.

650s
Arab traders take Africans to China.

1440
Portugal begins slave trade.

1500s
First enslaved Africans brought to Americas by Spanish.

1772
British court outlaws slavery.

1787
Sierra Leone founded as home for freed slaves.

1800s
European nations abolish slavery.

1804
Haitian independence.

1821
Liberia founded as refuge for freed slaves.

1888
Brazil ends slave trade.

number of Ethiopians visited Italy, Spain, and Portugal, and official representatives from Ethiopia spoke at several important church conferences in Europe.

The greatest dispersion of Africans into Europe started when Europeans began exploring the world in the 1400s. Europeans formed direct links with the caravan trade in gold across the SAHARA DESERT, which led to a larger number of Africans visiting and settling in European cities. Some of them became interpreters and guides for Europeans exploring Africa. The Portuguese, disappointed by the amount of gold they obtained in the African trade, began trading in African slaves in the 1440s. Soon both enslaved and free Africans were at work in farms, mines, workshops, and armies in Portugal and Spain.

The voyage of English mariner William Hawkins to West Africa in 1530 led to an increase in the number of Africans in England. In 1556 Queen Elizabeth I complained that there were too many "blackamoors" in the country and suggested that they be returned to Africa. By the 1800s the African population in England had risen to about 15,000. Many of them were poor and unwelcome. The number of Africans living in France increased as the French share of the slave trade grew. Officially, France did not permit SLAVERY, but it emerged there anyway. Africans could also be found in Italy, Eastern Europe, Turkey, and Russia, though little is known about the African diaspora to these areas.

The position of Africans in Europe was precarious. Although laws in Europe did not recognize slavery, those of European colonies in Africa, Asia, and the Americas did. As a result, enslaved Africans taken to Britain and France from the colonies were often kept as slaves in Europe. This situation continued until 1772, when a British court declared that Africans in Britain could no longer be legally held as slaves. During the early 1800s, European nations gradually outlawed and ended the slave trade, changing the legal status of all Africans in Europe to free people.

Before that time, not all Africans in Europe had been enslaved. A few African students lived there, especially after the mid-1700s when African rulers began sending their sons to schools in Europe to learn the language and commercial skills needed for conducting business with Europeans. Some of these students became involved with the European abolition movement. One, Ottoban Cugano, wrote a book called *Thoughts and Sentiments on the Evil and Wicked Traffic of the Slavery and Commerce of the Human Species* (1787), which stirred debate about the slave trade.

AFRICANS IN THE AMERICAS

Africans arrived in the Americas with the Europeans. From the early days of European exploration of North, Central, and South America, Africans were present. However, it was the slave trade that led to the greatest movement of Africans to the Americas. As a result of that forced migration and later waves of immigration, millions of Africans came to live in the Western Hemisphere. Today the majority of the people of Panama, Barbados, Haiti, and Jamaica are of African descent, but Brazil and the United States have the largest African American populations. In

varying degrees, the African diaspora has played a role in shaping the social, cultural, and political fabric of all of these places.

African Migrations. By 1800 an estimated 10 million Africans lived in the Americas. Most were enslaved Africans and children born to them in captivity. About 2 million African Americans were in the United States, and this number doubled by the late 1800s. Another 2 to 3 million lived in Brazil, which continued the slave trade until 1888. By that time, Brazil's African population had increased by millions.

Most Africans brought to the Americas by the slave trade came from the region between present-day GHANA and CAMEROON and from the area around the mouth of the CONGO RIVER. However, smaller numbers of Africans also arrived from the eastern coast of the African continent, long dominated by the Arab slave trade and colonized by the Portuguese.

Africans were usually captured by African kings, sold to slave traders, and packed on ships bound for the Americas. Some shiploads included enslaved Africans who spoke the same or related languages, came from the same areas, or belonged to the same ethnic groups. This made communication among the prisoners possible and, in some cases, led to acts of resistance such as shipboard revolts. Records of these mutinies show that the prisoners sometimes spent days plotting them. Occasionally, African women who served as cooks on the ships helped prisoners plan their mutinies by passing on information gathered from the European crew.

A New Culture. Amid the horrors of the slave ships and the dangerous voyages across the Atlantic Ocean, Africans forged friendships that lasted into the system of slavery in the Americas. These relationships formed the beginning of a new culture, blending elements from different African homelands that would endure and continue to develop during the slavery period and beyond.

During the 1600s and 1700s, blacks adopted the terms *African* and *Ethiopian* as identifying labels. Slave masters renamed Africans, but many individuals tried to keep their original names. Although American laws made it a crime to speak African languages and practice African religions and customs, many enslaved people did so in private moments. In time, however, the Africans learned European languages spoken in the Americas and adopted some elements of European culture.

Africans in the Americas were unified by the relationships formed on slave ships and by the continuing use of their languages and customs. These bonds provided a strong base for freedom movements, which sometimes led to uprisings or to the establishment of communities for fugitive slaves. In the 1500s a black community called Coyula arose in Mexico; in 1603 black pearl divers revolted in Venezuela.

In the French colony of Haiti the struggle of enslaved Africans for freedom reflected the combination of African and Western cultures. It began in 1791 when an African named Boukman attracted a group of loyal followers and succeeded in turning the Africans against the slaveholders. Toussaint L'Ouverture, a Haitian-born African, joined Boukman and organized a guerrilla* war. The war led to Haitian independence in

* **guerrilla** type of warfare involving sudden raids by small groups of warriors

207

Diaspora, African

* **nationalism** devotion to the interests and culture of one's country

* **abolitionist** person committed to ending slavery

* **ritual** religious ceremony that follows a set pattern

* **divination** practice that looks into the future, usually by supernatural means

1804. The second independent American republic in the Western Hemisphere (after the United States), Haiti became a symbol of African freedom in the diaspora.

These freedom movements reveal the beginnings of African nationalism* in the Americas. Africans did not want just revenge or escape from slavery. They sought control over their communities to promote their own values, goals, and traditions. Africans in the Americas made enormous contributions to the economic development of their countries and also fought for justice. Some became spokespeople for the idea of a larger African identity and, like African American abolitionist* Frederick Douglass, even traveled abroad to promote freedom for blacks in other parts of the world.

African Institutions. As Africans adapted to life in the Americas, they established churches, schools and other organizations that paralleled those of European-American society. Scholars are still investigating the history of these institutions to see how far they incorporated African ideas and traditions and how much they were influenced by European models.

African culture shaped many aspects of life in black communities in the Americas. Place names, speech patterns, proverbs and folktales, types of food preparation, decorative styles, personal adornments, beliefs, and ritual* practices are a few examples. Areas that once had widespread slave-based plantation economies, such as the Caribbean and the southeastern United States, are the historic heartland of African-influenced culture. However, the influence has spread far beyond this heartland as a result of the movement of African descendants after the Civil War and more recent international migrations. In addition, non-African people have adopted elements of African style and culture.

Scholars have identified certain aspects of culture in the Americas as African. For example, the divination* systems known as Santería in Cuba and Candomblé in Brazil are so similar to practices of the YORUBA people of NIGERIA that the African connection is clear. But other aspects of African American culture are not as easy to link to African sources. Scholars have long debated, for example, whether some types of African American social organizations, such as mother-centered families, are survivals of African traditions or were shaped by conditions in the Americas. Moreover, blacks in the Americas have sometimes "re-Africanized" themselves, seeking contact with or knowledge of Africa to strengthen their sense of African identity.

Religion. Throughout the Americas, religion reflects various forms of African influence. Many of the Africans who came to the Americas worshiped local gods and ancestors. Others were Christians, and some practiced hybrid religions, mixing Christian elements with traditional African beliefs. These people and their American descendants created a complex religious legacy that includes faiths that are specifically African and African influence in other religions.

Some religions in the Americas are distinctly African in their beliefs and practices—Candomblé in Brazil, and Sèvi Iwa (voodoo) in Haiti.

The Million Man March, held in Washington, D.C., in 1995, attracted more than 800,000 participants. It aimed to promote unity and spiritual renewal among Americans of African descent.

The gods of these religions have recognizable counterparts in African societies. African-inspired forms of ancestor worship also continue to be practiced on Caribbean islands and among the descendants of escaped slaves in the South American nation of Suriname.

European influence has also been strong. In parts of the Americas colonized by Roman Catholics from Europe, Africans often came to identify their gods with Catholic saints and to use some Catholic symbols and rituals. Most practitioners of Candomblé and Santería consider themselves Roman Catholic as well. In addition, some followers of Candomblé and other African-inspired religions claim Native American sources for their practices.

African influences also appear in American religions that do not view themselves as specifically African. In various African American Protestant churches, for example, the importance of dancing and of being "filled with the Holy Spirit" can be viewed as versions of African sacred dance and SPIRIT POSSESSION.

Religious practices are among the visible contributions of sub-Saharan* Africa to American civilization. Yet many African elements have been touched and transformed by European and Native American practices and beliefs. In a process that began centuries ago with the arrival of the first Africans on American shores, these different traditions—African, European, and American—are constantly combining and influencing one another in different ways.

* **sub-Saharan**   referring to Africa south of the Sahara desert

THE RETURN TO AFRICA

Africans in the diaspora remained attached to Africa, and many longed to return there. Numerous Africans lost their lives attempting to resist capture in their homeland, during slave-ship mutinies, or in revolts against enslavement. Some, however, succeeded and returned to join their families in Africa. Still others returned as businesspeople, teachers, and missionaries.

One early phase of the return to Africa began in Great Britain. By the late 1700s, that country's growing black population included many freed slaves from the United States who had fought for the British during the American Revolution. Abolitionists developed the idea of resettling these and other blacks in Africa. The hope was that the returning Africans would establish a society that would promote Christianity, the abolition of the slave trade, and Western principles of government. In 1787 a group of more than 400 Africans left Britain to found SIERRA LEONE, and by the mid-1800s, their descendants had brought the country's population to about 70,000. Many of the inhabitants were former captives freed from slave traders by the British. A group of people known as CREOLES emerged there, blending Western and African beliefs, customs, and language. As teachers, missionaries, and employees of the colonial governments, Creoles extended the influence of the diaspora across much of West Africa.

Free Africans in the United States made their own plans to return to Africa. The U.S. Navy seized American slave ships and delivered their cargoes to the African colony of LIBERIA, which was founded in 1821. By 1870 Liberia had more than 20,000 settlers. The majority came from the United States, and they patterned their political and social institutions after American ones. On declaring independence in 1847, Liberia became the second African nation to win international recognition (after Ethiopia) and the first whose leaders were part of the African diaspora.

In both Sierra Leone and Liberia the descendants of the returned Africans established governments that ruled over the indigenous* population. As in Africa's European colonies, the indigenous peoples were treated as inferiors. Several prominent African Americans went to Liberia and made significant contributions there. One of them, Edward BLYDEN, emphasized the importance of African languages and culture and developed ideas about the blend of African and Western culture.

* **indigenous**   native to a certain place

During the 1800s people of African descent from Brazil, Cuba, the Arabian peninsula, and India also returned to Africa. In modern times a two-way movement developed, with diaspora Africans returning to Africa and people from Africa migrating to other nations to work or study. These links contributed to a global sense of African identity and helped inspire the independence movements in Africa during the mid-1900s.

AFRICAN CULTURAL INFLUENCES OUTSIDE AFRICA

African traditions spread by the diaspora have influenced world culture in various ways, most notably in art and music. Artistic influences, particularly art forms created by people of African descent in the Americas, range from African-style painting and sculpture, masks carved in Yoruba style in Brazil, and a Cuban tradition of costumed dance that echoes the rituals of many peoples of West Africa.

Africa's greatest impact on world culture, however, has been through music. In the Americas, African traditions gave birth to many new musical forms, such as black gospel, blues, jazz, calypso in Trinidad and the West Indies, reggae in Jamaica, and samba in Brazil. African American music began to be recorded in the 1920s. By the mid-1900s records had made their way to Africa, where they inspired urban musicians to adopt some African American styles and blend them with traditional African ones.

African musicians have continued to borrow from African American music. In turn, American and European popular musicians have adopted the sounds of African popular music. Today, Africa is part of the world of popular music. The influence of African and African American music has shaped much of modern jazz, rock and roll, and pop music. (*See also* **Art; Dance; Ethnic Groups and Identity; History of Africa; Humans, Early; Music and Song; Negritude; Refugees; Religion and Ritual.**)

Dingiswayo

**1770s–1816
Chief of the Nguni
confederation**

Dingiswayo was the last chief of the Nguni confederation of southern Africa before Europeans colonized the area. According to legend, Dingiswayo became chief by killing his brother because he believed that his brother was not the rightful ruler. After assuming power, Dingiswayo combined several related kingdoms into a unified confederation. He then appointed subchiefs from those kingdoms to help him oversee the union.

Dingiswayo also introduced a military system in which young men preparing to be warriors spent a great deal of time together before their initiation. His goal was to develop a sense of fraternity among the warriors that would make them trustworthy companions in military campaigns. One of those brought up under this system was Shaka, the son of the ZULU chief. After the chief died, Dingiswayo sent Shaka to claim the Zulu throne. In 1816 Dingiswayo was killed by a follower of one of the subchiefs, and the confederacy began to fall apart. Shaka later took over as chief and reunited the confederacy under his own leadership. (*See also* **Shaka Zulu, Southern Africa, History.**)

Diop, Alioune

Diop, Alioune

1910–1980
Writer and cultural leader

* **ideology** set of concepts or opinions of a person or group

The Senegalese writer Alioune Diop played a major role in changing the way the French-speaking world viewed Africa. Born and educated in SENEGAL, Diop worked as a professor and represented the colony in the French Senate. In 1947 he started *Présence africaine*, which became the most influential French-language journal on Africa.

In *Présence africaine*, Diop tried to reshape the European image of Africa and to emphasize the continent's significance in world affairs. Diop was afraid that Africa was all but invisible when it came to world politics and that its people had become "disinherited" by other world leaders. His goal was to completely redefine the role of the African continent on the world stage. The journal consistently attacked colonialism without identifying itself with a particular philosophy or ideology*. In addition to his writing and journalism, Diop was active in promoting African literature and art in the Société Africaine de Culture he founded. He also played a major role in organizing the first and second International Congress of Black Writers and Artists (1956 and 1959), the first World Festival of Negro Arts (1966), and the Festival of Black and African Arts and Culture (1977). (*See also* **Publishing**.)

Diop, Cheikh Anta

1923–1986
African scholar and political leader

* **carbon-14 dating** method of determining the age of ancient objects by measuring the decay of radioactive carbon

Cheikh Anta Diop was an accomplished historian, physicist, archaeologist, and linguist who championed the cause of African independence and explored the roots of African culture and civilization. Born to a Muslim family in SENEGAL and educated in both Africa and France, Diop had an unusual background from which to examine Africa's colonial experience.

While doing graduate work in Paris, Diop became involved in the anticolonial movement and helped to organize the first Pan-African Student Conference in 1951. He also began to research the origins of civilization in Africa. He wrote a doctoral thesis that argued that ancient Egypt was a black African civilization. It took nine years for the Sorbonne—France's most prestigious university—to assemble a panel of scholars to judge the thesis, which earned Diop a doctor of letters degree in 1960. Diop then returned to Senegal where he set up a laboratory for carbon-14 dating* and founded several political parties.

Diop devoted his academic and literary career to defining Africa's identity, which had been shattered by years of European colonial rule. His books trace Africa's contributions to classical Greek culture and examine the relationship between Islam, Christianity, Judaism, and Egyptian religious thought. He argued that European colonial rulers had been racist and violent because they came from male-dominated societies. According to Diop, female-centered societies—which he claimed originated in Africa—were more humane. He believed that together Africans could repeat the great achievements of their distant past.

Diop received many honors during his lifetime, and at the first World Festival of Negro Arts in 1966, he was named one of the two scholars "who exerted the greatest influence on Negro thought in the twentieth century." (*See also* **Africa, Study of; Egypt, Negritude**.)

Diseases

Poverty and the scarcity of adequate health services have combined to make disease a particularly severe problem throughout Africa. Africans have to deal with many of the same illnesses that affect people in other parts of the world. They suffer from infectious diseases such as measles, lifestyle-related illnesses such as cancer and heart disease, and sexually transmitted diseases (STDs). However, social and economic conditions in Africa make the treatment and prevention of these diseases more of a problem than in wealthier, more industrialized nations. Moreover, certain diseases exist only in Africa, and various factors such as climate and traditional ways of living make it especially difficult to keep them under control.

INFECTIOUS DISEASES

* **virus** microscopic organism that can only live and reproduce within the cells of other living things

* **parasite** organism that feeds on the body of another organism

* **vector** organism that carries disease-causing substances from one body to another

Africa is home to a wide variety of infectious diseases caused by viruses* or parasites* that live in monkeys, rats, or other animals known as hosts. Flies, mosquitoes, and other agents known as vectors* transmit the diseases to humans.

Africa has some infectious diseases that appear nowhere else in the world and appears to be the source of numerous diseases found on other continents. Over the centuries, these diseases were spread through trade and travel. The SLAVE TRADE, for example, brought various African diseases to the Americas.

In modern times, the ease of travel has allowed infected people and livestock to carry additional viruses and parasites from Africa to other parts of the world. Mosquitoes and other animals that act as disease vectors have also found their way to other continents by way of airplanes and ships.

Parasitic Diseases Limited to Africa. One of the most common parasitic diseases in Africa is trypanosomiasis, or sleeping sickness. Often fatal, sleeping sickness is caused by a single-celled microorganism that lives in wild animals and is transmitted to humans and cattle by the bite of the tsetse fly.

Treatment with drugs can cure most cases of sleeping sickness, and the spread of the disease can be controlled by eliminating tsetse flies near populated areas. However, sleeping sickness remains a serious problem in rural areas and in nature preserves protected from human settlement.

* **savanna** tropical or subtropical grassland with scattered trees and drought-resistant undergrowth

Sleeping sickness is found mostly in Africa's savanna* regions, which are home to the game animals that carry it. Although a serious problem for humans and domestic animals, the disease has helped preserve wildlife herds in Africa by discouraging the expansion of human settlement in the savanna. It has also played a role in controlling the spread of the desert into savanna areas by limiting the livestock herds that graze on grasslands.

Leishmaniasis, another African parasitic disease, causes sores and disfigurement of the face. Some forms of the disease are found in South America and Asia, but one variety appears only in Africa. A common host animal for the disease is the hyrax, a cave-dwelling rodentlike animal. Sand flies feed on the blood of the hyrax and transmit the disease to humans.

213

Diseases

Several parasitic diseases are transmitted by worms. The loa loa worm carries a disease called loaisis that causes swelling of the skin and allergic reactions. The small worm enters the bloodstream of humans through bites from a type of large horsefly. It can often be seen crossing under the thin membrane that lines the inner surface of the eyelid in an infected person.

Parasitic Diseases of African Origin. A number of parasitic diseases found around the world originated in Africa. Perhaps the most widespread of these is malaria, now also a major health problem in Asia and South America.

The parasites that cause malaria, a disease characterized by recurring cycles of severe chills, fever, and sweating, are carried by Anopheles mosquitoes. Each year more than a million children—mostly in Africa—die from malaria. It is the leading cause of death among African children.

Most adults who live in areas of Africa where malaria is common have developed a great deal of natural immunity, or resistance, to the disease. Vaccines to prevent malaria exist but are not widely available to Africans. The vaccines may also damage naturally acquired immunity. Various drugs are used to treat malaria, but the malaria parasites have developed resistance to some of them. Most efforts to prevent malaria focus on eliminating mosquito-breeding areas and using mosquito netting to protect potential victims.

Parasites that live in small water-dwelling snails cause a disease called schistosomiasis, or bilharziasis. Once confined to central Africa, the disease was spread to the Americas by the slave trade and now occurs in many places that lack piped water supplies or that rely heavily on irrigation. Humans become infected by bathing, washing, or working in water containing the snails and their parasites.

Health experts estimate that schistosomiasis affects 200 million people worldwide, most of whom live in Africa. A single dose of a drug called praziquantel can cure schistosomiasis, and the snails can be killed with chemicals. The best long-term solution, however, is providing safe water supplies and educating people about how to avoid exposure to the parasites.

One of the most serious parasitic diseases in Africa is onchocerciasis, or river blindness, which is caused by a certain species of worm. The worms are carried by blackflies that breed in rivers and streams of rain forests. River blindness causes severe disfigurement of facial skin and often leads to permanent blindness. Over 30 million Africans suffer from river blindness, and in some areas about one third of the adult population has been blinded by the disease.

River blindness came to the Americas with the slave trade and is now widespread in Central America and South America. A drug called ivermectin provides an effective treatment for the disease, but eliminating breeding areas for the mosquitoes that carry the disease has dramatically reduced infection rates in many areas of Africa.

Viral Diseases Limited to Africa. Lassa fever, which is carried by rats, is found mainly in West Africa. This viral disease causes fever,

bleeding, swollen face and neck, and liver failure. The rats that carry lassa fever live in thatched-roof huts in rural areas, making it difficult to control the spread of the disease. Researchers are currently working on a vaccine.

Two of the most frightening viruses in Africa are the Marburg virus and the Ebola virus. The Marburg virus causes an extremely serious, often fatal disease characterized by severe internal bleeding. Little is known about the source of infection, but it seems to be transmitted by direct contact with an infected person.

Similar to the Marburg virus, the Ebola virus also causes severe internal bleeding and is usually fatal. It is spread by contact with the blood of an infected person, by infected needles, and through sexual contact. The host animal for the virus has not been identified, but bats are suspected.

So far there have been only occasional outbreaks of Marburg and Ebola in Africa, but experts fear the possibility of epidemics in the future. There is no vaccine or known treatment for either virus, and the only way to stop their spread is by keeping infected individuals in quarantine.

Viral Diseases of African Origin. Although first identified in Cuba, Central America, and the United States, yellow fever originated in Africa, where the hosts are tree-dwelling monkeys. Mosquitoes in forested areas transmit the virus to humans, who bring the disease back to populated areas. There it is spread by *Aedes aegypti,* a common species of mosquito. Yellow fever causes a yellowish discoloration of the skin, internal bleeding, and vomiting. A highly effective vaccine is available that gives lifelong protection against yellow fever, and control of the disease is also achieved by eliminating mosquito habitats.

The viral disease AIDS was identified in the United States in 1981. However, research has shown that the first human cases occurred in central Africa at least as early as 1959. Researchers believe that HIV, the virus that causes AIDS, originated in African monkeys or apes. Among human populations, HIV is spread by sexual intercourse or contact with contaminated blood. Mothers can also pass HIV to unborn children during pregnancy or while breast-feeding their infants.

In most cases it takes a number of years for HIV to develop into AIDS. As it progresses, AIDS destroys the human immune system, which normally protects the body against infectious disease. Death is often caused by secondary infections that occur after the breakdown of the victim's immune system. Drug treatments have helped prolong the lives of some people with AIDS, but a cure for the disease has not yet been found.

In the early years, African officials paid little attention to AIDS, but the seriousness of the problem soon became evident. The number of cases of AIDS in Africa has skyrocketed, with infection rates in some major cities in central and eastern Africa reaching 25 percent of sexually active adults. Because of the high death rate, the absence of an affordable and effective treatment, traditional sexual practices, and the lack of effective health education, AIDS threatens to be a devastating public health problem in many parts of Africa in the coming years.

The insects that carry the disease known as river blindness breed in fast-flowing water. As a result, the disease is prevalent along rivers with heavy rapids, such as the Nile, the Congo, and the Volta. This girl is helping a man infected with river blindness.

DISEASES WITH SPECIAL FEATURES IN AFRICA

A number of diseases that exist within and outside of Africa occur in somewhat different forms or circumstances in Africa. These differences can be traced mostly to factors such as climate, geography, and the behavior and customs of people likely to be affected by the disease.

Infectious Diseases. During the 1960s measles was the leading cause of death among West African infants. Widespread malnutrition contributed to the development of pneumonia, diarrhea, and other secondary infections in children with measles. Other complications from measles led to blindness, deafness, and mental retardation. Vaccines now available have helped reduce the danger from measles in urban areas, but the disease is still a major problem in remote areas.

Meningitis is another viral disease that has been much more devastating in Africa than in the West. At one time, periodic epidemics of the disease killed as many as 15,000 people. Antibiotic drugs have been effective in controlling meningitis, but parts of Africa—particularly the northern savanna region stretching from BURKINA FASO to SUDAN—still experience epidemics from time to time.

Two common infectious diseases related to animals, hydatid disease and trichinosis, also have special characteristics in Africa. Hydatid disease is caused by a worm that lives in dogs and is transmitted through their bodily waste. It is most common in the Turkana region of KENYA, where working mothers often use dogs to look after their children, than anywhere else in the world. Hydatid produces large growths in the liver that can be treated either with surgery or drugs.

Trichinosis, caused by eating tainted meat from pigs, attacks muscle tissue, including the heart, and can cause heart failure. In Africa, trichinosis infects wild pigs, but not domestic pigs. Taboos* against eating wild pigs have helped to control the spread of the disease.

Sexually transmitted diseases (STDs), such as syphilis and gonorrhea are widespread in Africa. Lifestyle and attitudes toward GENDER ROLES AND SEXUALITY play a major role in this problem as does the high proportion of young people in Africa. A significant part of the population falls in age groups most affected by STDs—men 20 to 30 years of age and women 15 to 25. Moreover, African men tend to marry later than men in the West. In the meantime, they may have sex with prostitutes who may carry STDs. In addition, many men move to urban areas to find work, and when they return home they may bring STDs back to their wives. Many men are also reluctant to use condoms.

With few doctors and little access to health care, education about and treatment of STDs in Africa lags far behind the West. As with other diseases, Africa's poverty contributes both to the development and spread of STDs and to the difficulty of preventing and curing the diseases.

* **taboo** religious prohibition against doing something that is believed to cause harm

NONINFECTIOUS DISEASES

The leading cause of death in industrialized countries is coronary heart disease, caused by a high-fat diet, lack of exercise, and cigarette smoking. In Africa heart disease is almost unknown, even among people who have a high-fat diet. But rheumatic heart disease, which is now rare in the West, is the most common cause of heart failure in Africa. One reason may be that rheumatic heart disease is associated with poverty and a certain type of bacterial infection—both widespread in Africa.

Cancer occurs in Africa as well as in the West, but the most common types are different. Lung cancer, for example, has been rare in Africa, though it is on the rise now as more Africans are smoking. Another type of cancer found more frequently in the West than in Africa is prostate cancer, which affects only men. The low incidence of this disease in Africa may be related to diet. However, cervical cancer is more common in Africa than in Western countries. The high rate of this type of cancer, which affects women, seems to be associated with early sexual activity and multiple pregnancies. Another type of cancer that is common in the West but almost nonexistent in Africa is skin cancer caused by too much exposure to the sun. In Africa, solar cancers are almost unheard of because there are built-in protective mechanisms in African's pigmented skin. Scientists learn a great deal about tumors by studying the factors that make some cancers common in Africa, but not in the West. (*See also* **AIDS, Healing and Medicine, Health Care, Pests and Pest Control.**)

217

Divination and Oracles

Divination and
Oracles

Throughout much of Africa people turn to divination for guidance in resolving their troubles. The act of divination involves advice, an explanation, or a prediction for the future—all of which are considered messages from the spiritual world. Many Christian and Muslim Africans do not see divination as conflicting with their faiths. Their approach to understanding life and solving its problems combines divination, religion, and other elements such as modern medicine.

Diviners and Their Methods. Diviners, the men and women who perform divination, are believed to be spokespersons for spiritual forces, including supernatural beings and the dead. Some people are selected at birth to become diviners; they may be descended from or related to other diviners. Other individuals are identified through religious or magical rituals or after recovering from a particular illness. Diviners are sometimes thought to have spiritual twins of the opposite sex. To bridge the gap between the earthly and spiritual worlds, a male diviner may dress in women's clothing or a female diviner in men's clothing.

Two main types of divination are practiced in Africa. Revelatory divination explains past misfortunes, and predictive divination foretells likely future events. Diviners rely on various methods, and some may use more than one technique.

Often diviners act as mediums, channels of communication between the earthly and spiritual worlds. This may involve entering a trance in which the diviner is thought to be taken over by a spirit or deity*. The diviner then passes along or acts out a message. In southeastern Burkina Faso, for example, a spirit has no tongue but communicates through a diviner's hand gestures. Some spirit mediums are associated with the shrines of major African cults*, such as the cult of Mwali in southeastern Africa and the cult of Ngombo in southern Democratic Republic of Congo and Angola. In other cases, a diviner may act as a medium without being possessed by a spirit. He or she may enter a trance and, upon waking, tell of a vision or a journey into the spirit world.

* **deity** god or goddess

* **cult** group bound together by devotion to a particular person, belief, or god

Dreams can be viewed as forms of divination. The TUAREG of North Africa believe that the spirits of the dead roam near graves and sometimes carry news to the living. To obtain a vision of the future, a person may sleep on a grave.

Diviners often interpret physical signs as spiritual messages. Among the Dogon people of Mali, for example, diviners trace a grid or set of lines in the dust outside the village at sunset. Over it they sprinkle grain to attract the pale fox, an animal that moves about by night. The following morning, the diviners read messages in the fox's tracks across the grid. Other diviners keep items in a special basket, bag, or cup. These items include seeds, insects, and parts of animals or birds. Manufactured objects that are important in daily life or associated with myths and symbols may also be used. The diviner observes the movement or arrangement of these items and interprets it to provide the message.

Purposes of Divination. People consult a diviner to discover the causes of a misfortune such as a difficult conflict, a disaster, a great loss, a mysterious illness, or even death. Divination is based on the idea that human relations can be the cause of such troubles. The diviner's mes-

Two Dogon diviners in Mali interpret a spiritual message by examining marks in the sand.

sage is expected to reveal the people or issues involved in the problem and to restore peace of mind. It may suggest a course of action.

A type of divination called an oracle may be used to determine guilt. In such cases, the diviner calls on an invisible force to arrange or move special items, such as horns, rattles, or gourds. The diviner might also poison a fowl, ask a series of yes-or-no questions, and interpret the movements of the fowl as answers to those questions. Sometimes the diviner will ask spirits or recently dead members of the community to respond to the questions of the oracle.

A diviner claims to be neutral in the process of divination, merely an instrument through which the spirits speak. His or her interpretations are respected. Oracles generally reinforce public opinion and the beliefs, values, and morals of the society. At the same time, they may reveal feelings of envy and an underlying power struggle within the community. Most traditions of divination operate at the level of family or community and have little to do with politics. In some cases, however, divination clearly serves to support political authority. (*See also* **Religion and Ritual, Spirit Possession, Witchcraft and Sorcery.**)

DIVORCE

See *Marriage Systems.*

Djibouti

The tiny country of Djibouti is located at the southern entrance to the Red Sea. Although the landscape is mostly flat and barren, several mountain ranges cross the northern part of the country. The climate is extremely hot; during the dry season temperatures can reach 113°F.

Djibouti's economy is based mainly on its role as a trading center for goods traveling to and from Africa on the Red Sea and Indian Ocean. It has a modern port and a railroad connection to ADDIS ABABA, the capital of ETHIOPIA. Apart from these commercial activities, however, the economy is not strong. Because most of the land is not suited for agriculture, Djibouti depends on imported food. It has little industry and unemployment ranges from 40 to 70 percent. Furthermore, a flood of refugees from the war-torn nations of Ethiopia, ERITREA, and SOMALIA has strained Djibouti's resources and increased its need for foreign aid.

The main ethnic groups in Djibouti are the Issa of the south and the Afar of the north. Other peoples include ARABS, recent immigrants from northern Somalia, and French citizens who hold many key government posts. Most of the population lives in or near the city of Djibouti, the nation's capital and major port.

A former French colony, Djibouti became independent in 1977. For many years President Hassan Gouled Aptidon and his party ruled the country. Most of Gouled's support came from the Issa people, which led to discontent among the Afar. In 1991 an Afar guerrilla* force of about 3,000 began a civil war against the Gouled regime*. Gouled responded by holding multiparty elections for the presidency and legislature in 1992 and 1993. Charging that the election system was unfair, oppo-

* **guerrilla** type of warfare involving sudden raids by small groups of warriors

* **regime** current political system or rule

Republic of Djibouti

POPULATION:
451,442 (2000 estimated population)

AREA:
8,500 sq. mi. (22,000 sq. km)

LANGUAGES:
French, Arabic (both official); Afar, Somali

NATIONAL CURRENCY:
Djibouti Franc

PRINCIPAL RELIGIONS:
Muslim 94%, Christian 6%

CITIES:
Djibouti (capital), 383,000 (1999 est.); Ali Sabieth, Dikhil, Tadjoura, Obock

ANNUAL RAINFALL:
Less than 5 in. (127 mm)

ECONOMY:
GDP per capita: U.S. $1,200

PRINCIPAL PRODUCTS AND EXPORTS:
Agricultural: goats, sheep, camels, cattle, coffee
Manufacturing: dairy products, mineral water bottling, port and maritime support, construction
Mining: salt extraction
Economy is based mainly upon services and commerce.

GOVERNMENT:
Independence from France, 1977. Parliamentary government limited to no more than 4 political parties. President elected by universal suffrage. Governing bodies: Assemblée Nationale; Council of Ministers (appointed by president).

HEADS OF STATE SINCE INDEPENDENCE:
1977–1999 President Hassan Gouled Aptidon
1999– President Ismail Omar Guellah

ARMED FORCES:
9,600 (1998 est.)

EDUCATION:
Literacy rate 46%

nents of the government refused to participate. Nevertheless, Gouled and his party declared victory. Gouled then seized the opportunity to attack and crush the armed opposition. He continued to dominate Djibouti's politics and government until 1999, when his nephew, Ismail Omar Guellah, was elected president. (*See also* **Climate, Colonialism in Africa, Trade, Transportation**.)

Du Bois, W.E.B.

1868–1963
Father of Pan-Africanism

William Edward Burghardt Du Bois was a leading champion of equality for blacks in the United States and elsewhere. An African American born in Massachusetts, Du Bois attended college and earned a Ph.D. degree from Harvard University. In the early 1900s, he became a black civil rights leader. Du Bois was known for his view that social change could be achieved only through active protest. In 1909 he helped create the National Association for the Advancement of Colored People (NAACP), which became a leading civil rights organization in the United States.

Du Bois was also the founder of Pan-Africanism, a movement aimed at unifying blacks throughout the world in protest against racism and colonialism. He believed that people of African descent everywhere had common interests and should work together to improve their place in society. However, he campaigned against the ideas of fellow Pan-Africanist Marcus Mosiah GARVEY, who encouraged black Americans to go "back to Africa" to rediscover their heritage and build new lives there. Du Bois organized several Pan-African conferences in the 1920s and 1930s.

Du Bois wrote many books, including *Souls of Black Folk* (1903), *The Negro* (1915), *Color and Democracy* (1945), and *The World and Africa* (1947). Toward the end of his life, Du Bois moved to Ghana, where he renounced his U.S. citizenship. (*See also* **Diaspora, African, Negritude**.)

Éboué, Adolphe-Félix-Sylvestre

1884–1944
Colonial administrator

Adolphe-Félix-Sylvestre Éboué was a Creole official who served France in a variety of colonial posts during the early 1900s. He is most famous for bringing several French colonies in Africa into World War II to fight on the side of the Allies.

Born in French Guyana in South America, Éboué attended a school of colonial administration, where he formed friendships that were important to his future career. He served in the French colony of Oubangui-Chari in central Africa from 1909 to 1931 and then held posts in several of France's Caribbean territories. In 1939 Éboué was demoted and sent back to Oubangui-Chari—probably at the request of personal enemies. Yet this turned out to be a fortunate move for both Éboué and France.

When France was occupied by Germany in World War II, most of France's African colonies supported its pro-Nazi Vichy government. However, Éboué convinced CAMEROON and FRENCH EQUATORIAL AFRICA to

Éboué, Adolphe-Félix-Sylvestre

join the Allies and Charles de Gaulle's Free French forces in fighting against Germany. After Éboué's death, de Gaulle ordered that he be buried in the Pantheon of Heroes in Paris. He is the only black person ever to receive that honor. (*See also* **World Wars I and II**)

Economic History

* **sub-Saharan** referring to Africa south of the Sahara desert

* **precolonial** referring to the time before European powers colonized Africa

A lack of written sources makes it difficult to trace the early economic history of much of the African continent, especially sub-Saharan* Africa. What is clear is that Africans in precolonial* times had basic economic activities that provided them with the things they needed to survive. At the same time, however, many factors limited the kind of intensive economic development that occurred in Asia and Europe.

Much of Africa's recent economic history is linked to the period of European colonialism, from the late 1800s to the mid-1900s. The nations that colonized Africa saw the continent as a vast source of untapped wealth. Only after many false starts and much wasted investment would they recognize the forces that had held back the African economy for centuries.

PRECOLONIAL ECONOMIES

Africans provided for their own economic needs and traded among themselves long before they had contact with other peoples. However, scholars have different views on the nature of these early economic activities.

* **domestication** adopting or training plants or animals for human use

* **artisan** skilled crafts worker

Agriculture. Economic history begins with the appearance of agriculture and the domestication* of animals. These two developments pave the way for settled communities that not only provide for their basic needs but also produce surplus food for trade. In addition, agricultural surplus leads to the creation of specialized groups—such as traders and artisans*—who are not involved in food production. Food surpluses also stimulate trade and commerce between neighboring societies.

Africans living in the SAHARA DESERT had domesticated cattle as early as the 6000s B.C. African agriculture, which developed around the late 1000s B.C. in the SAHEL region, spread to southern Africa by the A.D. 100s or 200s.

For several reasons, the shift to agriculture did not always result in dramatic increases in productivity. First, the most common farming method was swidden, or slash-and-burn. This method, involving small parcels of land and little irrigation or fertilizer, usually produces low crop yields. Second, the poor soil and unpredictable rainfall found in much of Africa makes it almost impossible to count on consistent crops over a long period of time. Third, Africa's geography makes transportation of goods extremely difficult. The terrain in the interior is rugged and unhealthy for the large animals often used to haul goods. Moreover, most rivers in the interior are navigable only for short distances, and Africa has few natural harbors along its coasts for shipping cargo.

222

Much local commercial activity in Africa takes place in open-air markets like this one in Antananarivo, Madagascar.

Because of the problems in transporting goods to distant markets, farmers had little reason to produce surplus food.

Another factor that slowed agricultural improvement was the lack of population pressure on the land. Until recent times, the overall population of Africa remained fairly low, partly because of the presence of many disease-carrying organisms. Furthermore, Africa contained abundant open space. When the farmland near a village became less fertile, some inhabitants simply moved to new areas. The SLAVE TRADE, which flourished between A.D. 800 and 1900, removed as many as 20 million people from Africa, further decreasing the population. Finally, African cultural values, which placed little value on goods and money, did not promote the production of surplus food for trade.

The situation in North Africa was different. There irrigation along bodies of water such as the NILE RIVER made intensive cultivation possible. EGYPT grew into a prosperous society by the 3000s B.C. and developed numerous connections with the ancient Middle East. By the 400s B.C., the city-state of CARTHAGE in present-day TUNISIA became one of the leading commercial powers in the Mediterranean world. With the Sahara desert acting as a barrier to migration, densely populated societies grew up in the fertile areas of North Africa.

Trade and Commerce. Despite various difficulties, trade and commerce did occur in precolonial Africa. Scholars have uncovered evidence of early exchanges between farmers and cattle raisers. Members of these groups also traded with hunting, fishing, and metalworking peoples. Such trade, however, was mostly local.

In sub-Saharan Africa, trade with groups outside the region developed very slowly. As early as the A.D. 100s, merchants from Southwest Asia were trading along the East African coast. By the 500s, camel caravans began to cross the Sahara, creating commercial links between sub-Saharan Africa, North Africa, and the Middle East.

Trade developed more easily in North Africa. As early as the 400s B.C., Carthage was exchanging manufactured goods with people on the Moroccan coast and obtaining tin from northern France. Carthaginian merchants were a common sight in the marketplaces of ancient Greece. Early Egyptian commercial ties extended to the kingdoms of Sumer and Babylonia in the Middle East, and ancient Egyptians conducted regular trading expeditions to SUDAN and ETHIOPIA. The Romans obtained many goods from North Africa, including grain, olive oil, livestock, timber, and marble.

The most common early exports from sub-Saharan Africa were gold, slaves, and ivory. Items of lesser importance included timber, spices, vegetable oils, and rubber. For hundreds of years, Africa was the major source of gold for the Mediterranean region and South Asia. The search for gold also motivated the earliest European trading voyages to Africa in the A.D. 1400s. For Europeans, the importance of African gold declined after they began to explore the Americas and to develop gold mines there.

Slaves made up an important part of sub-Saharan Africa's trade with North Africa, the Middle East, and Asia during the Middle Ages. In the 1500s European plantation owners in the Americas became the main customers. After European nations abolished slave trading in the 1800s, Muslims took over the commerce. Islamic involvement in the African slave trade reached its peak during the 1800s and did not stop until toward the end of that century.

During the precolonial era, Africans generally exported raw materials in exchange for manufactured goods, primarily textiles, metal goods, weapons, and shells and beads. In some cases, Africans used imported products, such as iron bars, to make manufactured goods. Beads and shells often served as currency as well as consumer goods. By and large,

Oil Rich and Oil Poor

The major exceptions to the poor performance of African economies have been the oil-producing states of North Africa. Libya, the largest oil producer in Africa, has the highest per-person income on the continent. Since independence, Algeria has developed both its oil and natural gas industries, which have contributed to rapid industrialization. However, Nigeria, Africa's second-largest oil producer, has not benefited nearly as much from petroleum. This is partly because Nigerian oil revenues go to a small, powerful segment of the population, and partly because of corruption among government officials who oversee the industry.

* **exploit**   to take advantage of; to make productive use of

* **cash crop**   crop grown primarily for sale rather than for local consumption

Africa's foreign trade affected coastal peoples much more than those living farther inland. Few imported goods reached the interior.

COLONIAL AND POSTCOLONIAL ECONOMIES

By the beginning of the colonial era in the late 1800s, the market for many of Africa's exports had declined sharply. Some, such as slaves, were no longer in great demand. Others, such as vegetable oils, were being replaced by cheaper alternatives from other sources. However, colonialism led to a revival of exports from Africa as Europeans took for themselves what they previously had obtained through trade.

The Role of Exports.   At first, the European nations that colonized Africa gave private companies the rights to exploit* the continent's natural wealth. Most of these companies, however, failed because of the high cost of setting up mines or plantations and of building roads and railroads to transport products.

By the early 1900s, European governments had stepped in to administer the colonies and oversee African exports. Over the next 60 years, trade and commerce between Africa and other parts of the world increased significantly. African mining was highly successful. By the mid-1930s, Africa supplied almost all the diamonds, half of the gold, and about one-fifth of the copper sold worldwide. Other important mineral exports included manganese, asbestos, and phosphates used in fertilizer.

The increase in exports helped stimulate the development of new manufacturing and service industries in Africa. In western Africa these new businesses were largely in the hands of Africans, but in eastern Africa they were dominated by Asian immigrants. Few of the new industries developed into large-scale companies. In southern and central Africa, the growth of mining and manufacturing led to a greater demand for food.

The colonial powers' agricultural efforts, however, were much less successful than the mining operations. The large plantations were often no more efficient than smaller farms. Moreover, colonies with agriculture-based economies often focused on a small number of crops and suffered when demands for those products dropped. In many areas, African peasants became skilled at growing and selling cash crops*. Rural incomes and standards of living were higher in places that featured small-scale farming rather than plantation agriculture.

The human cost for the colonial powers' focus on exports could be high. Governments and private companies often resorted to harsh methods, including forced labor, to ensure production. Africans were often denied access to land and to employment in skilled positions. In the late colonial period, a huge gap developed between urban and rural incomes.

The Postcolonial Economy.   In the early years after independence, most African economies continued to grow fairly well. However, the difference in incomes between urban and rural populations led to increased migration from the countryside to the cities as people

225

Economic History

searched for economic opportunities. By the mid-1960s, increased government spending on education resulted in large numbers of educated but unemployed youths in cities.

Under pressure to provide more jobs, many governments expanded their role in the economy. Bureaucracies* grew and government-owned and operated businesses multiplied. Most of these businesses were highly inefficient, employing far more people than they could reasonably afford. To increase revenues, leaders began to restrict imported goods that competed with locally produced items. They also kept the value of their currencies artificially high compared to foreign currency. In the long run, however, these policies reduced the price of exports and caused export earnings to shrink.

The effect of these postcolonial economic policies was dramatic. Between the late 1960s and 1980, agricultural exports fell by one-third. Mineral exports fared better, but in some countries they fell by up to 40 percent. Low prices for crops and minerals during the 1970s made the problem worse by lowering revenues for the goods that were exported. Personal incomes fell and unemployment soared, reducing government tax revenues.

To balance their budgets, African nations borrowed large sums of money from other countries as well as from institutions such as the World Bank and the International Monetary Fund. By the late 1980s, African economies were in serious trouble as their debts mounted and economic growth continued to decline.

The combination of reduced tax revenues, declining export earnings, staggering national debts, and growing political and social unrest forced African leaders to rethink their economic strategies. At the same time, nations and institutions that had lent money began to demand changes in the way African nations did business. Lenders forced many African countries to adjust the value of their currency to reflect its true value in the world marketplace. They also demanded an end to import restrictions and price controls. Many state-owned enterprises became private companies, and the size of government payrolls was cut. Even spending on social programs was reduced to help balance government budgets.

So far these new strategies have had little effect on African economies. Business owners have lacked confidence in the ability of governments to bring about change, and the production of goods has not increased significantly. Investors have been uncertain about Africa's commitment to economic reform. As a result, foreign investment in the continent has not grown as much as it has in other parts of the world.

Both lender nations and African leaders hope that reform policies will eventually improve the continent's economic outlook. (*See also* **Colonialism in Africa; Development, Economic and Social; Fishing; Forests and Forestry; Hunting and Gathering; Labor; Livestock Grazing; Markets; Minerals and Mining; Plantation Systems; Trade; Transportation; West African Trading Settlements.**)

Index

Page numbers of articles in these volumes appear in boldface type.

Index

Index

Bornu, **1:90–91**, 2:178, 4:36
Botha, Louis, 4:48
Botha, Pieter W., 4:53
Botswana, **1:91–94** *(map)*
    AIDS in, 1:14
    famine relief program in, 2:149–50
    geography and economy of, 1:91–92
    hereditary rank in, 1:147
    history and government of, 1:92–93
    Khama, president of, 1:92, **2:185–86**
    peoples and cultures of, 1:93–94
Botswana National Front (BNF), 1:93
Boudiaf, Mohammad, 1:22
Boukman, 1:207–8
Boumédienne, Houari, 1:21, **1:94**
Boundaries in Africa, **1:94–95**
Bourguiba, Habib, **1:95–96**, 1:161 *(illus.)*, 4:123
Bouteflika, Abdelaziz, 1:22
Braide, Garrick Sokari, **1:96**, 3:189
Brazil
    African population in, 1:207
    architectural influence of, 1:59
Brazza, Pierre Savorgnan de, 1:97, 175 *(illus.)*, 176, 2:74, 81, 4:117
Brazzaville, **1:97**
Bread, 2:66
Brewing, 2:68
Bridewealth, 2:194, 3:63–65
Brink, André, **1:97**
Britain. *See* Great Britain
British colonialism, 1:156–60
    architectural influence of, 1:59
    Asante attacks during, 1:15
    and Asante Union, 1:69
    in Bornu, 1:90–91
    in Cameroon, 1:114, 116
    and Cetshwayo, 1:126
    in Egypt, 2:18
    and Fante state, 1:15
    in Ghana, 1:108, 2:94
    in Kenya, 2:180–81, 3:120
    languages during, 2:207–8
    law in, 2:211
    Lugard, administrator during, 3:31–32
    Mau Mau opposition to, 3:67–69
    in Mauritius, 3:74
    myths justifying, 4:171
    in Nigeria, 3:140–41, 141, 143
    and the Nile, 3:149
    and political freedom for colonies, 2:155
    Rhodes, Cecil, **3:212**
    Saint Helena, **4:5–6**
    and "scramble" for Africa, 1:153
    in South African Republic, 1:5

    in Sudan, 4:67–68
    in Tanganyika, 4:82–83
    Thuku, Kenyan political leader, 4:90
    in Togoland, 4:93
    in Uganda, 4:129–30
    in Zambia, 4:164
British Creoles, 1:185
British Somaliland, 1:158
Broad-leaved savannas, 2:3, 4
Brong people, 2:98
Brotherhoods, Islamic, 4:15
Bruce, James, 4:115
Bubi people, 2:26
Buganda, 4:129, 130
    Kagwa, prime minister of, **2:176**
    Mutesa II, ruler of, 3:115, **3:115**
Building materials, 1:54, 2:138
Bulsa people, 2:97
Bunyoro, 4:129
Bunyoro-Kitara, 2:175
Burial, 1:191–93 *(illus.).* See also Funerals
    in ancient Egypt, 2:11–12
    of Malagasy people, 3:39
    pole sculptures, 1:64
    in pyramids, **3:196–97**
Burkina Faso, **1:98–102** *(map) (illus.)*, 4:96
    cultivation in, 1:11 *(illus.)*
    geography and economy of, 1:98
    history and government of, 1:99–102
    Mossi people, **3:96**
    peoples and cultures, 1:100 *(illus.)*, 102
Burton, Sir Richard Francis, **1:103**, 3:149, 4:116
Burundi, **1:103–8** *(map)*
    geography and economy of, 1:103–4
    history and government of, 1:105–7 *(illus.)*
    peoples and culture of, 1:104–5
    and Rwanda, 3:218
Bushman (San) people, 2:186
Busia, Kofi A., **1:108–9**, 2:95
Buthelezi, Gatsha, 4:54
Buyoya, Pierre, 1:106–7
Buzzer instruments, 3:113
Bwiti cult, 3:208 *(illus.)*
Byzantine Empire
    in Egypt, 2:15–16
    Ethiopian monks from, 2:38

C

Cabinda, 1:25, **1:109**
    art of, 1:28

    forestry in, 1:27
    petroleum in, 1:27
Cabora Bassa, 3:103, 4:162
Cabral, Amílcar Lopes, **1:110**, 2:110, 111, 3:172
Cabral, Luis, 2:111
Caesar, Julius, 1:147
Caillié, René, 4:116
Cairo, **1:110–11** *(illus.)*, 2:140
Cairo Declaration on Human Rights in Islam, 2:141
Calendars and time, **1:112–13**
Calligraphy, 1:68–69 *(illus.)*
Camara Laye, **1:113–14**, 3:25
Camels, 4:42
    dromedaries, 1:32, 33 *(illus.)*
    race, camel, 1:85 *(illus.)*
Cameroon, **1:114–18** *(map)*
    as British colony, 1:156
    folk dance masks of, 3:66 *(illus.)*
    as French colony, 1:162
    geography and economy of, 1:114–15
    as German colony, 1:163
    history and government of, 1:115–18
    maize grown in, 1:12 *(illus.)*
    peoples and cultures of, 1:116 *(illus.)*, 118
Cameroon National Union (CNU), 1:117
Camp David Accords, 3:93
Canary Islands, **1:119**
Cancer, 1:217
Candomblé, 1:208, 209
Cape Colony, 1:158, 4:137
Cape Coloured People, **1:119**, 1:185, 2:48, 4:49
Cape Malays, 1:185
Cape Town, **1:120**, 4:102 *(illus.)*, 138
Cape Verde, **1:120–22** *(illus.)*
    and Guinea-Bissau, 2:110, 111
    Pereira, president of, **3:172**
    as Portuguese colony, 1:165
Capitalism
    as development model, 1:199
    and labor organization, 2:197
Caravans, 3:29 *(illus.)*
Cardoso, Mãe Julia da Silva, 1:180
Carnivals. *See* Festivals and carnivals
Carthage, **1:122**, 3:214, 215, 4:123
Carved figures, 1:61, 62
Carving, 1:183, 184
Casamance (Senegal), 4:15
Casbah, 1:143
Casbah of Ait Benhaddou, 3:94 *(illus.)*
Casely-Hayford, Joseph, 3:23
Cash crops, 1:10–11
    labor needed for, 2:199
    and shortage of food crops, 1:13

Index

Clubs, dance, 1:189
Coal, 2:21, 3:77 *(map)*
Coastal ecosystems, 2:1
Coastal fishing, 2:63–64
Cocoa, 1:10, 4:7
Coetzee, J. M., **1:150**
Coffee, 1:10, 3:217, 218, 220
Cokwe people, 2:48
Cold War
    expansion of African studies during, 1:4
    political financial aid during, 1:201
Colenso, John William, **1:151**
Collection of Vocabularies of Central African Languages (Barth), 1:77
Collections, art, 1:61–62
Colleges and universities, 2:7, 9
Colonial festivals, 2:62
Colonialism in Africa, **1:151–67**
    (map)
    by Belgium, 1:155–56
    and ethnic division, 2:44
    by France, 1:160–63 *(illus.)*
    by Germany, 1:166–64
    by Great Britain, 1:156–60
    history, 2:131–33
    and independence movements, 2:153
    by Italy, 1:164, 165
    land ownership in, 2:202
    modern ethnic conflict resulting from, 2:90, 91
    overview of, 1:151–55 *(illus.)*
    by Portugal, 1:165–66 *(illus.)*
    protests against, 3:46
    societal impact of, 1:154, 155
    by Spain, 1:166–67
    and ethnic groups, 4:118
Colonial period, 1:4. *See also specific topics, e.g.:* French colonization
    Arabs in Africa during, 1:39–40
    architecture in, 1:58–59
    in Bénin, 1:81
    boundaries set during, 1:95
    in Burkina Faso, 1:99
    in Cameroon, 1:115–17
    cinema during, 1:136
    currency during, 3:89
    in Democratic Republic of Congo, 1:174–75
    development in, 1:198
    Diop, political leader during, **1:212**
    economies during, 1:225
    education during, 2:5–7
    Emin Pasha, governor during, **2:20–21**
    forestry in, 2:73
    in Gabon, 2:81

    government during, 2:106
    in Guinea, 2:108
    history of Africa during, 2:133–34
    Indian communities during, 2:157
    Ivory Coast during, 2:167–68
    in Kenya, 2:180
    labor systems during, 2:197–98
    law in, 2:210–13
    of Libya, 3:14
    literature in, 3:19
    mining during, 3:78–80
    in Mozambique, 3:100–1
    in Niger, 3:133
    in Rwanda, 3:217
    in Senegal, 4:13–14
    in Somalia, 4:41–42
    in Tanzania, 4:82–83
    theater during, 4:87
    in Togo, 4:92, 93
    trade during, 4:104
    transportation in, 4:106–7
    urban development in, 1:139–41
    in Zambia, 4:164
    in Zanzibar, 1:77
Color, symbolism of, 3:119
Coloured People's Congress, 4:52
"Coloureds," 1:36, 185
Columbus, Christopher, 1:119
Coming-of-age rites, 2:158
Commercial fishing, 2:64–65
Commoners, 1:144
Communal labor, 2:199
Communism, 1:82, 101, 2:34, 4:54, 99
Communist Party of South Africa, 4:49–50, 54
Communities
    age linked to status in, 1:144, 145 *(illus.)*
    European, **2:54–56**
    Indian, **2:157**
    Islamic, 1:55, 146
    Lebanese, **3:2**
    respect for elders in, 1:5
    small villages, 2:102–3
Community development, 1:201–2
Comorian (Ngazija) people, 2:48
Comoro Islands, **1:167–68**, 3:64 *(illus.)*
    as French colony, 1:163
    wedding dress/adornment in, 3:64 *(illus.)*
Company of Merchants Trading to Africa, 3:198
Compaoré, Blaise, 1:101–2
Compounds (architecture), 1:53
Conakry, **1:169**
Concessionary companies, 2:74–75
the Condominium, 4:67

Confederation of Tribal Associations of Katanga, 4:119
Congo Basin, 1:172
Congo (Brazzaville), **1:169–72**
    Brazzaville, capital of, **1:97**
    as French colony, 1:162
    history, government, and economy of, 1:169–72 *(illus.)*
    land and people of, 1:172
    as part of French Equatorial Africa, 2:75
Congo Free State, 1:155, 171
Congo (Kinshasa), 1:156, **1:172–77** *(map)*
    economy of, 1:176–77
    history and government of, 1:173–75
    Kinshasa, capital of, **2:191–92**
    masks of, 1:66
    peoples and cultures of, 1:177
    Tshombe, president of, **4:119**
Congo River, 1:173, **1:178–79**
Congress of Democrats, 4:52
Conrad, Joseph, 1:175
The Conservationist (Gordimer), 2:101
Constitutional monarchies, 2:191
Construction, 1:55, 2:138
Conté, Lansana, 2:109
Contract farming, 2:200
Convention People's Party (CPP), 2:94, 95, 3:149
Conversations with Ogotemmeli (Griaule), 3:116
Cooking, 2:67 *(illus.)*, 108
Copper, 3:77 *(map)*, 79
Coptic Christianity, 1:112, **1:179**, 2:16, 4:77
Coral reefs, 2:1
Corn, 1:10
Coronary heart disease, 1:217
Correia, Mãe Aurélia, **1:180**
Cosmetics, 1:87
Costa, Manuel Pinto da, 4:7
Côte d'Ivoire. *See* Ivory Coast
Council for the People's Salvation (CSP), 1:101
Covilhã, Pedro da, 4:114
Crafts, **1:181–84** *(illus.)*
    basketry, 1:181, 184 *(illus.)*
    beadwork, 1:181–82 *(illus.)*
    carving, 1:183, 184
    jewelry, 1:182 *(illus.)*
    pottery, 1:182–83
    textiles, 1:183
Creole languages, 2:203, 205
Creoles, **1:185–86**, 1:210, 2:26, 49, 74, 4:23
Crops, 1:8–11
    in Angola, 1:27
    cash *vs.* food, 1:13

Index

Index

Index

of Mali, 3:52–54
of Mauritania, 3:70–73
of modern Egypt, 2:15–20
of Morocco, 3:91–93
of Mozambique, 3:98–102
of Namibia, 3:121–23
of Niger, 3:133, 134
of Niger River and Delta, 3:136–37
of Nigeria, 3:139–44
of North Africa, 3:153–60
and oral tradition, **3:165–66**
of pastoralism, 3:29–30
of plantations, 3:176–77
prehistory to Iron Age, 2:123–25
of Réunion, 3:211
roots of colonialism in, 2:131–33
of Rwanda, 3:216–20 *(illus.)*
of Sahara desert, 4:2
of São Tomé and Príncipe, 4:7
of Senegal, 4:12–15
of Sierra Leone, 4:21–26
since independence, 2:134–36
  (illus.)
society, trade, and urban development, 2:125–27
of Somalia, 4:41–44
of South Africa, 4:48–54
of Southern Africa, **4:56–59** *(illus.)*
of Sudan, 4:66–70
of Swaziland, 4:77–78
of Tanzania, 4:82–83
of Togo, 4:92–95
of Tunisia, 4:121–23
of Uganda, 4:128–32
of Western Sahara, 4:145, 146
of Zambia, 4:164–65
of Zanzibar, 4:168
of Zimbabwe, 4:171–75
The History of the Yorubas (Johnson), 2:174
HIV, 1:14, 215, 4:55, 165
Hodgson, Sir Frederick, 1:70
"Homelands" (South Africa), 1:37
Hominids, 2:142–45
Homo erectus, 2:144–46
Homosexuality, 2:89–90
Horn of Africa, 1:164, 2:29, 30, 32, 4:40, 41
Horses, 1:32
Horton, James Africanus, **2:137,** 3:126
Horus (Egyptian god), 3:118 *(illus.)*
Hospitals, 2:120, 121–22
Houphouët-Boigny, Félix, **2:137,** 2:166–69 *(illus.)*
Hours, 1:113
Households
  as family units, 2:57–58
  slaves in, 4:13
  in small villages, 2:103

Houses and housing, **2:138–40**
  in Bénin, 1:82 *(illus.)*
  Islamic laws for, 2:210
  for migrant workers, 2:200–1
  rural, 2:138
  urban, 2:139–40 *(illus.)*
Hova people, 2:51
Human rights, 1:36, **2:140–42**
Humans, early, **2:142–47** *(map)*
  ancestors of, 2:142–45 *(illus.)*
  archaeological evidence of, 1:48–51
  emergence of modern from, 2:146–47
Hunger and famine, **2:147–50** *(illus.)*
Hunger season, 2:69
Hungry rice, 1:9
Hunting and gathering, 2:87–88, 102, **2:150–51**
Hut Tax, 4:23
Hutu people, 1:104–7 *(illus.),* 2:92, 3:216–20 *(illus.)*
Hydatid disease, 1:217
Hydroelectric power, 2:21, 22

I

Ibadan, **2:151**
Ibibio people, 2:50
Ibn Battuta, Abu Abdallah
  Muhammad, 2:133, **2:151,** 3:85, 4:90, 113
Ibn Khaldun, 4:125
Ibo people, 2:50
Ibrahim, Abdullah, 3:110
Identity, sense of. *See also* Ethnic
  groups and identity
  and age, 1:5
  Diop's work on, 1:212
Idiophones, 3:114
Idris I, 3:14, 92, 197
Idris II, 3:92
Ifni, 1:167
Ifriqiya, 4:121–22
Igbo (Ibo) people, 2:50, **2:152,** 3:137
  gender roles in, 2:88
  masks of, 1:65
  scarification among, 1:87
Igbo Ukwu (archaeological site), 1:46
Igboland, 1:2, 3:139–40, 140
Ijaw people, 2:50
Ijo (Ijaw, Kalabari) people, 2:50
Ile-Ife, 1:139
Illegal housing settlements, 2:140
Illnesses. *See* Diseases
IMF. *See* International Monetary Fund
Imhotep, 3:196
Imperialism, 1:153. *See also*
  Colonialism in Africa

In Darkest Africa (Stanley), 4:64
In the Fog of the Season's End (La
  Guma), 2:197
Inan, Abu, 3:159
Indentured labor, 2:198
Independence movements, **2:152–56.**
  See also Nationalism
  in Afrikaner Republics, 1:5
  in Algeria, 1:20–21, 78–79
  in Angola, 1:28–29
  in Belgian Congo, 1:174–75
  in Botswana, 1:92
  of Cape Verde, 1:120
  Chilembwe's activities in, 1:131
  Diop's influence on, 1:212
  early roots of, 2:152–53
  in Egypt, 2:19–20
  ethnic cooperation/conflict related
    to, 2:91
  in Ghana, 2:94–95
  in Guinea-Bissau, 1:110
  and independence era, 2:154–56
    (illus.)
  and Indian communities, 2:157
  in Kenya, 2:180–83
  in Mali, 3:52–54
  Mau Mau role in, 3:67–69
  in Mauritania, 3:71
  missionaries, role in, 3:84
  in Morocco, 3:92–93, 105
  in Mozambique, 3:86, 101–2
  in Namibia, 3:122
  and neocolonialism, 3:130–31
  Nkrumah, leader of, 3:149
  in Senegal, 4:14
  in Sierra Leone, 4:23–24
  in Sudan, 4:68–69
  Tshombe, leader in, 4:119
  and unions, 4:134
  and World War II, 4:159
Independent ICU, 2:176
Indian communities, **2:157**
Indian Ocean, coastline of, 2:1
Indigenous government, 2:102–6
Indirect rule, 1:156, 157, 159
Indo-Arabic number system, 4:160
Industrial and Commercial Union
  (ICU), 2:175–76, 4:49, 50, 134
Industrial Revolution, 2:131–32, 4:32
Industry, *For specific countries, see
  under* Economy
  fuel used by, 2:22
  labor, industrial, 2:200
Infancy, 1:128, 129 *(illus.)*
Infectious diseases, 1:213–17, 2:119
Informal labor, 2:201
Inheritance
  Islamic law related to, 2:165
  of kingship, 2:190
Initiation rites, 1:130, **2:158–59**

Index

Index

Index

Index

Index

S

Index

countries included in, 1:51
decorative arts of, 1:68
ethnic groups and identity in,
    1:74, 2:46–47
European settlements in, 2:55
history of, **4:56–59** *(illus.)*
Islam's influence in, 2:128–29
Khoisan people in, 2:186–87
law in, 2:213
literature in, 3:22
music of, 3:110–11
Ndebele people in, **3:129**
painting in, 1:67
rock art in, 3:212–13
sculpture of, 1:64–65
Shona people in, **4:20–21**
Southern African Development
    Community (SADC), 2:99, 100
Southern Rhodesia
    as British colony, 1:158, 159
    Central African Federation,
        1:122–23
Southern Sahara, 1:162–63
South-West Africa, 1:163–64
Soviet Union, 2:34, 35, 3:129
Soweto Massacre, 4:52
Soybeans, 4:174
Soyinka, Wole, 3:23, **4:59–60**, 4:89
Spanish colonialism, 1:161, 166–67
    of Equatorial Guinea, 2:24, 25
    Western Sahara, **4:145–46**
Spanish Guinea, 1:166, 167
Spanish Sahara, 1:166, 3:93
Speke, John Hanning, 1:103, 3:149,
    4:116, 129
Spirit possession, 3:210, **4:60–61**,
    4:87
Spirits, 3:207
    as agents of illnesses and cures,
        2:115–17
    of dead people, 1:192
    and divination, 1:218
    of forests, 2:73
    in religions, 1:102
Sports and recreation, **4:61–64** *(illus.)*
Sports clubs, 4:62
Squatter settlements, 2:139, 140
Stanley, Henry Morton, 1:174, **4:64**,
    4:115–17 *(illus.)*
    in Congo Free State, 1:155
    and Emin Pasha, 2:20
    exploration of Congo River by,
        1:178
    and Kinshasa, 2:191–92
    Livingstone and, 3:30–31
States
    definition of, 2:104
    formation of, 2:130–31
    government/political systems of,
        2:104–6

STDs. *See* Sexually transmitted diseases
Steppes, 1:149
Stevens, Siaka, 4:24
Stone Age, 1:42, 43
The Stone Country (La Guma), 2:197
Storck, Henri, 1:136
The Story of an African Farm
    (Schreiner), 3:24, 4:9
Strasser, Valentine, 4:24
Structural adjustment programs,
    1:199–201
Study of Africa, **1:3–4**
Sub-Saharan Africa
    Afro-Arab relations in, 1:40
    AIDS in, 1:14
    ancestor beliefs in, 1:194
    ancient Egypt's links with, 2:12–14
    art of, 1:60
    calendar in, 1:112–13
    Christianity in, 1:132
    cities and urbanization in,
        1:139–42 *(illus.)*
    dance in, 1:188, 190
    early exploration of, 1:3–4
    food staples in, 2:65–66
    funeral practices in, 1:191–92
    Ibn Battuta's accounts of, 2:151
    kingship in, 2:188
    lack of written history in, 1:41
    misery index standing of, 1:199
    mountain ecosystems in, 2:2
    precolonial trade in, 1:224
    regional problems in, 2:99
Subsistence farming, 1:26–27
Succession, kingly, 2:190
Sudan, **4:64–71** *(map)*
    art of, 1:62–63, 67
    British government in, 1:159, 160
    economy of, 4:70–71
    ethnic groups and identity in, 2:40
    geography of, 4:65–66, 68 *(illus.)*
    history and government of,
        4:66–70
    Islam in, 2:162
    Khartoum, capital of, **2:186**
    Mahdi, religious leader in, 3:44
    and the Nile, 3:148, 149
    peoples and cultures of, 4:71
Sudan People's Liberation Army
    (SPLA), 4:69
Sudanic Empires of Western Africa,
    3:136–37, **4:72–74** *(map)*
Sudanic people, 2:36–37
Suez Canal, 1:154 *(illus.)*, 3:125,
    4:74–75
    British control over, 2:19
    Egyptian shares in, 2:18
    sale to Britain of, 1:159
Sufism, 1:188, **4:75**

Sukuma people, 1:67, 2:53
Sumanguru Kante, 4:76
Sundjata Keïta, 3:52, 58, 3:165, 4:73,
    4:75–76
Sunni Ali, 3:52, 4:73, **4:76**
Sunni Muslims, 4:126
The Suns of Independence (Kourouma),
    2:195, 3:25
Supreme Council for Sport in Africa,
    4:63
Susenyos, **4:77**
Susu people, 2:53
Swahili coast
    Arab influence on, 1:37–38
    origin of communities in, 1:50–51
Swahili language, 1:168, 2:44, 204,
    206, 208, 3:19, 20, 24
Swahili people, 2:53, 184, **4:77**
    decorative arts of, 1:68
    first towns built by, 1:76
    literature in, 3:21
    music of, 3:110
    Shaaban, writer of, 4:19
SWAPO. *See* South West African
    People's Organization
Swati language, 4:79
Swazi people, 1:158–59, 2:53, 158
Swaziland, **4:77–79**
    as British colony, 1:158–59
    as constitutional monarchy, 2:191
    hereditary rank in, 1:147
    Sobhuza I and II, kings of, **4:39–40**
Swidden (slash-and-burn) agriculture,
    1:222, 2:72
Symbols and symbolism
    of animals, 3:210
    in architecture, 1:55
    on currency, 3:182
    of kings, 2:104, 188–90, 189

T

Taarab music, 3:110
Tabarmar Kunya (Kano and dan
    Gogo), 4:89
Taboo and sin, **4:79–80**
    as cause of sickness, 2:118
    food, 2:69
    sexual, 2:89
Tafari Benti, 2:34
Tafawa Balewa, Abubakar, **4:81**
Taitu, Empress, 1:3
Tales From a Troubled Land (Paton),
    3:168
"Talking drum," 3:106
Tamacheq language, 4:120
Tananarive, 1:36
Tandja Mamadou, 3:134

252

Index

Index